W0081095

Political Ecospatiality

Political Ecospatiality offers a new perspective on subaltern struggles and raises the issue of how people with limited lobbying power can still organize to defend their honour or livelihood–environmental ecospatial systems. The book narrates and analyses the historical and contemporary situations that shape and reshape the strategies and practices of larger livelihood–environmental and identity politics in Kerala by drawing parallels from the rest of India and the Global South. By employing Kerala as an example, it engages with and broadens debates in political economy, political ecology, and subaltern politics. The book moves through six ecospatial conflicts and assembles four key ideas – right-making/state-making, transverse solidarity, spatio-temporal-agential coalescence, and subaltern modernity – and applies them as analytical tools to form an overall framework of political ecospatiality. These narratives are primarily constructed using the innovative method of on-the-spot ethnography.

K. Ravi Raman is a member of the state planning board, Government of Kerala, and founding director of the International Institute of Migration and Development, Thiruvananthapuram. He is the author of *Global Capital and Peripheral Labour: The History and Political Economy of Plantation Workers in India* (Routledge, 2010) and *Kerala, 1956 to the Present: India's Miracle State* with Tirthankar Roy (Cambridge University Press, 2024).

Political Ecospatiality

Livelihood, Environment, and Subaltern Struggles

K. Ravi Raman

Shaftesbury Road, Cambridge CB2 8EA, United Kingdom

One Liberty Plaza, 20th Floor, New York, NY 10006, USA

477 Williamstown Road, Port Melbourne, VIC 3207, Australia

314–321, 3rd Floor, Plot 3, Splendor Forum, Jasola District Centre, New Delhi – 110025, India

103 Penang Road, #05–06/07, Visioncrest Commercial, Singapore 238467

Cambridge University Press is part of Cambridge University Press & Assessment, a department of the University of Cambridge.

We share the University's mission to contribute to society through the pursuit of education, learning and research at the highest international levels of excellence.

www.cambridge.org
Information on this title: www.cambridge.org/9781009337397

First published 2024

Printed in India by Avantika Printers Pvt. Ltd.

A catalogue record for this publication is available from the British Library

ISBN 978-1-009-33739-7 Hardback

Contents

Acknowledgements vii

1 What Is Politics Proper? Why *Political Ecospatiality* Matters? 1

2 Birlas in Communist Kerala: Clash and Consensus as Subaltern Narratives 31

3 Occupy Muthanga: Land, Forest, and Reinventing Indigeneity and Identity 67

4 Dalits and the Global Cola: Water, Power, and Resistance 99

5 Politics, Epistemology, and Environmental Modernity: Anti-endosulfan as Ethical Practice? 126

6 Caste, Land, and the State: What If Chengara Took the Place of Muthanga? 151

7 Pombilai Orumai: Plantation Dalits, Intersectionality, and Power 176

8 Ecospatiality: Right-Making/State-Making 198

Index 228

Acknowledgements

Thirty-five years is a short period within the political history of a state; however, it spans the prime years of the academic life of an individual scholar. The progression of struggles narrated in this monograph coincides with my initiation as a young radical and through my scholarly adult life since I joined the Centre for Development Studies Thiruvananthapuram in 1985. I was able to participate in most of these struggles though some of the struggles had a much earlier beginning and have continually published papers and articles on these movements over the years, both while I lived in India and while on scholarships and visiting/honorary fellowships in the UK. My long stint at the University of Manchester (2005–2008) and shorter periods spent in Oxford (1999), Cambridge (2011), and SOAS London (2010–13) helped me sharpen some of the earlier versions of my writings and thoughts. The professorial fellowship at the Nehru Memorial Museum and Library, New Delhi (2015–16), helped me improve the early version of manuscripts. Three reviewers of Cambridge University Press have provided helpful comments on various chapters, and I found them very constructive.

I am grateful to those who were supportive of my writings while in the field and also during my placements in academic institutions. It is perhaps humanly impossible to list them as I am conducting this study over decades. However, a few names deserve special mention now. First of all, I wish to express my deep gratitude to A. Vasu Mayilamma, C.K. Janu, M. Geethanandan, Sabina Plackanam, Laha Gopalan, and Gomathy Sebastian; they were active leaders of the protests and movements narrated in this monograph. My discussions with academic scholars, including Bruce Kapferer, Heather Bedi, the late David Washbrook, Barbara-Harris-White and John Gledhill, on varying occasions, were very helpful.

I am grateful to Tirthankar Roy, Vinita Damodaran, Indrajit Roy, and Mahesh Rangarajan, who have always been helpful. I greatly value the benefits received from K.T. Rammohan, V.K. Ramachandran, B. Ekbal, K.P. Kannan, K. Venu, J. Reghu, P.T. Thomas, the late M. Kunhaman, M.M. Khan, K. Govindaraj, Vilayodi Venugopal, Shibu Natesan, T. Prasadan, Ajit Dayanandan, Subrahmanian N, Nisar Kizhakkayil, N.K. Ravindran, Moidu Vanimel, C. Surendranath, R. Ajayan, Vazhur Soman, Pyarelal Raghavan, C.K. Brahmaputran, and C. Jayakumar. I have greatly benefited from my discussions with the new generation scholars, particularly Labeeb Muhammed, Reghunathan M., Bipin Chandran, Benna Fatima, and Dulhaqe S.

Sabeena Panicker, my wife and critic, has always been a constant presence with her comments and helpful suggestions.

1

What Is Politics Proper?

Why *Political Ecospatiality* Matters?

Much before the Western radical youth 'invented' Occupy politics of 2011 (Occupy Wall Street, Occupy St Paul) in the West, inspired largely by the Arab Spring,[1] there were instances in the Global South where precarious workers and communities unleashed their agency with unpredictable outcomes. What Hardt and Negri (2012)[2] attribute to Occupy politics – their imaginations, revolts, slogans, movements and insistence on democracy as characteristics of multitudes – was also relevant for the subaltern struggles in the Global South. It is remarkable how the multitudes, both in the West and in the Global South, though spatially and temporally distinct, declare historically evolved truths through imaginative interventions towards a more egalitarian way of living. In South Asia, they also practised it as social movement identity politics in a world where corporates, often with the support of the state, threatened their rights to the commons, including their traditional environmental rights to land and water resources, and their human right to a decent living,[3] thus bearing wider connotations than the Western-style Occupy protests. Latin American and African resistance movements such as the Landless Workers Movement in Mexico and Zapatistas/Chiapas in Brazil, and those in Buen Vivir (Ecuador), Cochabamba (Bolivia), the Estallido Social (Social Uprising) in Chile, and Ongoni (Nigeria) share similar traits in the way they assert and attribute new meanings to land rights, autonomy, food, water, environmental sovereignty, and identity. As a critical complement to the earlier-mentioned literature, the present monograph examines the livelihood, environmental, and identity struggles of the marginalized with a focus on Kerala, the state known for its twin legacies: the communist experiments and social development.

More on Premises

The protests, struggles, and movements in the Global South challenging corporate capital and the state, and even the mainstream male-led trade unions, take the form of what I would refer to as ecospatial struggles, resulting in the conceptualization of political ecospatiality in which 'eco' represents the varying dimensions of critiques of economics and ecology/environment and 'spatiality', the power relations ingrained in the social body politic (see Raman 2020b; Peluso and Watts 2001; Wapner 1996; Lefebvre 2011; Massey 1994; Harvey 2000). Political ecospatiality in this context refers to the rationale of the ecospatial struggles from the margins – why they are being fought, how they are being organized, and what is to be imagined – and is the lens through which I perceive the actual manifestations of ecospatial conflicts in the Global South. Ecospatial conflict is not the analytical framework; instead, it explains the types and dynamics of conflicts that are relatedly understood in terms of space, time, and agencies – a process of what I would call transverse solidarity through spatio-agential-temporal coalescence. Such historical events are further enhanced by what I would refer to as the 'right-making/state-making process', which implies that the state's everyday formation has been predominantly impacted by the subalterns' rights claims. What is prefigured is that right-making is a reciprocal process in which claim-making comes first, then right-making as state-making, and vice versa.

Right-making is seen as state-making and state-making as right-making in this two-way process, which need not always be linear.[4] Although the Marxist version of 'state' is typically thought of as an oppressive institution, we advance the argument that graduated social democracies are potentially capable of reducing harsh inequalities of wealth and power (Piketty 2021) which could be a significant step towards an imagined common wealth, often triggered by a series of protests and/or even just through a process of conscientization of the state from below. We might also ask how far the process of right-making/state-making come along and how far the ecospatial struggles have aided civil society–state synergy and in democratizing democracy. This right-making state-making process is a democracy project, both individually and collectively, for all the pluralistic agents involved. Additionally, it would suggest that right-making/state-making dialectics and the outcomes should be used to evaluate both state formation and state performance, particularly under neoliberal conditions. This narrative is developed through an innovative method: on-the-spot ethnography, which is employed in this way and is, to my knowledge, a first in the social sciences, including in anthropology. What is more significant for this author is the interconstitutiveness of subaltern power, the coming together of the closely related pre-existing identities from differences that makes politics proper possible or political ecospatiality a reality. The Indian state of Kerala, a state known for its exceptionality in terms of a communist government and social development, is used as the case study for the Global South. The struggles led by the subaltern non-upper castes – particularly the Dalits, the indigenous people, and the backward communities, including the minority Muslims and backward Christians – are augmented by their histories of oppression, deprivation and exclusion at multiple levels. This monograph's eight chapters are made up of these struggles and movements that have occurred since the state's formation in 1956 and the first communist regime that came to power in 1957.

As part of framing the ecospatial struggles and the consequent political ecospatiality,[5] I pose a few questions: First, what is politics proper as understood through the narratives of ecospatial struggles, or how is ecospatiality in itself of politics proper? Second, how best can one study livelihood-environment protest politics and resistance movements – spatially, agentially, temporally, or would it be by a combination of modes? Third, who could represent whom, and how do identities play a critical role in challenging the legacies of exclusion and oppression and the production of political ecospatiality as the imagined future? As no single episteme could truly encompass the whole as there are many modes of knowing things (see Foucault 1980, 2001), what is important is to understand the ecospatial reasoning for the collective meaning-making and right-making/state-making processes? This is in fact an attempt at an 'epistemological break' (Althusser 1969) which empowers our understanding of politics proper with the hybrid metaphor of ecospatiality enriched, mostly through on-the-spot ethnography/on-site ethnography.

Politics proper or what makes politics political[6] is rightly to be understood as a phenomenon of demos, those who do not have firmly held positions in the existing stratified social order. Political is that which emerges when the poor and the marginalized – 'a part of those who have no part' (Rancière 1999: 11) – not only claim that their voice be heard against those in power but that they be included in the public sphere on an 'equal footing', disrupting the natural order of dominance (Žižek 1998: 989). What is to be erased is the inequality of wealth and power by reinventing the political, in this case, through ecospatial protests and struggles and identifying ourselves with the true universality or, in Rancière's words, *universel singulier* (Žižek 1997: 49; Žižek 2008; also see Rancière 2001). Further, they should present themselves as the representatives of the whole without any privileged interest. It is important to understand to locate and identity ourselves with this politics proper as part of what Agamben (1993) would call the 'coming community' – a life different from today, particularly in the larger context of failures of efforts whether it was in Soviet communism, which was replaced by an oligarchic capitalism, or in the West where 'democracy were replaced by hyper-capitalism' (Kiøsterud 2021). Given that the marginalized communities – the Gramscian subalterns[7] – are always at odds with the hegemonic forces due to their conflict with the local caste system, the state and the larger capitalist system (Thorat and Newman 2010), it is vital to see this agential resistance as a window into the future.[8] Deriving insights from such contributions, this monograph develops the ideas further, in terms of subaltern power and practices for immediate goals and imagined futures.

First of all, in my framing, the constitutive principles of political ecospatiality would include the conditions of living of those economically, ecologically, and spatially marginalized – those outside of the hegemonic *chaturvarna* (the four-fold caste order) of the Hindu caste system, and the minority Muslims and backward Christians. It is also constitutive of state and state spaces, so also the 'relations of power stretched out' (see Massey 1994: 2; see also Gregory 1994; Harvey 2000) in the larger capitalist system. By bringing 'subaltern counterpublics' to the fore, Fraser, for instance, opened up the possibility of a subaltern counter-discourse and a recognition of their 'identities, interests, and needs' (Fraser 2014: 8–42, 129–156; Olson 2008), thus releasing their 'emancipatory potential' (Fraser 1997: 82; also see Ambedkar 1948) and also of subaltern modernity as its potential culmination as argued elsewhere by the author[9] – accomplished through transverse solidarity and politics, in order to reverse historical and contemporary forms of marginalities of exclusion. Subalterns belonging to the oppressed castes, therefore, must engage with the integration of class and castes as well as the question of development. When seen through the perspective of 'modernity as liberation' (Wallerstein 2000) – the triumph of humankind over oppressive forms of privilege and authority and resistance against hegemonic forces – it becomes all the more imaginative and creative.

For us what is equally important is to decode the stretching-out process in which both the interaction and 'intra-action' are interlinked to generate the imagined 'agential realism': 'an appreciation of the intertwining of ethics, knowing, and being' (Barad 2007) but with a difference. In contrast to the posthumanist/new materialist understanding of social practices, the agency is attributed more to humans as it is only through the conscious interaction with humans and the entangled power relations, and with nature as well, that the desired change could be materialized.[10] The purpose of agency – in this context, the subaltern agency – is to overcome the hegemonic social forms in order to pursue a common aim; any other interpretation is depoliticizing the very purpose of agential activism (Noys 2011: 12–13). Second, it is argued that it is the collective agency – the transverse solidarity – of not only those whose voices should be heard against the hegemonized power relations but also they themselves should be part of the processes of liberatory politics (Rancière 1999 [1995]; Žižek 1998; Santos 2014). This represents the capacity of a collective to present its universal agenda as incarnating the interests of the society as a whole – a collective meaning-making process – that is contested and ever-growing. Third, while I am in agreement with varying notions of solidarity,[11] I focus on the co-production of knowledge and practice – including the associated controversies – as a bottom-up resistance project and reconfiguring the hierarchies of knowledge and practice at multiple levels, primarily the spatial, agential, and temporal levels (Castree 1995).

Spatio-Agential-Temporal Coalescing

By spatial coalescing, I mean the combined effect of diverse movements that affect not only the place or location in which they emerge in response to an apparently local issue at a specific point in time, but also other locations of struggles having an impact on an entire region or a nation state or even beyond, as a whole. Often, these struggles are networked and intertwined in countering the hegemonic forces (see Featherstone 2008; McCarty 2012). When and where people come together and act, and we appear to others as others appear to us, Arendt (1958: 198–199) demonstrates how the 'space of appearance' becomes a political endeavour. When political activities are 'structured around place in form but stretch in sub-stance to embrace space', as Lefebvre (1991) notes, the place–space dialectics – which is also latent in that work – becomes all the more liberating. As Harvey (2000: 38) has effectively explained how capitalism has exploited its capabilities of 'spatial manoeuvring to thwart place-bound proletarian/socialist revolutions', we also do have diverse places of worker and public mobilization as spaces of resistance and identity creation challenging power hierarchies (Kohn 2003; Howarth 2006; Lefebvre 1991; Nash 2001). While 'spatial' is 'social relations stretched out' (Massey 1994: 2) and 'spatial' and 'spatiality' share many characteristics in common, the latter lays more emphasis on the subjective and objective dimensions as interactive processes.

While not exactly physically overlapping, save on rare instances, there is a significant agential merging as the initiatives and participants of the various movements borrow and share the fundamental idea of social and environmental justice and work towards such objectives. This is closely related to how identities, especially those of caste and gender, come together to create an agential plurality of indigenous communities, Dalits, minority communities, poor Muslims, and backward castes, all of which have the 'general attribute of subordination' (Guha 1982: vii), and which stand out in the larger process of state-driven developmentalist modernization. This 'agential realism' – a relationship that emerges through entanglements, subject positions, and discourses with the potential for new material conditions (see Barad 2007) – when unleashed through subaltern struggles cannot be engulfed by hegemonic forces. In addition to the aforementioned, the consolidation of the many resistance movements, even within a single region, demonstrates a commitment to the original conception of enlightenment. This process of historical coalescence suggests that the past gives the present strength, and to that extent, ecospatiality becomes historical through the temporal coalescence of agents and spaces. The Silent Valley campaign, the first significant environmental effort in India after independence, was to save the only unaltered evergreen woods in the country located in the Kerala region of the Western Ghats. People from all walks of life came together to oppose the state-led developmentalism that was envisioned as only being possible by razing at least 89 square kilometres of forest. The Kerala State Electricity Board persevered with the hydropower project in 1976, but the campaign with scientific intellectuals and the organizational presence of Kerala Sastra Sahitya Parishad (KSSP) – the people's science movement – mobilized against the proposal, forced the state to withdraw,[12] and pops up in every environmental, political ecological, and 'post-development' (Blake 1986; Bryant and Bailey 1997; Moore 2015; Escobar 1995; also see Watts 1983; Watts, Mason, and Appel 2015) struggle in India. The temporality has local dimensions as well: it also entails reconstructing the present and the future as potential alternatives. This broadens and deepens the very notion of politics proper as evolved through history and time, constituting a historically ecospatiality practice (Sewell 1996).

As understood in this monograph, transverse solidarity/interconstitutiveness of subaltern power towards ecospatial struggles denotes a collective agency that operates within the arena of social difference, but aiming at a broader community than their immediate origins in terms of class, caste, and gender. It implies an equivalence among different 'subject positions' based on antagonism to a particular configuration of political and economic power: the state, the corporates, or even the mainstream male-led trade unions. It was Badiou that pointed out that subjects become political when they create events – as trans beings (see Hallward 2003; Badiou 2004, 2018), even in the absence of any premediating agency. One cannot predict the outcome of such events, but what is often authentic is the post-event declaration. As a result of the production of ecospatiality through transverse solidarity, the multiple sites of power, such as production, consumption culture, and the market, and thereby the state and civil society, are transformed. Socially concerned individuals, non-governmental organizations (NGOs), public institutions, and media organizations – both local and global – find themselves unable to remain unbiased and become drawn towards the bottom-up movement, which is in turn enlarging it even further. This emergent transverse solidarity (TS) not only enlarges the space between civil society and the state, as described by Melucci (1989: 71), but also constantly seeks to educate and mobilize its constituents to come into this solidarity with all its own complexities and conflicts. Also, not only the subaltern in general but the subaltern womanhood was being reclaimed through imaginative fights and resistance, a continuation of the wider challenge of universal womanhood (see Butler 1999 [1990]; Spivak 1987). This has implications for social reproduction of labour and Dalit epistemic agency (see Guru and Sarukkai 2012) challenging the intersectionality of exploitation and oppression (see Collins 1990), thus responding to the Spivakian challenge, 'Can the subaltern speak?' and reaffirming that the subaltern as Dalit female is also no longer in the shadow. In many ways, the strategy of dissent is that of self-organizing by the mis-organized (Raman 2020a), and thereby turning away from the non-representational, hegemonic organizational forms – thus creating an alternative to the traditional Marxist perspective that worker and peasant communities cannot act on their own but must be represented (see Santos 2014; Fraser 2014), which also enriches a decolonial critique (see Said 1978; Mignolo 2000; Quijano 2000) on Western epistemology from the Global South.[13]

While writing a foreword to Frantz Fanon's *The Wretched of the Earth*, Jean-Paul Sartre stated that a people's misfortunes snowball to become their courage. Laclau and Mouffe (1985: 125), while developing their radical democracy project, asked: when would a peasant identity get kindled? They point out that 'a peasant working on the land would not in the normal course of things refer to himself or herself as a peasant but would become a peasant – begin to articulate an identity as peasant – at precisely the moment at which a landlord comes along and says "I am selling this land, get off the land"'. This threatened expropriation of the land brings to the fore certain aspects of everyday life that are explicitly linked to land dependency for survival, and thus form the initial basis for the construction of a new and more politicized peasant identity. It becomes a political and articulate identity, something to connect with through positioning, something to strive for. This may also happen when the commons are appropriated to the effect of depriving livelihood to those on the edge. This is exactly what happened in the case of Kondha tribes in the Niyamgiri hills in Odisha in October 2004. The state signed an agreement with the multinational Vedanta Alumina, a subsidiary of Sterlite Industries (India), to mine bauxite deposit from the Niyamgiri hills jointly with the Orissa Mining Corporation, violating the livelihood and the human rights of the local indigenous people (see Sahu 2008). Their struggles gained momentum after the police killing of 13 poor people who were protesting against Vedanta's Copper Sterlite Industries in Thoothukudi, Tamil Nadu. Thus emerged a slogan, 'Polluter and Killer Vedanta Quit India] (CDRO 2019).

Like land resources, if the water or forest resources are enclosed or misutilized, and if it threatens not only the immediate livelihood but also the larger environment, the local inhabitants may come forward to reclaim their rights. In this context another ecospatial struggle was the Chipko movement in the early 1970s. Tensions started to build when a Gandhian workers' cooperative, which began working as a source of livelihood with local forest resources, was denied local resources when the collusive deal between the hegemonic forces – the private company and the contractors as 'outsiders', and also the state – threatened not only their livelihood but also entire forest ecologies, driving them to hug all those trees giving birth to the Chipko (to hug the tree) movement.[14] Both ecology and economics intertwined, and class, caste, and gender overlapped, gravitating a wide variety of social groups, the Gandhians, the poets, the intellectuals, and the activists (see Gadgil and Guha 1994; Bankoti 2018; Ramesh 2015), and, more importantly, the movement grew to the extent of the Save Himalaya campaign. Yet another significant movement was that of the anti-dam campaign of the Narmada Bachao Andolan (NBA) led by the potential displacement of the people in the Narmada Valley (see Omvedt 1993; Dwivedi 1998; Nilsen 2008), which helped generate a new livelihood environmental consciousness and politics in India.

Why Kerala in the Global South?

The Indian state of Kerala, however, is illustrative and exceptional. Dalits and indigenous people in the state of Kerala, known for its social development and communist experiments, practised forms of resistance unique to Kerala, both as a survival strategy and as politics of identities. I would assert that the question of identity plays a key role in movement politics in Kerala as in the Global South wherein the Dalits and Adivasis, and also the backward communities, with their shared origins – outside of *cahturvarna* and leading a deprived political, material, and social life – come together to manifest their self-assertion, demanding that they be heard and represented. It is specifically in this context that the state of Kerala holds a unique place within India and the Global South for various reasons. Kerala has a socially expressive lineage of various groups (castes and religious) claiming rights to state and non-state resources – both the Hindu and the colonial state – right from colonial times. Such claims have their roots in missionary activism, renaissance movements and articulations on the streets through organizations as well as through literary expression, and Kerala has also passed through various phases of resistance as modernity. In other words, with hegemonic forces transitioning from imperialism to caste and state dominance as interactive forces, the state has travelled through several overlapping periods of subaltern modernity as resistance, of which three phases are particularly relevant (Raman 2017). The fourth stage is currently in progress.

In the earliest phase, indigenous groups known as the Kurichias and Kurumbas challenged the alien norms and enclosures of the British authorities and the military apparatus in Wayanad's hill tracts in 1812 using their traditional weapons as a form of subaltern resistance, signifying the first stage of modernity. The caste system as practised in India was typical of ecospatial practices of exclusion. The Dalits and those outside the *chaturvarna* were tied to feudal land relations; in the Adivasi regions, they were even transacted along with land transfers. By and large, most of those outside the caste hegemony were stuck with low-paying menial jobs without any upward mobility. As the caste Hindus not only practised distance pollution but also considered the mere seeing of a non-caste Hindu as polluting, the Dalits and other oppressed communities remained invisibilized by the hegemonic Hindu state of Thiruvithamkur. Nineteenth- and early-twentieth-century Kerala saw the peak of oppressive caste Hindu practices but such ordering and discourses associated with the same were challenged by the powerful reformers from outside of the *chaturvarna*. The first major enlightening revolt came from the *avarna* women in Thiruvithamkur who were barred from covering their breasts and chest. They defied these caste orders and the associated spatial material inequality and distributional injustice and claimed equal rights by covering their bodies (see Yesudas 1975). More than that, this was their attempt to embrace the ideas of modernity and collective consciousness of self-dignity. Despite a series of violence and torture from caste Hindu elites, these subaltern women continued to resist the caste order between 1813 and 1859. This movement led by the Nadar women came to be known as Channar revolt or *marumarakkal samaram*. It is the counter-discourse power represented by Narayana Guru (1856–1928), Ayyankali (1863–1941), and other visionaries that triggered the second phase of modernity, which was also strengthened by missionary activism challenging the norms of the Hindu state (Chandramohan 2016). As Osella and Osella (2000: 9–10) explain, the Ezhavas, inspired by Sree Narayana Guru, repudiated their nineteenth-century selves and created an enlightened modernity through a 'dialogue between local ideas of justice and equality and European-derived notions of modernity and reform'. *Swadeshabhimani*, the paper established by Vakkom Abdul Khader Moulavi in 1905 under the editorship of Ramakrishna Pillai, used cutting-edge press technology imported from England and made the birth of critical print modernity during this phase.

The first industrial workers trade union in Alappuzha was organized by one of Narayana Guru's disciples, Vadappuram Bava, on 31 March 1922, after Narayana Guru's encouragement, in continuation of his early preaching of education and organizing. It was much before the formation of a communist-led All India Trade Union Congress (AITUC) in the state. A monthly journal, *Thozhilali* (the Worker), was also published by him to address workers' concerns. their rights and material improvement. The association and the publication were the first to intervene in the right-making process for workers subjected to merchants from the local and colonial spheres. It also proved to be the embryonic form of the communist movement in the state. Ayyankali, the leader of the Pulayas, the former slave castes, not only challenged the caste Hindus when place–space exclusion was practised by the caste Hindus in using public roads, schools, and so on, but also forbade his communities from tilling lands owned by the caste Hindus unless Pulaya children were admitted to schools, a decision which drastically transformed the ecospatial exclusion practised by Hindus.[15] Anti-colonial, anti-feudal struggles such as the Malabar rebellion in 1921 (Panikkar 1989), the Kayyur–Karivellur–Kavumbayi protests and revolts in the 1940s (see Kurup 1988: 35–45; Radhakrishnan 1980), the temple entry movement in Thiruvithamkur, and other subaltern movements and protests including the Punnapra Vayalar revolts all constituted the desire for socialist modernity, a higher form of egalitarian existence (see Kusuman 1977; Jeffrey 1981) The evolving social formation and the civil society were embedded in grassroots uprisings, protests, and movements with more hope than despair.

In parallel to these reform protests, there was the *aikya Kerala* movement (literally United Kerala Movement) encompassing students, peasants, and various political parties, originally initiated by the Kerala Pradesh Congress

Committee from the 1920s onwards. This movement and campaigns for united Kerala were strengthened by the communist parties in alliance with almost all social and political forces and culminated in the formation of the state, as part of the Reorganization Act, 1956, on linguistic lines, which desired a linguistic nationality and autonomy within the federal setup (for more details, see Namboodirippad 1984). As part of the greater decolonizing movement and an anti-Hindu state at another level, the Congress Socialist Party was founded in 1934; this was followed by the creation of broad alliances of agricultural tenants in the north, landless industrial workers in the south, and newly formed transverse solidarities among the oppressed groups of the dominant religions (Hindus, Muslims, and Christians). This, in fact, proved to be the main base of the communist party immediately predating the formation of the state: in 1956, the two princely realms of Kerala, Kochi and Thiruvithamkur, and the Malabar region of the Madras Presidency were brought together to form the state, marking an overlapping stage – third in its sequence – in its modernity with the first communist government in power in 1957 in India (see Isaac 1985; Heller 1999; Jeffrey 2010; Lieten 1982; Menon 2007).[16]

This was in fact the culmination of the process of state-making as right-making, right-making as state-making: the oppressed and the marginalized challenged both internal and external colonialisms – the Hindu state and the colonial state – with egalitarian and ethical aspirations. The social formation that thus emerged in Kerala has taken shape in such a way that no social injustice will be tolerated by the people on the margins. The renaissance values as imbibed by the communist party in power can ill afford the violation of human rights or social injustice and if the state still fails in protecting them, no option was left for the marginalized other than to challenge the discourse power, often by sharpening identities of their own. This is what happened in most of the situations giving birth to protests and movements in the post-state-formation phase, challenging the hegemonic power relations.

Despite being led by the Communist Party of India, the acceptance of Nehruvian developmentalism by the newly formed state of Kerala – the state's first chief minister, E.M.S. Namboodirippad, acknowledged that he had taken lessons in communism from Nehru – marks the beginning of democratic polity. However, this phase of modernity remained incomplete as the land reforms in Kerala favoured the tenants rather than the tillers of the land themselves. In other words, while the credit for the protection of *kudikidapukar*s (hut dwellers) goes to K.R. Gowri Amma's Agrarian Relations Bill of the first communist government and the abolition of landlordism to the Achuthamenon-led government in 1970, the radical communist parliamentarian A.K. Gopalan still had to continue with his imaginative 'land grab' struggles to identify surplus land and bring it to the government's attention. The land reforms bill was originally the result of efforts taken by the E.M.S. Namboodirippad ministry (March 1967 to November 1969) when K.R. Gowri Amma was the revenue minister. Due to the twists in the coalition politics, the government fell and the same was implemented under the government led by the Achuthamenon ministry.[17] The actual tillers remained landless and so also materially deprived and politically marginalized with everyday forms of livelihood and identity struggles. There were winners and losers in these struggles from below, but they also marked one of the highest peaks of resistance in modern history as and when state-led and corporate-driven developmentalism (see Ferguson 1990) grew more intense.

This manuscript has yet another dimension in the sense that it critiques the stated view that Kerala is epoch-making and that Kerala's forms of resistance were something unique and require further qualification rather than casually presenting it to the readers. First, it is important to comprehend that Kerala has a political lineage of leftist movements, which stemmed from the activism of socially expressive groups and the deliberate organization of left party politics, particularly in the post-state-formation phase. The left-oriented state and its developmentalism have advanced the experience of what is called the Kerala model of development (see Drèze and Sen 1993, 1995; Franke and Chasin 1992, 1994 [1989]; Heller 1999; Kannan 1995; Parayil 2000; Ramachandran 1997; Kurien 2000; Roy and Raman 2024) but with its own kind of ecospatial outliers impacting on Dalits and Adivasis, who became the hardcore activists of the new subaltern social movements (Kurian 1995, 2000; Raman 2010a, 2010b, 2010c; 2020a; 2020b; Rammohan 2008; Mannathukkaren 2021). Second, Kerala's exceptionality has already been integrated into larger narratives, but the very struggles have demonstrated that the concept of 'model state' itself is problematic. In other words, Kerala is exceptional at one level – when it comes to its average state-wide performance with the given indicators such as education and health – but it is not free from the material deprivation and aspirations of Dalits and Adivasis. Third, the frequency of livelihood–environmental struggles in Kerala is much greater than similar movements in India or the Global South and this is despite the fact that Kerala outshines all other regions in terms of social development. Fourth, Kerala's environment has become increasingly fragile over the years, beginning with the plantation monoculture pattern practised under colonialism, and heavy pressure on land, and the current high levels of urbanization with all the attendant consequences on the livelihood–environmental nexus of the common people. This gains importance against the backdrop of the emerging debate on the extent to which the livelihood–environmental risks are human-made (see Beck 1992, 1999; Roy 2012; Raman 2020b; Roy and Raman 2024), what resources corporate capital, both with and without the help of the state, encloses, and how the state responds to ecospatial struggles and movements that are often scaled up in terms of identities as well, which cannot be understood in a linear sense as 'won' or 'lost' or sustained or abandoned (Hall 1991, 1996). No matter whether in Europe or the Global South, resistance and claim-making is incomplete, so is modernity (see Habermas 1987), while the subalterns forward the agenda of egalitarian struggles (see Mignolo 2000; Quijano 2000; Santos 2014; Raman 2017), as shown by Kerala to the Global South.

The monograph attempts to answer these concerns by narrating six major struggles that have occurred in Kerala since the first communist government (1957–1959), some of which have been termed successful and some remaining unresolved even now. The manuscript is thus about ecospatial livelihood–environmental and identity politics in Kerala and it narrates and analyses the historical and contemporary situations that shape and reshape the strategies and practices of larger environmental and identity politics in the state by occasionally drawing parallels from the rest of India and the Global South. The primary concern of this book project is thus to understand the story behind these livelihood–environmental resistance movements, what relationship they had with state-led developmentalism on the one hand and Kerala's own distinctive history on the other in terms of social resistance by the historically vulnerable social sections such as Dalits and indigenous communities (Adivasis), and what connections they bear with similar movements elsewhere in India and the Global South. By employing Kerala as an example, I also hope to engage with and broaden debates in political economy, political ecology, and subaltern politics.

Onsite/On-the-spot Ethnography: A Word

In terms of method, the study is reflexive at three levels. First, I have had an opportunity to participate in most of the struggles narrated in this monograph, mostly as a critical participant or as a sympathizer with an occasional physical presence. While I was active in supporting struggles such as those in Mavoor and Plachimada, my critical participant observation in other struggles such as

Chengara and Munnar enriched me with first-hand information on movement politics and its trajectories as I travelled to the sites with the objective of conducting on-the-spot ethnography of the particular struggles/events. This onsite/on-the-spot ethnography (Raman 2020a) differs from the practice adopted by the otherwise rich ethnographic tradition in organization scholarship (see Marcus and Fisher 1986). While an ethnographer is familiar to the research participants, the on-the-spot ethnographer is present in their midst to observe first-hand the 'diagnostic events' as referred to by Moore (1987: 730). Moore agrees with Foucault (1971) that while no single episteme could truly encompass the whole wide picture, there are many modes of knowing things capable of unravelling multiple meanings as and when we juxtapose competing events and ideas. It is my belief that on-the-spot ethnography helps in the understanding of diagnostic events by challenging the multiple hierarchies at various sites of struggle. I was able to interact directly with the protesting communities, and occasionally exchange ideas with them. While in the traditional mode of doing ethnography, the ethnographer's presence is a familiar sight for the research participant, 'on-the-spot ethnography' encourages communication and exchange of ideas between the two, as the latter participates first-hand in the processes of struggle, albeit in a limited fashion. My own social positioning in terms of caste, in that I am a male belonging to the larger category of other backward communities but still outside the Hindu caste hierarchy embodied in the *chaturvarna*, rendered me in a unique position as both observer and experiencer.

Second, as the study is integrationist and trans-disciplinary in terms of drawing insights from theoretical strands on post-colonial theory, political economy and ecology, and social reproduction crisis and identities, it offers unconventional explanations on a range of issues such as the nature of identities and the politics and nature of the state. The analytical distinctiveness of the study also provides a renewed understanding of the history, economy, and political anthropology of state formation and its transformation (see Scott 1985, 1990; Skocpol 1985) and a reformulation of the notion of civil society (see Gramsci 1971; Held 1993) and ecospatial resistance. Both the state and civil society, the latter with the subalterns playing a key role, mutually reinforce power through struggle and consent (see Gramsci 1971; also see Graeber 2013; Holloway 2002). Marginalized groups first recognize that if they do not engage in struggles, they do not become political subjects and do not play politics properly. Rather than leading to a new era of democracy with political pluralism and freedom of the press, the Arab Spring has replaced it with autocratic and religious fundamentalism in many regions, attributable to an absence of ideological clarity and enlightened imagination. Nonetheless, potentialities of both the Arab Spring and Occupy protests are still present, just as they are in Kerala's theatres of resistance.

Chapters and Chapter Summaries

The chapters are by and large organized chronologically. While some movements had their origins in the early post-state-formation years, others took shape in the new millennium, and some of them coexisted in various time periods. Importantly, some struggles also had colonial origins although they manifested only much later. Following the introductory chapter, 'What Is Politics Proper? Why Political Ecospatiality Matters?' the remaining seven chapters are arranged as follows.

Chapter 2: Birlas in Communist Kerala – Clash and Consensus as Subaltern Narratives

The first of the two water narratives relates to the pollution of the Chaliyar river in the early 1960s owing to pollutants discharged from the Birlas' rayon factory in the Kozhikode district of Kerala. It was on the government's initiative that the factory was set up in Mavoor. The Birlas had been attracted to the state by the prospect of a continuous supply of raw material, namely bamboo, for its pulp and fibre division, and were assured by the then communist state of industrial peace. However, once factory operations were underway, the local people began feeling the effects of toxic wastes generated by the plant. Moreover, events took an unexpected turn as factory operations began to deplete the natural resources of the region, endangering the livelihood of the indigenous communities. Equally important was the persistent protest by the workers for higher wages and salaries and better working conditions. This forced the people of Mavoor, Vazhakkad, and other neighbouring villages to launch their own protest movement with the support of the wider civil society, ultimately leading to the closure of the factory in 2001. This chapter is more about the total disregard for local livelihood concerns by Indian big capital that violated environmental standards, workers' rights, ethical development, and sustainable development, which, however, is counterbalanced by the generation of much-needed employment opportunities and income through tax collection. The chapter deals with the multiple ways in which the Indian big capital destroyed local life and how the local communities and people dealt with it through their protracted struggles, as the actual and potential benefits of extraction industries like rayon were overshadowed by the unscientific management of the manufacturing processes.

Chapter 3: Occupy Muthanga – Land, Forest, and Reinventing Indigeneity and Identity

On the day of Onam – the harvest festival of Malayalis – in 2001, hundreds of Adivasi families descended from the forest peripheries in Kerala to the state secretariat in the capital Thiruvananthapuram and pitched 'refugee huts' in protest against mass starvation deaths within the communities in a firm assertion of their land rights. This chapter deals with the struggles led by the Adivasis for the restoration of alienated lands. What they sought was their right to livelihood resources – land for the landless. They demanded a settlement outside the controversial Kerala Restriction on Transfer by and Restoration of Lands to Scheduled Tribes Bill, 1999, passed by the state legislative assembly, which repealed the original Kerala Scheduled Tribes (Restriction on Transfer of Lands and Restoration of Alienated Lands) Act, 1975. The Adivasi Dalit Samara Samithi (ADSS) affirmed that as many as 45,000 adivasi families were landless in the state. The movement escalated into an occupation of the Muthanga Range of the Wyanad Wildlife Sanctuary and brought the attention of the state to wider constitutional rights of the indigenous communities. This reinvention of politics, however, led to violent clashes with the armed police, with casualties on both fronts. I plan to elaborate on this episode as one of several in the world that mark the rise of a political consciousness that could be called indigeneity.

Chapter 4: Dalits and the Global Cola: Water, Power, and Resistance

The chapter explores the conflict between Coca-Cola and the local communities. The state of Kerala welcomed the multinational to its northern district of Palakkad in 2002 which, in a re-enactment of history, turned out to be a major livelihood issue for the local population. While Coca-Cola and PepsiCo have often been the target of attacks in many countries, particularly Colombia, Guatemala, Zimbabwe, the Philippines, and also in their home country, the United States, in protest against poor working conditions, in India the issues raised were related to environmental degradation and the contents of the drinks. The villagers of Plachimada were joined by social activists and NGOs protesting against the 100-odd cola-manufacturing units across the country, turning the Cola Quit Plachimada movement into a nationwide Cola Quit India movement. The present case offers insights into how a boycott introduces an element of challenge, and boycott politics becomes an expression of solidarity. As the chapter directly addresses the issue of privatization of water rights, the narrative is situated in the wider context of privatization of water resources and commoditization by global capital. Yet the chapter warns that no linear narrative could be drawn from this regarding the wider process of globalization as is usually done by scholars as the anti-cola movement was a struggle in its own right without much reference to the usual anti-globalization stance.

Chapter 5: Politics, Epistemology, and Environmental Modernity – Anti-endosulfan as Ethical Practice?

Another major environmental campaign that rocked the state of Kerala was the movement against the use of endosulfan on state-owned cashew plantations. Media reports such as 'Life Cheaper than Cashew' highlighting the health consequences of the aerial spraying of the pesticide helped build up public awareness of the serious consequences of this practice. Two of the local village *panchayats* passed a resolution demanding that the state desist from its aerial spraying of pesticides while highlighting the negative consequences of spraying; they also began to exercise their power as decentralized administrative units that are vested with the right to speak on behalf of their local communities, a right guaranteed by the Indian constitution. The mobilization of the local communities and the public outcry in Kerala became so strong that the government was forced to declare a ban on the use of endosulfan, which was also reflected in the discussions and debates at the Stockholm conference; this was followed by a decision in May 2011 to phase out the use of almost all pesticides in the state. However, the anti-edosulfan struggles have opened up spaces for new knowledge controversies (Whatmore 2009: 587–598; Foucoult 1980), conflicts, and legal tussles in Kerala.

Chapter 6: Caste, Land, and the State – What If Chengara Took the Place of Muthanga?

The chapter outlines the trajectories of the Dalit land struggles in the state with a focus on the occupation of a rubber plantation in Chengara, owned by one of the industrial conglomerates in India that had colonial origins. Apart from critically examining the land reforms passed by the leftist governments in the state, the chapter also addresses how caste and landlessness are interrelated and why the dominant political forces including the left are reluctant to push ahead with these reforms, particularly when the colonially evolved plantation capitalism continues to enjoy large areas of land under its control. This reluctance helps us understand the movement and, equally, the success of the Dalit families in this instance offers new insights into the nature of subaltern mobilization and strategy. While there were various similarities and dissimilarities between the Muthanga–Chengara occupations and other movements in India (such as the Chipko movement), particularly on the question of non-violence and the potential of imagined territories, this chapter highlights the livelihood–land struggles primarily by the Dalit communities. The local struggles for land resources and their implications are further explored by situating them in the wider context of Latin American and African resistance movements (Ecuador, Bolivia, Nigeria, and so on) towards autonomy, food sovereignty, and identity. More importantly, the historical origins of the Muthanga–Chengara movements are explored by situating the same in the state formation and the communists coming into power in 1957 and how subaltern rootedness of agency against the state and corporate capitalism forms the core of the analysis.

Chapter 7: Pombilai Orumai – Plantation Dalits, Intersectionality, and Power

The chapter on Dalit feminitude examines the strikes in the Kanan Devan plantations in Munnar and explores how they challenged the traditional understanding that workers themselves are not self-representable and are hence to be represented and through this how they challenged the capitalist and patriarchal forms of exploitation/oppression. It has been argued that the new 'destitute power' first challenged their own male-led trade unions by peeling away from them, thereby opening up a new politics of becoming, and simultaneously taking on the Tata-controlled Kanan Devan Hills Plantations Company Private Limited (KDHP). The chapter also explains why the claims made by the company for its refusal to offer higher bonuses and wages do not stand scrutiny and how corporate capital transfers crisis to the workers while refusing to share their prosperity with them. The historically marginalized and vulnerable social sections who are more suppressed intersectionally (see Crenshaw 1991; Raman 2020a, 2020b; Mies and Shiva 1993; Spivak 1988) began to assert their basic livelihood and egalitarian rights; the exclusionary processes involved can also be explained in terms of the changes in global capitalism. Yet the resolution is in the form of ground-level mobilization, and it was the victims who first came forward and got themselves identified in terms of a shared history of the intersectionality of exploitation and oppression. The chapter concludes that there has been an erosion in the right to have rights in the plantations, but the present struggle brings hope through self-assertion, when the trade unions have depoliticized themselves and corporate capital has intensified its exploitation/oppression.

Chapter 8: Ecospatiality: Right-Making/State-Making

By the time I completed the narratives of the struggles from the margins in the Indian south, we have been driven to a global existential crisis by the Covid-19 pandemic with the new normal uncertain as never before. The spatial material inequality, distributional injustice, and ecospatial exclusion, as noted earlier, have wider implications, as society and place–space dynamics are inextricably intertwined. The burden on the poor and the intersectionally marginalized social sections continues to be a key concern for Kerala, notwithstanding the state's accomplishments to date in controlling the Covid-19 outbreak as well as the natural dangers of the 2018 and 2019 floods. Instead, it is a state that both engages in and articulates the principles of an ethical and equitable future state. In order to interact with the idea of political ecospatiality, the concluding chapter situates the important conceptual tools. It also addresses the questions I raised at the beginning of the chapter, such as what constitutes politics in its true sense and why ecospatiality counts.

In spite of the right-making/state-making process as evolved through anti-colonial and anti-feudal struggles was briefly interrupted when the first communist state was toppled by the federal government's abuse of power, the state-making primarily under the left legacies continued but remained challenged by the subalterns through ecospatial struggles, allowing the state to remake itself in more egalitarian ways. This is further explored in the contemporary context of Kerala, which helps us to reinforce the fact that those involved in various struggles, such as the struggle for land resources, livelihood–environmental sustainability, and the recognition of identities, have no reason not to continue with their protests in more democratic ways. However, this is seen as a process of conscientization of the state from below and the very shaping of the state towards egalitarian forms of existence through an ever evolving right-making/state-making process primarily under the left legacies. While the Western Occupy movements faded away fast, the indigenous and Dalit occupy movements refused to do the same; while the Occupy movements do not challenge either the state or corporate capital directly, as is evident from their slogan that they are challenging the growing inequalities – we the 99 per cent – the indigenous and Dalit Occupy movements directly challenge the state and the combined forces of state and capital, and even trade unions. In other words, the struggles that we find in this part of the world are more about livelihood, environment, and identities, which, in turn, demands the presence of an 'effective state and its imaginative forms', not as 'governance-beyond-the state' as post-political critics often argue. Rather, it is a state that not only engages with but also articulates practices of an ethical and egalitarian future state. The question with which I begin this monograph, what is politics proper and why ecospatiality matters, gains all the more relevance in these contemporary times of crisis – natural and existential – as post-Covid-19 capitalism the world over is more aggressive and predatory. In this regard, Kerala offers alternatives and contributes to enlightening the Global South with the concepts of political ecospatiality and right-making as state-making; however, the question of where we are now remains unresolved.

Notes

1. The first major Occupy protest to receive widespread attention, Occupy Wall Street in New York City's Zuccotti Park, began on 17 September 2011; this was followed a large number of Occupy protests, first in the United States and then in Europe and the United Kingdom. The Occupy sites in Washington, DC, and St Paul's at London – where this author had the chance to participate – were evicted by the police and led to the simultaneous rise and disappearance of the protests. The Occupy Protests worldwide were demanding democracy as against the corporate engulfment of the world and socio-economic inequality. These movements were inspired by the Arab Spring, a series of uprisings and armed rebellions across the Arab world beginning with Tunisia and spreading across Libya, Egypt, Yemen, Syria, and Bahrain, demanding a change in the government. See Achcar (2016); for a recent survey of global protests, see Ortiz, Burke, Berrada, and Cortes-Saenz (2022); Fabian (2022); also see della Porta (2017) and Davenport and Armstrong (2004).
2. Drawing insights from Baruch Spinoza, Michael Hardt and Antonio Negri (2005) expand the notion of multitude as a theory of political subject challenging

the Empire. The multitude has found its expression in the occupy protests. For details see Hardt and Negri (2000, 2009, 2012).

3. There exists a vast body of literature on the area which includes Desai (2015); Baviskar (1997); Guha (1992, 1995); Rangan (2003); D'Souza (2002); Guha and Martinez-Alier (1997); Wood (2007) and Pathak (2020).
4. This is how I would reformulate Charles Tilly's classic statement in the context of European history that 'war made the state and the state made war' (Tilly 1975: 42).
5. L.D. Wyse constructs the notion of 'ecospatiality'/'ecospatial orientation' as a way of comprehending place in simultaneously ecological and geographical terms, which is noteworthy, but confined to literary criticism with a focus on twentieth-century literary representations in the United States. See Wyse (2021).
6. Varying notions of politics, political, and politics proper are explored by various scholars (see in particular Badiou 2018; Rancière 1999; Schmitt 1996; Laclau and Mouffe 1985; Hardt and Negri 2005; Žižek 1997). Inspired from Foucault's notion of 'biopolitics' and Arendt's notion of ' right to have rights', Agamben (1998) has radicalized the notion of politics in *Homo Sacer* – which is not free from limitations – wherein *zoe* refers to life as bare physical survival and only *bios* can be considered as the base of the emerging politics; this has been further examined by Mbembe in *Critique of Black Reason* (2017). One common theme across such contributions is the extermination of the humans for the survival of the nation under authoritarian regimes wherein racism, class, capitalism, and so on, are used as political tools.
7. Gramscian political-cultural identities within the Subaltern Studies Project of South Asian and Latin American scholarship experienced several levels of subordination based on class, caste, and gender. *The Subaltern School of historiography emerged in India in the 1980s, inspired from Thompsonian task of writing history from below, as a response both to the elitist method of historiography and to Marxism with its emphasis on class and mode of production narrative in preference to identities*; see the 12-volume *Subaltern Studies: Writings on South Asian History and Society* (Delhi: Oxford University Press, 1982–2003), the first six edited by Ranajit Guha, the seventh volume by Partha Chatterjee and Gyanendra Panday, the eighth volume as essays in honour of Ranajit Guha edited by David Arnold and David Hardiman, and the remaining volumes edited by the editorial collective.
8. It is worth noting that there exist historiographies of popular protests in India that do not follow the subaltern studies trope, and even reject it (see Chandavarkar 1998; Gooptu 2001).

9. What the author considers crucial is treating resistance as modernity, as he has previously argued that there are many shades of modernity (see Raman 2017: 91–110) apart from the fact that it is often 'muddled' (see Chakrabarty 2011; Eisenstadt 2001; Roy 2016; Woodside 2006; Israel 2009), 'vexed', and even 'slippery' (Washbrook 2010).
10. For Marxist critiques of the posthumanist/new materialist reading of the social dynamics, see Choat (2011).
11. Through what will be referred to as 'chains of equivalence' (Laclau and Mouffe 1985) and 'politics of belonging' (Yuval-Davis 2004), 'transversal solidarity politics' will be realized through ecospatial struggles – which are in and of themselves political in nature – eliminating the concern for intra-group differences as outlined by intersectionality scholars (see Crenshaw 1991; Raman 2020a).
12. In response to the movements that were starting to spread throughout India, the Central government finally brought various reserve forests together – the Silent Valley (89.52 square kilometres), new Amarambalam (80 square kilometres), Attapadi (120 square kilometres) in Kerala, and Kunda (100 square kilometres) in nearby Tamil Nadu to form the National Rainforest Biosphere of 389.52 square kilometres.
13. Fraser's critique (2014) is that modernity in the Habermasian sense is elitist, leading to the spread of science and universality of reason with its incompleteness as a teleological condition. An equally important critique that Fraser makes is that Habermas does not provide space for the marginalized and the silenced. Santos (2016) too considers Habermasian universalism to be an 'imperialist universalism' and thus limiting with a fair degree of control over 'what it includes and excludes'. The process of 'sociology of emergences' and translation as conceived by Santos is by and large limited to processes within cultures and boundaries, which is restrictive in itself, and hence a stepping out from the confines of bordered cultures renders the concept more comprehensible and 'mutually intelligible'.
14. While there are several versions of the Chipko movement, a significant intervention is found in Guha (1989), Pathak (2020) and its critiques. For a critical review, see D'Souza (2002: 31–49); also see Saberwal (1999); Rangarajan (2006).
15. A number of leaders were involved in the renaissance movement, including Chattampi Swamikal (1853–1924), Poykayil Appachan (1879–1939), and so on.
16. It was the second ever communist government to be democratically elected, after communist success in the 1945 elections in the Republic of San Marino, a sovereign ministate in Europe.

17. Given the fact that ideas are the primary agents of change, the credit should go to the E.M.S. Namboodirippad ministry.

References

Achcar, G. (2016). *Morbid Symptoms: The Arab Uprising Five Years On.* London: University of California Press.

Agamben, Giorgio (1993). *The Coming Community.* Minneapolis: Minnesota University Press.

——— (1998). *Homo Sacer: Sovereign Power and Bare Life.* Translated by D. Heller-Roazen. Stanford, California: Stanford University Press.

Ambedkar, B.R. (1948). The untouchables: Who were they and why they became untouchables. *New American Ethnologist* 29 (4): 981–1002.Arendt, H. (1958). *The Human Condition.* Chicago: University of Chicago Press.

Arnold, David, and Ramachandra Guha, eds. (1995). *Nature, Culture, Imperialism: Essays on the Environmental History of South Asia.* Delhi: Oxford University Press.

Badiou, A. (2004). *Theoretical Writings.* Translated and edited by A. Toscano and R. Brassier. London: Continuum.

———. (2018). *Can Politics Be Thought?* Durham: Duke University Press.

Bankoti, T.S. (2018). *Chipko Movement.* New Delhi: Global Vision Publishing House.

Barad, Karen (2007). *Meeting the Universe Halfway: Quantum Physics and the Entanglement of Matter and Meaning.* Durham: Duke University Press.

Baviskar, Amita (1997). *In the Belly of the River: Tribal Conflicts over Development in the Narmada Valley.* Delhi: Oxford University Press.

Beck, U. (1992). *Risk Society: Towards a New Modernity.* London: Sage.

——— (1999). *World Risk Society.* Cambridge: Polity Press

Blaike, P. (1986). *The Political Economy of Soil Erosion in Developing Countries.* Oxford: Longman.

Bryant, R., and S. Bailey (1997). *Third World Political Ecology.* London: Routledge.

Butler, Judith (1999 [1990]). *Gender Trouble: Feminism and the Subversion of Identity.* New York: Routledge.

Castree, N. (1995). The nature of produced nature: Materiality and knowledge construction in Marxism. *Antipode* 27 (1): 12–48.

Centre for Science and Environment (2019). *State of India's Environment.* New Delhi: Centre for Science and Environment.

Chakrabarty, D. (2011). The muddle of modernity. *American Historical Review* 116 (3): 663–675.

Chandavarkar, Raj (1998). *Imperial Power and Popular Politics: Class, Resistance and The State in India, c. 1850–1950.* Cambridge: Cambridge University Press.

Chandramohan, P. (2016). *Developmental Modernity in Kerala: Narayana Guru, SNDP and Social Reforms.* New Delhi: Tulika Books.

Choat, Simon (2011). Science, agency and ontology: A historical-materialist response to new materialism. *Political Studies* 66 (4): 1027–1042.

Collins, P.H. (1990). *Black Feminist Thought Knowledge Consciousness and the Politics of Empowerment.* Boston: Unwin Hyman.

Coordination of Democratic Rights Organisations. (2019). *Tuticorin Massacre: A Corporate Developmental Terrorism.* Tuticorin: CDRO.

Crenshaw, K. (1991). 'Mapping the margins: Intersectionality, identity politics and violence against women of color. *Stanford Law Review* 43 (6): 1241–1299.

D'Souza, D. (2002). *The Narmada Daned: An Inquiry into the Politics of Development.* Delhi: Penguin.

Davenport, C., and D.A. Armstrong (2004). Democracy and the violation of human rights: A statistical analysis from 1976–1996. *American Journal of Political Science* 48 (3): 538–554.

della Porta, D., ed. (2017). *Global Diffusion of Protest: Riding the Protest Wave in the Neoliberal Crisis.* Amsterdam: Amsterdam University Press.

Desai, Manisha. (2015). *Subaltern Movements in India: Gendered Geographies of Struggle against Neoliberal Development.* Routledge Contemporary South Asia Series. New Delhi: Routledge.

Drèze, J., and A.K. Sen (1993). *Hunger and Public Action.* Oxford: Oxford University Press.

——— (1995). *India: Economic Development and Social Opportunity.* Oxford: Oxford University Press.

Eisenstadt, S.N. (2001). Multiple modernities. *Daedalus* 129 (1): 1–29.

Escobar, A. (1995). *Encountering Development: The Making and Unmaking of the Third World.* Princeton: Princeton University Press.

Fabian, K.P. (2022). *Arab Spring That Was and Wasn't.* London: Macmillan Education.

Featherstone, D. (2008). *Resistance, Space and Political Identities: The Making of Counter-Global Networks.* Oxford: Wiley-Blackwell.

Ferguson, J. (1990). *The Anti-Politics Machine: 'Development,' Depoliticization, and Bureaucratic Power in Lesotho.* Cambridge: Cambridge University Press.

Foucault, M. (1971). *The Order of Things: An Archaeology of the Human Sciences.* Translated by Alan Sheridan. New York: Random House.

——— (1980). *Power/Knowledge: Selected Interviews and Other Writings.* New York: Pantheon.

——— (2001). *Madness and Civilization*. Milton Park: Routledge.

Franke, R.W., and B.H. Chasin (1992). Kerala state, India: Radical reform as development. *International Journal of Health Services* 22 (1): 139–156.

——— (1994 [1989]). Kerala: Radical reform as development. *International Journal of Social Determinants of Health and Health Services* 22 (1): 139–156.

Fraser, N. (2014). Transnationalizing the public sphere: On the legitimacy and efficacy of public opinion in a post-Westphalian world. In N. Fraser et al., *Transnationalizing the Public Sphere*, ed. K. Nash, pp. 8–42, 129–156. Cambridge: Polity.

Gadgil, Madhav, and Ramachandra Guha (1994). *This Fissured Land: An Ecological History of India*. Delhi: Oxford University Press.

Gooptu, Nandini (2001). *The Politics of the Urban Poor in Early-Twentieth Century India*. Cambridge: Cambridge University Press.

Graeber, D. (2013). *The Democracy Project: A History, A Crisis, A Movement*. Bristol: Allen Lane.

Gramsci, A. (1971). *Selections from the Prison Notebooks of Antonio Gramsci*. New York: International Publishers.

Greenough, Paul, and Anna Lowenhaupt Tsing, eds. (2004). *Nature in the Global South*. New Delhi: Orient Longman.

Gregory, D. (1994). *Geographical Imaginations*. Sage: London.

Guha, Ranajit (1982). *Subaltern Studies I: Writings on South Asian History and Society*. Delhi: Oxford University Press.

Guha, Ramchandra (1989). Radical American environmentalism and wilderness preservation: A third world critique. *Environmental Ethics* 11 (1): 71–83.

——— (1992). *The Unquiet Woods: Ecological Change and Peasant Resistance in the Himalaya*. California: University of California Press.

Guha, Ramachandra, and J. Martinez-Alier (1997). *Varieties of Environmentalism: Essays North and South*. London: Earthscan.

Guru, G., and S. Sarukkai (2012). *The Cracked Mirror: An Indian Debate on Experience and Theory*. New Delhi: Oxford University Press.

Habermas, Jürgen (1987). *The Philosophical Discourse of Modernity: Twelve Lectures*. Translated by Frederick Lawrence. Cambridge: Polity in association with Basil Blackwell

Hall, Stuart (1991). Old and new identities: Old and new ethnicities. In *Culture, Globalization, and the World System: Contemporary Conditions for the Representation of Identity*, ed. Anthony D. King, pp. 41–68. Binghamton: State University of New York Press.

——— (1996). *Questions of Cultural Identity*. London: Sage.

Hallward, P. (2003). *Badiou: A Subject to Truth*. Minneapolis: University of Minnesota Press.

Hardt, Michael, and Antonio Negri (2000). *Empire*. New York: Harvard University Press.

——— (2005). *Multitude: War and Democracy in the Age of Empire*. London: Hamish Hamilton.

——— (2009). *Commonwealth*. New York: Harvard University Press.

——— (2012). *Declaration*. New York: Argo-Navis US.

Harvey, D. (2000). *Spaces of Hope*. Berkeley, CA: University of California Press.

Held, D. (1993). Democracy: Past, present and possible futures. *Alternatives* 18 (3): 259–271.

Heller, P. (1999). *The Labor of Development: Workers and the Transformation of Capitalism in Kerala, India*. Ithaca, NY: Cornell University Press.

Holloway, John (2002). *Change the World Without Taking Power: The Meaning of Revolution Today*. London: Pluto Press.

Howarth, D. (2006). Space, subjectivity, and politics. *Alternatives: Global, Local, Political* 31 (2): 105–134.

Isaac, T. (1985). From caste consciousness to class consciousness: Aleppey coir workers during inter-war period. *Economic and Political Weekly* 20 (4): 5–18.

Israel, Jonathan. (2009). *A Revolution of the Mind: Radical Enlightenment and the Intellectual Origins of Modern Democracy*. Princeton: Princeton University Press.

Jeffrey, R. (1981). India's working class revolt: Punnapry-Vayalar and the Communist 'conspiracy' of 1946. *Indian Economic and Social History Review* 18 (2).

Kannan, K.P. 1995. Public intervention and poverty alleviation: A study of the declining incidence of rural poverty in Kerala, India. *Development and Change* 26 (4): 701–728.

Kiøsterud, Erland (2021). Agamben and the ethics of abnegation. *Modern Times Review*. http://home.online.no/~ekio/index.cfm (accessed 7 May 2023).

Kohn, M. (2003). *Radical Space*. Ithaca, NY: Cornell University Press.

Kurien, J. (2000). The Kerala model: Its central tendency and the outlier. In *Kerala: The Development Experience*, ed. G. Parayil, pp. 178–197. London: Zed Books.

Kurup, K.K.N. (1988) Peasantry and the anti-imperialist struggles in Kerala. *Social Scientist* 16 (9): 35–45.

Kusuman, K.K. (1977). *The Extremist Movement in Kerala*. Trivandrum: Chaithram Publications.

Laclau, Ernesto, ed. (1994). *The Making of Political Identities*. London: Verso.

Laclau, Ernesto, and Chantal Mouffe (1985). *Hegemony and Socialist Strategy: Towards a Radical Democratic Politics*. London: Verso.

Lefebvre, H. (1991). *The Production of Space*. Oxford: Basil Blackwell.

Lieten, G.K. (1982). *The First Communist Ministry in Kerala, 1957–9*. Calcutta: KP Bagchi & Co.

Mannathukkaren, N. (2021). *Communism, Subaltern Studies and Postcolonial Theory: The Left in South India*. Milton Park: Routledge.

Massey, D. (1994). *Space, Place, and Gender*. Minneapolis, MN: University of Minnesota Press.

Marcus, G.E., and M.J. Fischer, M.J. (1986). *Anthropology as Cultural Critique: An Experimental Moment in the Human Sciences*. Chicago, IL: University of Chicago.

McCarty, Philip Curtis, ed. (2012). *Integrated Perspectives in Global Studies*. San Diego, CA: Cognella.

Mbembe, A. (2017). *Critique of Black Reason*. Durham: Duke University Press.

Melucci, A. (1989). *Nomads of the Present: Social Movements and Individual Needs in Contemporary Society*. Philadelphia: Temple University Press.

Menon, D. (2007). *Caste, Nationalism and Communism in South India: Malabar 1900–1948*. Cambridge: Cambridge University Press.

Mies, Maria, and Vandana Shiva (1993). *Ecofeminism*. Delhi: Kali.

Mignolo, W. (2000). *Local Histories/Global Designs: Essays on the Coloniality of Power, Subaltern Knowledges and Border Thinking*. Princeton, NJ: Princeton University Press.

Moore, S.F. (1987). Explaining the present: Theoretical dilemmas in processual ethnography. *American Ethnologist* 14 (4): 727–736.

Namboodirippad, E.M.S. (1984). Aikyakerala: Realization of a dream. In *Kerala Society and Politics An Historical Survey*, pp. 168–183. Thiruvananthapuram: National Book Centre.

Nash, K. (2001). 'The cultural turn' in social theory: Towards a theory of cultural politics. *Sociology* 35 (1): 77–92.

Noys, B. (2011). The discreet charm of Bruno Latour, or the critique of 'anti-critique'. Paper presented at the Centre for Critical Theory, University of Nottingham, 8 December.

Ortiz, I., S. Burke, M. Berrada, and H. Cortes-Saenz (2022). *World Protests: A Study of Key Protest Issues in the 21st Century*. New York: Palgrave Macmillan. Osella, F. and C. Osella (2000). *Social Mobility in Kerala: Modernity and Identity in Conflict*. London: Pluto Press.

Panikkar, K.N. (1989). *Against Lord and State: Religion and Peasant Uprisings in Malabar, 1836–1921*. Oxford: Oxford University Press.

Pathak, S. (2020). *The Chipko Movement: A People's History*. New Delhi: Permanent Black.

Parayil, G. (2000). *Kerala: The Development Experience*. London: Zed Books.

Peluso, Nancy Lee, and Michael Watts, eds. (2001). *Violent Environments*. Ithaca: Cornell University Press.

Piketty, T. (2021). *Time for Socialism*. New Haven: Yale University Press.

Quijano, A. (2000). Coloniality of power, ethnocentrism, and Latin America. *NEPANTLA* 1 (3): 533–580.

Ramachandran, V.K. (1997). On Kerala's development achievements. In *Indian Development: Selected Regional Perspectives*, ed. J. Drèze and A. Sen, pp. 205–356. Oxford: Oxford University Press.

Raman, K. Ravi, ed. (2010a). *Development, Democracy and the State: Critiquing Kerala Model of Development*. London and New York: Routledge.

——— (2010b). *Global Capital and Peripheral Labour: The History and Political Economy of Plantation Workers in India*. London and New York: Routledge.

——— (2010c). Transverse solidarity: Water, power, and resistance. *Review of Radical Political Economics* 42 (2): 251–268.

——— (2017). Subaltern modernity: Kerala, the eastern theatre of resistance in the Global South. *Sociology* 51 (1): 91–110.

——— (2020a). Can the Dalit woman speak: How intersectionality helps advance postcolonial organization scholarship? *Organization* 27 (2): 272–290.

——— (2020b). Ecospatiality: Transforming Kerala's post-flood riskscapes. *Cambridge Journal of Regions, Economy and Society* 13 (2): 319–341.

Ramesh, Jairam (2015). *Green Signals: Ecology, Growth and Democracy in India*. New Delhi: Oxford University Press.

Rammohan, K.T. (1991). Understanding Keralam: The tragedy of radical scholarship. *Monthly Review* 43 (7): 18–31.

——— (2008). Caste and landlessness in Kerala: Signals from Chengara. *Economic and Political Weekly* 43 (37): 14–16.

Rancière, Jacques (1999 [1995]). *Disagreement: Politics and Philosophy*. Minnesota: University of Minnesota Press.

——— (2001). Ten theses on politics. *Theory and Event* 5 (3). https://muse.jhu.edu/issue/2225.

Rangarajan, M. (2006). *Environmental Issues in India: A Reader*. Noida: Pearson Education India.

Roy, I. (2016). Equality against hierarchy: Imagining modernity in subaltern India. *Contributions to Indian Sociology* 50 (1): 80–107.

Roy, T. (2012). *Natural Disasters and Indian History*. New Delhi: Oxford University Press.

Saberwal, Vasant (1999). *Pastoral Politics: Shepherds, Bureaucrats, and Conservation in the Western Himalaya*. New Delhi: Oxford University Press.

Sahu, G. (2008). Mining in the Niyamgiri Hills and tribal rights. *Economic and Political Weekly* 43 (15): 19–21.

Said, E. (1978). *Orientalism: Western Conceptions of the Orient*. New York: Pantheon Books.

Santos, B. de Sousa (2014). *Epistemologies of the South: Justice against Epistemicide*. London: Routledge.

Schmitt, C. (1996). *The Concept of the Political*. Chicago: The University of Chicago Press.

Scott, J.C. (1985). *Weapons of the Weak: Everyday Forms of Peasant Resistance*. Yale: Yale University Press.

Sewell, W.H. (1996). Three temporalities: Toward a sociology of the event. In *The Historic Turn in the Human Sciences*, ed. T. McDonald, pp. 245–280. Ann Arbor, MI: University of Michigan Press.

Skocpol, Theda (1985). Bringing the state back in: Strategies for current research. In *Bringing the State Back In*, ed. Peter Evans, D. Rueschemeyer, and T. Skocpol, pp. 317–352. New York: Cambridge University Press

Spivak, G.C. (1987). *In Other Worlds: Essays in Cultural Politics*. London: Methuen.

——— (1988). Can the subaltern speak? In *Marxism and the Interpretation of Culture*, ed. C. Nelson and L. Grossberg, pp. 271–317. Urbana, IL: University of Illinois Press.

Subaltern Studies I–VI (1982–89), ed. Ranajit Guha (Delhi: Oxford University Press); vol. VII (1992), ed. Gyanendra Pandey and Partha Chatterjee (Delhi: Oxford University Press); vol. VIII (1993), ed. David Arnold and David Hardiman (Delhi: Oxford University Press).

Thorat, S., and K.S. Newman, eds. (2010). *Blocked by Caste: Economic Discrimination and Social Exclusion in Modern India*. New Delhi: Oxford University Press.

Tilly, Charles (1975). Reflections on the history of European statemaking. In *The Formation of the National States in Western Europe*, ed. C. Tilly, pp. 3–83. Princeton: Princeton University Press.

Wallerstein, I. (2000). *The Essential Wallerstein*. New York: New Press.

Wapner, Paul (1996). *Environmental Activism and World Civic Politics*. Albany: State University of New York Press.

Washbrook, David (2010). Intimations of modernity in South Asia. *South Asian History and Culture* 1 (1): 125–148.

Whatmore, Sarah J. (2009). Mapping knowledge controversies: Science, democracy and the redistribution of expertise. *Progress in Human Geography* 33 (5): 587–598.

Woodside, Alexander (2006). *Lost Modernities: China, Vietnam, Korea, and The Hazards of World History*. Cambridge, MA: Harvard University Press.

Wyse, L.D. (2021). *Ecospatiality: A Place-Based Approach to American Literature*. Iowa: University of Iowa Press.

Yesudas, R.N. (1975). *A People's Revolt in Travancore*. Thiruvananthapuram: Kerala Historical Society.

Yuval-Davis, N. (2004). Borders, boundaries and the politics of belonging. In *Ethnicity, Nationalism and Minority Rights*, ed. S. May, T. Modood, and J. Squires, pp. 214–230. Cambridge: Cambridge University Press.

Žižek, Slavoj (1997). Multiculturalism, or, the cultural logic of multinational capitalism. *New Left Review* 1 (225): 28–50.

——— (1998). A Leftist Plea for 'Eurocentrism'. *Critial Enquiry* 24 (4): 988–1009.

2

Birlas in Communist Kerala

Clash and Consensus as Subaltern Narratives

Nehruvian developmentalism reigned supreme in newly independent India in the 1950s and 1960s, and it was against this backdrop that the Soviet-inspired Communist Party came to power in Kerala in 1957, a year after state formation, creating history as the first democratically elected communist government[1] in the world. It epitomized a smooth transition to power for the communists, based on the premise of peaceful coexistence as legitimized by Khrushchev in post-Stalinist USSR.[2] While Nehru found inspiration in the Soviet principles of socialism, E.M. Sankaran Namboodirippad, the first communist chief minister of Kerala, in turn, admitted to having borrowed Marxism from Nehru, along with which he would also have been persuaded to open up the newly formed Kerala to state-driven developmentalism. The industrial road was thus extended from Delhi to Kerala with the left government facilitating the entry of Indian capital, the Birlas, to the state by establishing the Gwalior Rayons Silk Manufacturing (Wvg.) Company Ltd, Mavoor, on the outskirts of Kozhikode, which soon became a hub of industrial activity with the company setting up a rayon factory that attracted a huge mass of industrial workers. With hundreds of thousands of jobs on offer, the factory provided fresh employment opportunities for the families in the region; however, the initial euphoria gave way to protests when the pollution of the Chaliyar River by factory effluents became evident, virtually destroying the livelihoods of large numbers of families and rendering the water unusable, eventually forcing the Birlas to leave the state. Although the company did shut down its factory, it left in its wake devastated bamboo forests and a state economy that had suffered heavy losses by supporting the business venture; their departure was thus welcomed by the public even though it meant the loss of livelihood for a huge number of workers.

Mapping Resources: Agreements after Agreements

Surveying and mapping were key instruments of colonialism that remained in use in state-driven development projects in collaboration with big capital, as in the case of bamboo resource mapping and indigenous livelihood in Nilambur-Waynad facilitating the territorial enclosure of resources for the Indian big bourgeoisie in Mavoor. The communist government appointed Sivarajan, the then assistant conservator of forests, to survey the availability of bamboo resources and also assist the state in establishing resource territorial borders for the proposed rayon pulp factory (see Sivarajan 1959). This was followed by agreements after agreements allowing the Indian big capital to expand its empire in the Western Ghats with far-reaching implications on livelihood–environment ecosystems. The Government of India has also taken measures for resource planning for the promotion of paper and pulp industry.

The original agreement between the Kerala government and the Birlas signed on 3 May 1958 was historic as it assured the company access to sufficient raw materials – bamboo in particular – at nominal prices, and the use of land and water on terms favourable to the company. The agreement permitted the company to set up a 100-tonne-per-day rayon-grade pulp manufacturing factory in Mavoor on the banks of the River Chaliyar. The company would have 'the exclusive rights and license for a term of 20 years' to fell and cut bamboo from the reserved forests of the Nilambur valley.[3] As per this master agreement, the government was committed to supplying 1,60,000 tonnes of bamboo every year as raw material to the factory at a minimal rate of INR 1 per tonne. A year before the commencement of factory operations in 1963, and now with an expansion plan to produce 200 tonnes per day of rayon-grade pulp – which was double the amount originally proposed – the company observed that the raw material requirement as agreed upon with the government would be inadequate, which would be met by felling more trees and removing bamboo from 'additional contract areas' (ACAs) in Nilambur valley.[4]

Grasim sought a number of supplemental agreements with the state government and kept enclosing more and more forest areas with the intention of increasing production and accumulation of surplus. With a commitment of 2 lakh tonnes annually (by adding 40,000 tons to over and above the original 1,60,000 tons) and the inclusion of the forest divisions of Wayanad, Kozhikode, Nenmara, and Palghat, the first such supplemental agreement was signed with the state on 6 August 1962. Additionally, the state consented to allow the company to harvest and remove additional amounts of bamboo, if any, from the contract areas (CAs) and ACAs to support the factory's potential to produce up to 200 tonnes of pulp per day. In an intriguing turn of events, the government also gave the Birlas permission to buy private forests of 30,000 acres from Nilambur Kovilakam in order to grow the captive plantation and transform those lands into the species of raw materials needed for the plant, particularly eucalyptus. Further, the government also agreed not to acquire such areas for a minimum period of 60 years, which, however, was violated by the state but only for public gain.

The private forests purchased by the Birlas was thus vested in the government after the Kerala Private Forests (Vesting and Assignment) Act of 1971 was passed. Though the Act was challenged by the Birlas and was invalidated by the High Court, it was reinstated by the Supreme Court in the government's favour. The government and the firm were embroiled in disputes and arbitration proceedings. The latter intended to increase the plant's capacity and calculated that it would need 3.60 lakh tonnes of raw materials to operate at full capacity, and the state gave the permission to clear and purchase as much more bamboo as was needed for the plant's capacity expansion, in addition to the committed amount. If this was not available, the corporate capital was also allowed to access it outside of the CAs and ACAs. While the government was generally committed to providing 2 lakh tonnes per year to the Birlas, especially in light of the proposed Hindustan Newsprint Ltd under the public sector by the Government of India, what the state government was actually doing was allowing the company to enclose and extract bamboo and eucalyptus resources outside the original CAs.

The company shall have the exclusive right, liberty, and licence to extract and remove the entire quantity of bamboo available in the CAs at a marginally increased price, at INR 1.67 per tonne. The state also allowed the company to enclose forest areas outside of the CAs worth an increased quantity of 20,000 tonnes with a marginal increase in prices – at a rate ranging from INR 2.78 to INR 36 per tonne, depending on weighment and the day of felling. The state further assured eucalyptus from state plantations to make good the deficit of the total agreed quantity of 2 lakh tonnes at a rate of INR 22.50 per tonne. The state also committed that if bamboo areas had to be destroyed for silvicultural purposes, limited to 100 acres, the government would replant the areas so destroyed with pulpwood plants, again to feed Grasim Industries (Government of Kerala and Grasim Industries 1958).

Paradoxically enough, the government failed to formulate any rules and regulations either for allotment of areas, felling practices, collection of raw materials, or any kind of monitoring and evaluation of extraction of resources.

For almost one and half decades, these were completely left with the company. The third supplemental agreement was thus the outcome of setting the rules and regulations agreed upon, which was signed on 20 November 1976. In the following years, two major developments took place, which were not in favour of the Birlas. First, in 1978, the Kerala government passed the Kerala Forest Produce (Fixation and Selling Price) Act of 1978, which stopped all subsidies for Grasim Industries. This led Grasim Industries to enter into disputes and arbitrations in various courts, also along the lines of labour disputes, which precipitated into a long lockout between 1985 and 1988, inviting A. Vasu (popularly known as GROW Vasu) to lead the historic workers' struggle against the Birlas (see Ram Mohan and Raman 1988, 1989). This was a historic movement in which several unions were involved in protests and struggles in front of the factory. Second, with the establishment of Hindustan Newsprint Limited (HNL) in the public sector in Kerala, Grasim Industries for the first time had to face a major competition for its raw materials in the state and for its products in the country. Some of the decisions to settle the lockout, forming the fourth supplemental agreement signed on 27 October 1988, at one level allowed further extraction of resources at cheap rates – 2 lakh tonnes of wood per annum, a combination of bamboo and eucalyptus. Almost 80 per cent would be eucalyptus and the remaining 20 per cent bamboo at a subsidised rate of INR 250 per tonne – as against the market price of INR 2,000 per tonne – besides squeezing job rights, including a ban on labour strikes for a five-year period, the details of which we will explore soon. Evidence suggests that Grasim Industries was actually procuring bamboo and eucalyptus much more than what was originally agreed upon, which was also a source of conflict between the Forest Department and the Grasim management.

Emergence of the Modern Factory Complex

In 1960, the Kerala government acquired 136.26 acres of land next to the Chaliyar River from private landowners and gave it to Grasim Enterprises. The Birlas finally had 320.78 acres of land in possession and ownership for the factory alone after acquiring additional 50.90 acres in 1964, 0.91 acres in 1965, 50 acres in 1977 through the government, and the company itself buying 82.37 acres as and when it required. (see Government of Kerala/Kerala State Planning Board 1997: 32), which also involved dispossessing the local populace. The resultant primitive accumulation in the Marxist state, however, was legitimized through compensation for their lands, except in some cases of dispute with the local households.[5] It was agreed that if the land was not used for industrial purposes, it would be taken back by the government. The affected village was structured along semi-feudal lines with caste Hindus and a few prominent Ezhavas owning most of the lands, while the Muslim community sought livelihood through fishing and small trade, and so also the Dalit communities from whom the agricultural workers were drawn (see Vidhyadharan 2009). The setting up of the factory and the associated construction work began to transform the entire village and the agrarian community with the development of roads and infrastructure, leading to the gradual emergence of a township in Mavoor (Government of Kerala/Kerala State Planning Board 1997: 12) with not less than INR 92 lakh in wages circulating every month. The now famous Mavoor road was constructed on the initiative of the company. The physical infrastructure of the company involved officers' quarters, a power house, a hospital, an English medium school, and a labour colony, with the foundation stone for the latter (Vidhyadharan 2009) being laid by V.V. Giri, the then Governor of Kerala, who, in his public speech, advised that it should not be called a labour colony but to no avail, until Murkoth Ravunni, a retired civil servant, took charge of the administration of the company and later introduced labour-friendly reforms: temporary workers were made permanent, and in the newly renamed 'labour quarters' a new room was added in each residence (Vidhyadharan 2009: 184).

The Birlas' Kerala venture in Mavoor – Grasim Industries – consisted of three divisions: a rayon-grade pulp division, a viscose staple fibre (VSF) division, and a paper plant. The company started operations with the rayon-grade pulp division and the others followed as part of its expansion. The factory began functioning in 1963 with an original capacity of 100 tonnes per day with a capital investment of INR 18 crores (1 crore = 10 million), the first major industrial establishment in the state. The installed capacity was increased to 200 tonnes per day and production was extended to the manufacture of VSF in addition to pulp.[6] The factory, however, was functioning below the capacity in processing 130–140 tonnes of bamboo and eucalyptus a day as the government was able to supply only 116,000 tonnes of raw material. The plant was one of its kind in the entire world as the pulp produced was sourced from bamboo, as opposed to various species of wood in other parts of the world. The company proudly claimed this as a success story of Indian technology, which, however, turned into a disaster when taking into account the entire consequences of the factory operations and the pollution it generated, which I shall explain soon.

The Birlas also acquired 30,000 acres of private forest land towards raising an industrial plantation of eucalyptus. It was reported that in the initial years, 2,500–3,000 acres of natural forests were turned into eucalyptus jungles every year (see Sridhar 2000). There was a ruthless exploitation of forests leading to a diminution in the supply of bamboo and eucalyptus; apart from its environmental effects and loss of biodiversity (see Raman 1998), the indigenous people for whom the bamboo forests were their only source of livelihood were left unsupported; yet the company continued to demand more resources, and the state continued to comply until it reached a point where it could no longer honour its commitment to the company. The factory also drew water in huge quantities – about 68 million litres per day: 48 million for the pulp division and 20 million litres for the fibre division (see Vidhyadharan 2009) – which it sourced upstream from the Chaliyar River free of cost. This was at a time when the entire Calicut water supply scheme was using only 45 million litres per day.

The paradox of the social democratic welfare state with a corporate bias was thus brought home to the general public. This was more evident with respect to resource subsidies as noted above. As early as 1860, the price of 1 tonne bamboo was INR 5 (Cleghorn 1860: 20), but as late as the 1950s, the paper industry in India was provided bamboo at the throwaway price of INR 1 per tonne while the open market price was over INR 2,000 per tonne. This was also the case with the rayon industry in Mavoor with the rate fixed for the Birlas being INR 1 per tonne, and remaining so for more than a decade; when the second supplement agreement was signed in 1974, the rate was marginally increased to INR 1.67,[7] which was far below the open market price of around INR 2,000 per tonne (see Sridhar 2000); even in the 1980s, bamboo prices were raised only to INR 200–500 per tonne, when market prices were well over INR 5,000 per tonne (Gadgil and Guha 1992: 199). Moreover, as mentioned earlier, while the Birlas drew water free of cost, the rest of the town had to pay for the use of water from their own river – yet another example of how social democracy worked in the state in its initial years. More importantly, the livelihood sources of those communities on the river banks – particularly the Muslim traditional families for whom fishing and associated activities were the sources of livelihood – were destroyed as the factories began to pollute the river water. The company began to claim that the state had always been defaulting on the agreement. The state, however, maintained the view that it was able to supply sufficient raw material as it wanted to make every effort to offer jobs to its youth, and this was legitimized by the fact that Kerala had one of the highest rates of unemployment in the country. A major development that occurred in 1974 was the passing of the

Water Act (Prevention and Control of Pollution) Act by the Indian Parliament, which made it mandatory for any factory that discharges effluents into a water body to obtain permission to do so from the State Pollution Control Board and follow the standards laid down by the Board. This also made it mandatory to establish state-level Pollution Control Boards, which led to the setting up of theKerala State Pollution Control Board (KSPCB). However, despite the favourable concessions and support from the state government and pollution control institutions, the Birlas failed to continue their operations in Kerala as conflicts over various issues – three major issues in particular – emerged, all substantiating our position that it was subaltern ecospatial resistance that became the marker of modernity: the politics proper.

Conflicts over Water Pollution

Once factory operations were under way, the local communities began feeling the ill effects of toxic wastes generated by the plant. The water treatment was primitive as there were no scientific pollution control measures in place. Water contaminated with black liquor was allowed to flow back into the Chaliyar without any waste treatment (Surendranath 2000).[8] The untreated effluents of the factory were being discharged into the river at two locations, Elamaram and Chungapalli, which together amounted to 40 million litres, leading to the virtual death of the river and thereby seriously jeopardizing the livelihood of the people on the banks of the river, along a 21-kilometre downstream stretch as it was in this part of the river that the effluents freely mixed with the seawater, turning the river into a 'black soupy cesspool'. This made the lives of the local inhabitants extremely unsustainable, and they began to articulate what exactly was going on in Mavoor: if it was 'thick black smoke from the factory chimney', 'waves of foul smell, coming on and off, as if a septic tank has been kept open', 'thick, viscous liquid with a lot of wood chips in it', 'lot of sluggish and dead fish in the river' (see George and Krishnan 2002: 11). This became a primary source of conflict, and the villagers of Vazhakkad launched their first agitation against the company in 1963, the first major environmental struggle in the state. Further, the local economy was adversely affected, particularly impacting on those who earned their livelihood through fishing, collection of lime shells, and so on. The consequences of the consumption of polluted water were further compounded when the local communities began to experience a deterioration in their health as a direct result of it. Apart from the rise in deaths due to cancer amongst the local communities, there was also a sharp rise in mortality due to heart and lung diseases, including tuberculosis and asthma (Government of Kerala/Kerala State Planning Board 1997: 31) – more than 200 in a short period of five years in the early 1990s alone – and the local communities attributed the same to the pollution of the Chaliyar River.

Though the management did not miss the opportunity to deny allegations of dumping waste or polluting the river on several occasions, it was later compelled to promise to take all precautions and carry out all maintenance works to ensure that the effluent treatment plant was working properly,[9] discharge effluents directly into the sea by laying a pipeline, and also dig wells for drinking water supply for the villagers as an interim relief; nothing substantive was done until 1965, leading to a series of struggles and promises (see Damodaran 1981), eventually leading to the closure of the factory, though other reasons compounded the issue and hastened the closure.

Further scientific studies conducted by well-established institutions, including the State Pollution Control Board (SPCB),the state-run medical colleges, and so on, did not find a correlation between this rise in deaths and any factors other than the pollution of the river water, which remained a source of livelihood for those living in its vicinity. Meanwhile, various scientific institutions conducted studies highlighting the environmental hazards stemming from the factory's operations (see Seethi 2000, 2001). It was revealed that the levels of hazardous elements such as lead, chromium, and so on – mostly carcinogenic – were far beyond the safe limits in the Chaliyar River. A house-to-house health survey conducted by the Vazhakkad Grama Panchayat in 1995 reported that 213 people had died of cancer in the village in a short span from 1990 to 1994 and reported further that the cancer mortality rate in the village was very high.[10] The Sen Gupta Committee appointed by the Government of Kerala in 1996 had to give specific instructions to Grasim Industries to adopt clean pulping technologies with the intention of reducing carcinogenic pollutants in the effluents. The Committee on Environment headed by A.V. Thamarakshan of the state legislative assembly reported that out of the 98 workers of the pulp division who died during the period between 1989 and 1995, 20 deaths were due to cancer. The Public Accounts Committee headed by the legislative council member Aryadan Muhammed in December 2000 also reported several cases of violation of the Water Act, 1974, and the Air Act, 1981, and found lacunae in the functioning of the Kerala State Pollution Control Board (KSPCB) in preventing or controlling of water and air pollution and hazardous wastes in the state. The committee highlighted that with respect to many of the public-sector industries such as Travancore Titanium Products Ltd, Thiruvananthapuram, Fertilizers and Chemises Travancore Ltd, Cochin (FACT), Cochin Refineries Ltd, and Kerala State Drugs and Pharmaceuticals Ltd (Alappuzha), untreated effluent discharged to the sea and river was significantly high, causing heavy damages. When the news of the death of three workers caused by inhalation of noxious gases while they were repairing faulty valves on the pipeline came out on 23 June 1995, the protests reached a new phase with the workers of the company also joining the struggle against the inadequate pollution control measures.

While the SPCB in its studies indicated the presence of pollutants far in excess of the prescribed tolerance limits, which the Environmental Review Committee of the federal government acknowledged, neither the concerned industries nor the Board had taken any resolution. With respect to Grasim Industries, the Board found that the company did not take any safety measures for the storage and disposal of wastes and instead continued to utilize wastes for land filling, contravening the provisions of the Hazardous Wastes (Management and Handling) Rules, 1989 (see Muhammed 2000). The committee expressed dissatisfaction and did not find any justification for not taking the required legal actions against the errant companies, whether public or private. The committee observed that the issue was still grave in spite of the longstanding agitation by the local people (Muhammed 2000: 25). The committee also expressed dissatisfaction for not publishing the studies on pollution in river bodies and streams caused due to discharge from various sources during the various plan periods.[11] The Board too was concerned that the factory did not meet the stipulated standards for the treatment and discharge of effluents and initiated prosecution proceedings against the company; it observed that the factory's effluent-treatment plant was not capable of dealing with the large volume of toxic waste it generated every day. However, the company continued to deny such allegations as 'incorrect and untrue' and assured the Board that they would discharge the effluents only after treating the same to the parameters prescribed by the Board except for the colour.[12] The company asserted that it had not violated any provisions of the Act or Rules. When the Board refused authorization to the company upon noticing that the company had not provided adequate facilities for segregation of wastes and when it prescribed certain standards for disposal of effluents, the company was in a position to obtain a stay from the High Court in August 1997. Several organizations continued to campaign for the closure of the factory and joined the local communities in their struggle, and also sought compensation for the illnesses caused; some of the petitions, including those to the National Human Rights Commission (NHRC), offered fresh strength to the movements.[13]

As the protests gathered steam, the Grasim management initiated the construction of a bund in Elamarom, which was also out of their necessity as their own intake of water had become polluted by the effluents released from their own factory. This was further aided by the Public Works Department of the government, but this was not effective, as the reduction in the flow of water in summer from upstream only helped to accumulate and increase the concentration of effluents. This led to the idea of discharging effluents in lagoons or further away into the sea, the former being in those areas owned by local inhabitants which the company had made a failed attempt to acquire through provisions in the Kerala Land Acquisition Act. The remaining months witnessed confrontations between the company and the KSPCB, the former failing to meet the standards prescribed by the Board. The company attempted to install a boiler that had already been dismantled from the Birlas' own Nagda Rayon factory at Nagda, Madhya Pradesh, but the people's protest did not allow the company to do it.

While the idea of channelling the effluents to the sea by a 28-kilometre-long pipeline instead of discharging it in the river was raised in several meetings and the company often promised the same, no substantial progress was made. It was in this context that in December 1974, the home minister, K. Karunakaran, initiated a discussion in Trichur in the larger context of the Environmental Review Committee in which the management agreed – as per the Ramanilayam Accord – to install an effluent treatment system, and it was decided to discharge the fully treated effluents at Chungapalli, nearly 7 kilometres downstream from the factory by laying a pipeline from the factory site (Government of Kerala/Kerala State Planning Board 1997: 12–13). The original idea was to discharge waste water away into the sea through a 20-kilometre pipeline, which, however, did not come to fruition. As part of the accord, the length of the pipeline was reduced to 7 kilometres, after much delay, and on the instructions of the Board for Prevention and Control of Water Pollution.

But the management neither treated the effluents to the standards prescribed by the Board nor adopted any measures to carry the effluents to the prescribed space; the company instead argued that the standard prescribed by the Board was not in conformity with those laid down by the Bureau of Indian Standards. In 1977, the Estimate Committee of the Kerala Legislative Committee submitted its report in which it was highlighted that the management was 'adamant and arrogant' in not complying with the instructions of the SPCB. To quote:

> The Committee is of the opinion that the management has not taken any earnest effort to solve the problem even considering their moral obligation towards the people who are suffering a lot due to the pollution for the last fifteen years; the committee strongly recommends that prosecution proceedings should be taken against the management for not having complied with the instructions issued by the Board in implementing the pollution control measures.[14]

While agreeing in principle to invest in partnership with the government in the laying of the pipelines as suggested by the Board, the joint president of the company, however, adopted quite an arrogant approach. He asserted before the Estimate Committee (1977) that 'the company could not dance to the tunes of the Board in implementing the control measures'.[15] When asked whether the government had taken any steps to control the pollution of the Chaliyar River and the gas emissions from the factory, the industries minister responded that the suggestions from the Public Health Committee had been accepted by the management and that initial work was under way. The protests and struggles against the continued operation of the factory began with the local government representatives themselves taking an interest against the pollution. The Mukkam *panchayat* took the lead, with B.P. Unnimoyeen and K.A. Rahman, president and vice president of the *panchayat* respectively, succeeding in mobilizing the trade unions of the Indian National Trade Union Congress (INTUC), the All India Trade Union Congress (AITUC), and Swatantra Thozhilali Union (STU) to gather strength even as expert committees were constituted in an attempt to resolve the environmental conflict. In September 1973, an elaborate Chaliyar-Jala-Vayu Shudhikarana Committee (Chaliyar Air and Water Purification Committee) was formed which passed a strongly worded resolution that warned the chief minister of Kerala, the home minister, and the management of Gwalior Rayons that in the event of immediate and practical steps not being taken to prevent the severe air and water pollution from the fibre and pulp divisions of Gwalior Rayons, the people of this area would be prepared to organize a strong protest against the same (Chaliyar Samara Samithi 2007).[16] This was followed by a widening of the committee to form a larger general council, and, for the first time, the local members of the legislative assembly (MLAs) of various political parties were brought in and thereby it became a pressure group demanding the government to take action against the management and stop it from polluting the river by discharging in it untreated effluents and also curtail air pollution from the factories.

The struggle began with the formation of the Chaliyar Action Committee, which was led by K.A. Rahman, who himself was the president of the local *panchayat*, Mavoor. Much earlier than this, the CPI(M) under the leadership of Bepur MLA K. Chathunni Master, initiated awareness against Gwalior Rayons' water pollution in Chaliyar, but was unable to continue because the labour unions, including those under his leadership, were opposed to it. Rahman, supported by the Muslim League and the local communities, took on the role of the symbolic force opposing Grasim's slow killing of the Chaliyar River. The very fact that he was a people's representative made the mobilization of the local communities easier. His identity as a Muslim might also have given additional strength in collective meaning-making among the locals as it was the Muslim households, by and large, who were immediately affected by the river pollution. Mavoor and the banks of the Chaliyar became the centre of environmental activism, the first of its kind in Kerala. Several new organizations were formed such as the Chaliyar Samara Sahaya Samithi, the Chaliyar Human Rights Protection Samithi, and Jananeethi, all making increased demands on the government to enquire into the situation and take favourable action.

In response to the widespread public agitation, in which new organizations helped to intensify the struggles, the state was compelled to hear what the agitators were trying to raise and the first major discussion in the state legislative assembly on the issue of the pollution of the Chaliyar was held on 29 August 1968. Several members raised concerns regarding the lack of pure drinking water and also about the discharge of untreated water and waste from the factory (also see Government of Kerala/Kerala State Planning Board 1997: 28–29). The industries minister, T.V. Thomas, was of the view that an amicable solution would be arrived at, both on pollution and the supply of drinking water. However, the minister pointed out that this was not an issue confined to Mavoor alone, but affected Punalur as well where a state-run paper mill was in operation, as also all locations where such industries operated; the issue, he pointed out, was not new and was, in fact, as old as the industries themselves. He was of the view that in such cases, the industries should be given a grace period to seek solutions to the challenges; otherwise, the popular demand for setting up factories and industries would become a farce.[17] It was pointed out that apart from the two legally accepted outlets, which were capable of treating barely half of the effluents, there were many illegal effluent outlets through which the untreated effluents were discharged into the Chaliyar River (see George and Krishnan 2002). The local communities, however, realized that the tidal waves would bring back the effluents upstream, and so the pipeline too was yet another failed experiment. The local communities even went to the extent of demolishing the bund at Elamaram, expecting that the new bund would be constructed at Chungappalli or the pollution would be reduced by restricting the production of pulp and fibre.[18]

By December 1980, Gwalior Rayons had commissioned the 6.4-kilometre outlet near Chungappalli after closing all other unauthorized outlets, and after the Board found that the effluents had prohibitively high levels of biochemical oxygen demand (BOD), the company had to install additional treatment units to achieve the standards prescribed. With respect to air pollution, the study team found that although the factories did have chimneys to dispose of the gases from inside the factory, there were no adequate arrangements to dispose of the residual sulphur dioxide escaping from the sulphuric acid plant, thereby resulting in serious air pollution. Further, the pipeline to Chungappalli was prone to leaking and breaking, and thereby contaminating the Chaliyar, which invited protests from the local communities, stopping any repair of the same. The management on one occasion had to invite the local police for protection but miserably failed in the High Court, which passed the verdict that the banks of the Chaliyar, once a health resort, have virtually become a hell on earth.

> At least for one decade, the people there are suffering. The Petitioner Company has liberally contributed to this. If the State Government and the Kerala State Board for Prevention & Control of Water Pollution had taken effective steps, this could have been prevented long ago. The Rayons is an industry where the margin of profit is not only comfortable but considerable. It is to be remembered that one of the pollutants here is nothing other than mercury. Then what is the magnitude of the threat to life caused by the effluent discharged from the Petitioner's factories, I need not say. Life, especially human life, should not be so cheap in this country.[19]

The question of pollution and the gradual death of the Chaliyar River was raised in the state legislative assembly again. P. Seethihaji, for instance, pointed out that the Birlas were a bigger bourgeoisie than the state. He also drew the attention of the members and the chief minister to the fact that the children in the area were being exposed to particularly unhealthy conditions due to the pollution and gas emissions from the factory and requested state intervention as a matter of urgency. While acknowledging the extent of the hazards, the chief minister, P.K. Vasudevan Nair, explained that the issue dated back to the beginning of factory operations in 1962 and that the state-led Board of experts had suggested at the outset that the waste water be discharged 6 kilometres away in Chungapalli.

In its report to the Rajya Sabha committee, the company claimed that the knowledge or the know-how to treat the effluent from bamboo processing was not available; the presence of mercury was also challenged by R.N. Saboo,[20] the factory manager, who expressed his reservations in a personal interview, pointing out to this author that no mercury was used in the production of rayon. This could form a source of knowledge controversy, which in fact was raised in the context of endosulfan (Chapter 5), though not on mercury. The company also declared that there was no question of treating the effluent as there was no such law. When the water in the river proved sufficiently available, in a show of social responsibility, the company approached the National Environmental Engineering Research Institute (NEERI) to discuss the process to treat the effluent. It was suggested that the pulp was manufactured by treating bamboo with a certain amount of sulphuric acid and caustic soda and that the effluent was not harmful in the least, particularly when diluted in a large volume of water. Furthermore, the company maintained that the residual material that returned to the water was only lignin plus certain chemicals, and that 80–85 per cent of the chemicals used for production purposes was recovered by the factory processes and only 15–20 per cent of the chemicals remained in the water. KSPCB has stated that unfortunately the water in the river was not available in such large volume as to dilute the effluent; they used to put up a temporary bund right up to 1972. After that the bund was not allowed to be put up.

The government had taken the position in the legislative assembly that despite repeated suggestions and directives from the SPCB, the company had failed to comply with the standards prescribed by the Board, leading it to institute prosecution proceedings against the company in late January 1981,[21] which was unprecedented in its history. This was also the time when the company began to employ a new strategy, now against the workers, by reducing production and retrenching workers, in the name of the failure of the government to keep its promises to supply adequate raw materials, aspects I shall explain in section titled 'Conflicts over Natural Resources'. In 1992, in response to the repeated requests by the company for consent for discharge of effluents, the Board provided consent for discharging effluents from the factory through specified outlets with stringent conditions, including the collection of effluents on a daily basis and analysing the same to meet – not to exceed – the prescribed standards.[22] The overall impact was so significant that it aroused great opposition to the continued operation of this industry. This instigated the people of Vazhakkad and other neighbouring villages, with a predominantly subaltern Muslim population, to launch their own protest movement with the support of the wider civil society.

Conflicts over Natural Resources

The second major conflict between the company and the state was over the question of the supply of raw materials. The company was assured of forest resources, beginning with the Nilambur valley, and extending to the entire Malabar forests, as could only be expected. The government was not in a position to provide the agreed quantity of bamboo and hence was prepared to provide that factory with hardwood and eucalyptus instead. By 1963, nearly 17,300 tonnes of bamboo were harvested in Wayanad alone; the harvested bamboo in divisions such as Nilambur and Kozhikode was 15,656 tonnes and 4,650 tonnes respectively; a significant portion had already been transported to the factory. The agreement to supply bamboo covered a period of 50 years and the number of workers employed by the factory was 879 in March 1963. In 1968, the rate per tonne was hardly INR 1.67 in the form of seigniorage; the government stated that in Mysore, it provided bamboo at the rate of INR 1.25 per 3 tonnes; the industries minister was thus in effect rejecting the argument that bamboo was cheaper in Kerala, and also mentioned in the assembly that another rayon unit would be set up in Mysore rather than shifting the Kerala firm to Mysore, allaying the apprehensions expressed by members.[23] By 1976–1977, the rates charged for bamboo and eucalyptus were revised but still on terms that favoured the company.[24]

The state took particular interest in protecting the company and assuring the required raw materials in adequate amounts. To fulfil the agreed promises, bamboo and eucalyptus were raised by the Forest Department, followed by the Kerala Forest Development Corporation. The move to nationalize private forests prompted concerns among members of the legislative assembly as to whether the company would continue to get raw materials and whether the government had taken any precautions in this regard. P.S. Srinivasan, who was the minister for transport and electricity, however, reassured the members that the government had taken steps to protect the company from any adverse effects that might ensue from this legislation.[25] It was further stated that the government had also given permission to the factory to access softwood and firewood from private properties, and had also amended the rules to allow this. The factory could also collect firewood in advance from the Kozhikode division, and was given permission to transform wood from private properties and the rangers were given special powers to do this; further, trees could be harvested from places like Aralam and Kuthali, thus ensuring a steady supply of wood to the factory. Despite such a favourable approach adopted by the government, the Grasim management fielded a case against the government for non-compliance with the original agreement to provide 2 lakh tonnes of bamboo. The Birlas filed an arbitration demanding compensation worth INR 4 crores as per the agreement. It was in response to this that the government opted for a new agreement to supply 2 lakh tonnes of the raw materials at subsidized rates.

The Grasim management also had requested the government for an extra 20,000 tonnes of eucalyptus, which led to a discussion in the legislative assembly in February 1974 on the advisability of offering resources to the Birlas when there was a requirement for the public sector as well. The eucalyptus plantations raised by the government were not intended solely for the Birlas' plant, but also for the Hindustan Newsprint Limited (HNL) as a subsidiary of the Hindustan Paper Corporation, owned by the Indian government. The chief minister, C. Achutha Menon, refers to this in his reply to a concern raised by C.B.C. Warrier as to whether the Hindustan newsprint mill – that provided employment to 4,000 workers and which was under the public sector – would suffer a shortage of raw material if a long-term agreement with the Birlas was to be finalized. The chief minister stated that the government would be allowed to revisit the decision as and when the Hindustan Paper Corporation Ltd mills were in need of raw material.[26] However, while conceding that the Punalur paper mill was of utmost importance to the state in terms of employment and economy, Menon pointed out that it was to become functional only in 1977.[27] Hence, the eucalyptus supplies could be allocated to Grasim. Further, as the trees were 10 years old at that point, a timely harvest was essential as it would not have been fit for any other purpose beyond then.

With the state having persistently failed in keeping its promise to supply adequate amounts of raw materials as agreed,[28] and the rising tide of public opinion against the pollution of the Chaliyar River (Save Chaliyar Campaign 2011; Shaji 2008) and the workers' struggle, an aspect that we will turn to soon, against low wages and salaries, the Birlas adopted the strategy of closing down its factories despite the state having rejected the request from the management for the same.[29] In 1988, it was further agreed that the company would be provided bamboo or eucalyptus at INR 250 per tonne, and various other tax concessions such as forest tax and sales tax. While this agreement, which was renewed for five years, stood terminated in August 1999, a few months in advance, the company cleared all its dues as part of its usual tactics. By continuing to provide raw materials at discounted rates, the government capitulated to the company's interests. Compared to the market price of INR 775 and INR 1,000, bamboos and eucalyptus were offered at INR 426 and INR 463, respectively. Other species including acacia and casianna were also provided at discounted prices. According to the government's own admission, the company received a subsidy worth more than INR 8 crores in just two years from 1996 to 1998.[30] When considering the entire period of subsidy, which began with the factory's establishment in the early 1960s, the overall subsidy would reach hundreds of crores and the total resource loss would run into thousands of crores. At the time, socially concerned scholars and environmentalists sent warnings against this, but to no avail. On many occasions, it was also pointed out that the government supplied more resources to the company than originally committed – though denied by the company – at a price fixed lower than that of the forest department, and also at a price much less than what the government supplied at to the public sector Hindustan Newsprints, all leading to public debates and several legal disputes.[31]

Local protests continued and took several forms – meetings, discussions, and public seminars, mostly in the nearby *panchayats*. It also had its imaginative campaigns such as a boat campaign from Elamaram to Farook, mobilizing rural communities into the struggle. With the local communities and environmental activist-groups intensifying their protests, other agencies joined them in their demand to not renew the agreement with the Birlas. The Kerala Shastra Sahithya Parishad (KSSP) – the Kerala forum for science literature – which was responsible for spearheading the People's Science Movement in the state, for instance, pointed out that in providing raw materials, water from the Chaliyar, and electricity, all at subsidized rates, the government was losing more than INR 50 crores per year, and it was argued that no private company should be provided such levels of subsidies to the detriment of the local economy. The Centre for Nature Studies in Thiruvananthapuram and several NGOs continued to campaign against the outright violation of resource extraction and severe loss for the government. While the KSSP estimated the total loss over the years to the government in subsidizing resources to the range of INR 500 crores, it was as high as INR 2,500 crores in the estimation of the Centre for Nature Studies. The Kerala Forest Department (KFD) too, from time to time, highlighted the huge forest resource loss due to the heavy and unsustainable use of forest resources by Gwalior Rayons. KFD has always stated clearly that the long-term supply contracts at subsidized rates as that between the government and Gwalior Rayons have led to excessive harvesting from forests at unsustainable rates and to forest degradation with adverse effects on the larger environment. While this pressure from the public agencies intensified, the company sought to apply counter-pressure in order to negotiate terms of trade in its favour.[32] The public became increasingly cognizant of the fact that bamboo degradation eroded both the biodiversity of the forests of the Western Ghats and the livelihood of the artisan communities (see Gadgil and Guha 1992: 171–172, 198–200; Raman 1998).[33] While discussing the subsidized resources provided to the big industrial houses, it was pointed out by Gadgil and Guha that 'the subsidies cut across conventional political alignments' (1992: 186) and even Kerala under the communist government could not remain an exception. Rayon grade pulp manufactured at the time catered to the luxury clothing of the elite and the upper classes in India and abroad.

Conflict over Workers' Rights

One of the major attractions of the company and the reason behind the decision of the communist government to invite the Birlas to set up their factory in Mavoor was the immense potential for employment it brought, both to the local people and those outside the state. The company employed both permanent and contractual workers, but in a non-proportionate manner: roughly 6,000 workers were permanent and directly employed, and the remaining, numbering around 10,000, were indirectly employed on a contractual basis (see Ram Mohan and Raman 1988). The pulp division later expanded to employ over 4,000 workers. The second largest employment division was the paper division, with around 1,000 workers, followed by the fibre division, with 500 workers. Despite the fact that the workers in the rayon factory were paid reasonably good wages and salaries, the emergent unions were not ready to accept what the Birlas wanted to offer. This was made explicit by the workers who formed the first union, the Gwalior Rayons Pulp Factory and Construction Workers Union, which was inaugurated by the communist veteran K.P. Gopalan on 16 February 1961.

On the following day, a memorandum demanding a rise in wages was put forward, which, however, was accepted with a rise in wages by a quarter of a rupee. More importantly, it was also assured that the dependents of those who met with accidental death would be offered jobs in the company; both the agreements found favour with the agitating workers. On 12 February 1962, the union participated in the call for a collective protest by the AITUC, though the union was not formally affiliated with it. The fast in front of the factory was a great success. The protests also aired the concerns of the workers in relation to boilers and safety measures, the inadequacies of which had claimed the lives of two workers who were killed in industrial accidents in the factory on 22 January 1961 (see Vidhyadharan 2009). During this period, the Birlakkoottam Workers' Union was also formed under the leadership of comrade Elamaram Kareem, who was also the general secretary of the union. This also gave rise to new forms of struggles, including the gheraoing of senior officials, including the vice president of the factory, as the workers by that time had gained more political leverage with the participation of prominent communist leaders like A.K. Gopalan. Furthermore, when Gopalan refused to accept a personal invitation to meet the management,[34] it kindled fresh forms of class divisions between the communist workers and the newfound bourgeoisie in the state, although the latter had been invited to the state by the communist party itself.

Workers' strikes were common in the Mavoor factories in relation to disputes over wages, bonuses, and salaries (see Ram Mohan and Raman 1988, 1989); however, occupational and health aspects, too, figured in these discussions from time to time. For instance, there was a lockout in the pulp division from June 1973, which was left to adjudication; however, the government, the company, and the unions came to a consensus that a month's pay would be paid as advance to the workers while a final settlement was found over the next six months. When this strike in the pulp division was settled in December 1973, yet another strike broke out in November 1977, demanding a renewal of the long-term agreement on wages and salaries between the management and the unions, which had expired on 26 October 1975. Further discussions were held in 1977 to formulate an agreement, which met with no success, and it was in this context that the government came to a decision to take over the management temporarily through an ordinance, which turned out to be unsuccessful.[35] It was then decided to move the case in the Supreme Court, and the then labour and housing minister, Oommen Chandy, declared in the state assembly that the government would not abandon the 20,000 workers to the mercy of the Birlas. The understanding was that all efforts would be initiated by the government to avoid the workers' strike and hence there was no point in stopping the legislative steps to discuss the matter.[36] Moreover, this laid bare the internal contradictions within the Congress government in dealing with the workers' struggles, particularly when it also involved a conflict with Indian big capital. Neither did the communist party, when in power, succeed in settling the workers' issues or addressing the larger concerns of the sustainability of resources.

P.K. Vasudevan Nair, the Communist Party of India minister for industries and electricity, presented the case again in the assembly in 1978, recommending the takeover of Gwalior Rayon's (pulp division) management. Nair legitimized the ordinance for the takeover of the pulp division arguing that the nearly 20,000 workers in the factory were living a precarious existence for the past six months. Second, the neighbouring areas of Kozhikode and other towns were also feeling the deleterious effects with both the state and central governments incurring heavy revenue losses due to the non-opening of the factory. The factory had not been functioning since November 1977. However, the High Court rejected this ordinance on the grounds that as per the Indian constitution a person has the right to accumulate wealth and sell assets. Further, the person also has the right to run industries and trade. Hence, the ordinance was against the constitution. The High Court was of the view that even if it was not against the constitution, the state government would not gain permission from the president of India. In another context, the High Court stated that only the Indian Parliament had the right to pass such laws as it has repugnancy with the Industries Development and Regulation Act, 1952, and hence the state assembly did not have the legal authority to pass those laws.[37] The ordinance, however, was passed, and the company was taken over by the government; however, the company filed a petition against the ordinance. Moreover, the High Court directed the comptroller not to proceed with any further action.[38] The bill, Gwalior Rayons (Rayon Pulp Division) Taking Over of Management Bill, 1978, was finally passed on 2 August 1978,[39] but no substantial change followed.

When the company began to be sandwiched on one side by the protesting communities on account of river pollution and on the other by the workers with fresh demands, it skilfully shifted the public discourse, raising the point that it had to reduce production on account of shortage of raw materials. The company stated that the government failed in its promise to supply an adequate amount of raw materials and in their assessment, it had to retrench at least 1,418 employees, which invited the workers' wrath. Such strikes and lockouts continued till 1985, when the company closed down for three years, leaving the workers in the lurch, during which not less than 13 workers committed suicide. On the negotiating table, the government failed, as it agreed to reduce the benefits of workers and supply raw materials at subsidized prices. However, not all those unions were in agreement either with the left government or with the company management. A new history of workers' protest emerged in Kerala.

The disregard of the management for the workers' demand for decent living standards went unheeded, forcing them to go on strike, and this time round in an intensified form. From 7 July 1985, for instance, all the factory workers, irrespective of their union affiliations, and trade unions such as AITUC, INTUC, and the Centre of Indian Trade Unions (CITU) struck work, which lasted for 39 months. Around 2,330 workers in the pulp division, 1,180 workers in the fibre division, and the workers associated with the two units were on strike. They demanded that there should be a long-term agreement on the dispute, they should be awarded bonus payments for 1982–1983, 1983–1984, and 1984–1985, and the full employment of reserve workers. In a further development, the long closure of the factory for about 28 months, and the consequent lack of maintenance of the equipment, resulted in the leakage of chlorine from cylinders. Workers who attempted to repair the leaks took ill and were hospitalized. While answering questions on the closure of the factory and the leakage of hazardous gas, Gowri Amma, the industries minister, replied that the management was not keen on opening the factory because they got imported raw material, as was pointed out by other members. The government assured that it would be able to supply 16,000 tonnes of eucalyptus and 40,000 tonnes of bamboo at a rate that would be discussed. However, as the management was sceptical of this offer, since the state government had earlier requested the central government to take over the factory in Mavoor, it was suggested that the management should be demarcated, which was done.

Earlier, the state government had also requested the central government to take over the Mavoor factory but the centre had refused to do so. The factories were closed on 7 July 1985. In June 1987, the matter was again discussed in the assembly. However, with the factory having been closed for 23 months, despite several rounds of discussion between the Labour Department and the management, no amicable solution was reached. Aside from that, the company informed the public that it was ready to begin operations provided that it was supplied with raw materials, which meant that the ball was now in the government's court. The first position taken by the management was that the bonus question could only be settled based on the norms of the Bonus Act, that is, only when the factory makes a profit could it be shared. However, when the workers continued with their struggle, the management linked the bonus issue to the supply of raw materials. The management insisted that they could resolve the issue of bonus payments only if the government complied with its agreement with the company, that is, to supply the required amount of raw materials, and only then could the factory be reopened. Gowri Amma reported to the assembly that a decision was taken by the management to run the factory on the assurance of a minimum supply of 50,000 tonnes of raw material for five years from 19 February 1988.[40] No decision was arrived at either on the price of the raw materials or the wages and benefits for the workers, and the factory was shut down on 7 July 1985.[41] Gowri Amma stated that as per the Industrial Development Act, the central government alone had the authority to take over the factory and she urged a suspension of the hunger strike by the factory workers as it was a futile attempt at forcing a decision to reopen the factory.

The first major hunger strike – a Gandhian method of non-violent protest – now led by (Gujarat Rayons Workers Union) GROW leaders, Moyeen Bapu and A. Vasu, in Mavoor was begun on 26 January and ended on 20 February. Prominent feminist leaders like K. Ajitha, a former Maoist, too participated in the hunger strike.The demands raised during this 26-day-long fast were unmet by the government. Further, the chief minister, Nayanar, himself made it explicit that the Mavoor protest was a failure. The protestors had no choice but to renew their hunger strikes, that also within the space of a month. In fact, it was unusual in Kerala's history for the same person(s) to engage in a second lengthy hunger strike in the same month. Mavoor's struggle, however, was an exception. The second indefinite hunger strike was started on 18 March 1988 by Moyeen Bappu in Mavoor and A. Vasu in front of the secretariat in Thiruvananthapuram.

The 33-day-long strike came to an end on 19 April 1988, much longer than the hunger strike that Gadhi himself had carried out.[42] The GROW leaders were compelled to withdraw the strike since the government assured them an amicable agreement and there was an increasing demand and pressure from supporting organizations to discontinue the strike unto death, considering the worsening health conditions of the fasting leaders. The agreement was by and large in favour of the company management. The factory would be provided with the raw material at less than half the price that was being given then, and in the instance of its failure, the company would be given cash compensation as well. The agreement promised only a marginal increase of the wages, INR 32, to the workers. In addition, there was a wage freeze and strike holiday for the next five years (for more details, see Rammohan and Raman 1989). With regard to this tripartite agreement, E.K. Nayanar, the then chief minister, confessed that 'the government could not claim that it protected all the interests of the workers'. As one discussion continued without a resolution, Nayanar became so enraged that he even threw the files in Saboo's face and blamed him in both English and Malayalam (Vidhydharan 2009:179). Apart from this, the GROW leader A. Vasu has stated that it was 'a total surrender' by the workers and the institutionalised unions, including GROW. In an interview with the author, A. Vasu has stated that the petty bourgeois attitude of the supporting organizations, especially CRC-CPI (ML),[43] led by K. Venu, had a vital role in the withdrawal of the hunger strike.

Meanwhile the Chaliyar struggle was strengthening by itself with new organizations joining the movement. However, it took many years for the struggle to turn into a full-fledged movement, and despite the untimely demise of one of the leading activists of the Chaliyar Action Committee, K.A. Rahman, the former president of the Vazhakkad *panchayat*, who succumbed to cancer in January 1999, the movement gathered momentum until the forced closure of the factory in mid-2001. Rahman had based his campaign against the factory on the obvious rise in the prevalence of cancer in the region as a result of exposure to toxins discharged from the factory (Vijayamandhavan 2011). The movement entered its next phase after the death of Rahman, and was led by his son and the remaining villagers, many of whom were themselves affected by cancer. This caught the attention of environmentalists and activists from other parts of the state and the country as a whole, and the ensuing pressure led to the eventual closure of the factory.

In the words of M. Dharmajan, a former *panchayat* president and union leader of CITU, 'Every month Rs 92 lakh in wages used to circulate in this area' and after the closure of the factory, there is a virtual collapse of the economic activities in this area spreading the crisis even to the entire Calicut city.' On 5 April 1988, while the second hunger strike was going on, the government reported in the assembly that five workers had taken their lives due to the hardship and misery accruing from the prolonged closure of the factory. Field-level investigations conducted by this author revealed that the number of workers who committed suicide following the closure of the factory numbered more than a dozen, leaving their families to fend for themselves. The trade unions in alliance with the left-wing parties pressed for the opening of the factory in an attempt to retain its workforce as well as to avoid being branded as 'anti-industries'. Sadly, the established trade unions turned a deaf ear to these otherwise emergent environmental struggles of the local communities. The government also decided to supply the workers with free ration for weeks together. When previously the left-wing parties had requested the government to supply ration to the workers, the then Congress government had retorted that workers on strike should not be encouraged with a free supply of rations! The left government instead took a firm stand on the supply of free ration to the workers.[44]

The pressure tactics employed by the company continued and again came in the form of lay-offs. In May 1999, for instance, the company laid off first its pulp division, affecting around 650 workers, in the wake of the workers' struggles for not revising the wages and salaries from April 1988 despite the expiry of the wage agreement between the management and the trade unions. The fibre division was also laid off, on the grounds that there was an accumulated stock of fibre. The company used such tactics to buy time, in the knowledge that the raw material agreement terminated in August, and with the plan to negotiate further subsidized supplies of raw materials. Meanwhile, the public debate on whether the Birlas would resume operations intensified. The workers, by and large, had very little expectation of this happening as there was huge pressure from environmentalists to close the factory down; further, there continued to be no guarantee that the company could be supplied with the agreed quantity of raw materials.

The environmentalists and the Chaliyar Action Committee were confident that the factory would not be opened as they were prepared to intensify the protests. Further, the changes brought in by economic liberalization already allowed the Birlas to import pulp and fibre at a cheaper cost, and the company also had opportunities to improve its production capacities in its branches in other states. On the other hand, there were some who believed that the company could still open on the basis of a further subsidy on the raw materials. This view was promoted by the company's response to the High Court direction that the polluted water in Chungapalli be further treated in three places with the installation of improved facilities for the treatment of the effluents. The Industries Department was also of the view that the factory should not be closed down as it provided much-needed employment and had brought a level of industrialization to the area but with the caveat that it should not be at an environmental cost. The department had also suggested that further improvements be taken up by the company including the installation of a chemical dosing tank. The need for a constant updating of laws and technology was stressed by the departmental representative, and it was also suggested that the SPCB should be given more independent powers to deal with defaulting industries. The company, however, finally closed down, with the workers and their trade unions accepting the compensation package offered by the management.

The company for the first time filed for permission for a closure application before the Government of Kerala in August 1999. However, the company was not allowed to do so as the reasons cited by the company, such as shortage of raw materials, were not 'genuine in public interest'. After getting permission on a closure application, the company attempted to transfer the ownership to a new company, called M/S Moonlight Chemfab Ltd Indore, but the workers' unions, particularly the Gwalior Rayons Employees Union (INTUC) and the CITU-led Gwalior Rayon Pulp & Fibre Factory Union, both in Mavoor, challenged the same by arguing that the company was trying to circumvent the provisions of industrial and labour laws.[45] While the workers' arguments for objecting to the closure of the factory yet also transferring the divisions from Kerala to Madhya Pradesh had the support of the Kerala government and turned out to be a failure, the protesting local communities continued their campaign for the closure of the factory, as we have seen in the section titled 'Conflicts over Water Pollution'.

Two major solidarity organizations, the Chaliyar Samara Samithi (CSS) and the Chaliyar Samara Sahaya Samithi (CSSS), continued to challenge the views of the government, first by saying that they had not been given a chance to represent their cause and, second, their reasons were different and thus had a claim to be heard 'before dismissing in haste the closure petition filed by the Company'.[46] The environmental organizations also exposed the true nature of the closure notice served by the company as it was a 'smokescreen to escape from the polluter's liability to compensate the damages already done to the workers, community and environmental health'. The company was trying to 'blackmail' the government to gain further supplies of subsidized inputs and further concessions in pollution-control norms. The government, be it left-wing or right-wing, was concerned most about the loss of employment due to the closure of the factory and requested the Birlas not to close the factory, expressing its willingness for yet another round of discussions. However, the decision was not to be changed. At one stage, the state entrusted the district collector to confiscate the lands owned by the Birlas, which was challenged by the company. The company, in another context, expressed its interest in starting a knowledge-based industry in Mavoor,[47] the latest development in the long history of Mavoor, an idea, however, that has yet to come to fruition.

The people's organizations have valid reasons for asking the government to allow the closure of the factory. They have highlighted the whopping loss of raw materials, the failure of the company to comply with the requirements of committee reports, and, above all, for ignoring the gross violation of law and natural justice with regard to the lives of thousands of people, including its own workers. As and when the workers themselves realized that their concerns should not be confined to jobs or job losses alone, the movement against Grasim Industries gained strength, as it was a unique coalescence of agencies involved, though, in different domains, they were all struggling for livelihood. They began to realize that livelihood sustainability would not be possible without sustaining the environment and society–nature relations.

A compensation worth four days' salary of the workers as well as the remainder of the service as per original contracts was decided to be distributed. An additional compensation worth INR 27,500 as part of the package was also agreed upon.[48] Other agreements included an ex-gratia grant of INR 10,000 to those who retired in the interim, a bonus payment for the ongoing year, which was fixed at 8 per cent, and the assurance that the workers would be awarded all legally binding payments, including provident fund, gratuity, and other allowances. Workers employed on compassionate grounds following the death of a family member on the payroll would be paid INR 1 lakh each. Dependents who were not yet employed would receive INR 3.5 lakhs, to be divided equally among the family members. The school for the children of the employees was to remain open for one more academic year, and the families of the school children were permitted to remain in the company quarters until the end of the school year; however, they were expected to pay a rental for their stay. Employees working in hospitals, cooperative stores, and so on, were not covered by this package.[49] On 28 June 2011, it was reported in the assembly that the government passed an order to acquire the land as the company was not functioning. However, this was challenged by the company in the High Court. The idea of starting new-generation industries came up at this time, which was being discussed between the government and the company. The latest development in the long history of struggles, contests, and debates on the Mavoor rayon factory appears to be positive: the present left-wing government has been planning to convert the vast acres of land now lying vacant either into an electronic hub or a biodiversity garden or even a space for Kerala's long-lasting demand to the centre – an All India Institute of Medical Sciences (AIIMS) – aspects yet to be opened up in Kerala debates. However, Kerala has not given adequate attention to how the forest resources such as bamboo could be rejuvenated to create livelihood and employment for a large number of marginalized communities, some of the aspects that the Chaliyar Action Council explored while submitting their demands to the government (Chundamannil 1986; Gadgil and Prasad 1978).

Concluding Remarks: Moral Economy Wins?

The struggle resulted in the formation of what could be called a 'transverse solidarity' (see Raman 2010), and varying phases of right-making/state-making processes. This solidarity – the agential coalescing – helped counter the corporate strategy of fragmenting the resistance in various contexts into environmental agitators and workers. A number of environmentally concerned activists and public figures, including E.N. Peethambaran Master, M.P. Veerendrakumar, Arundhati Roy, and Sukumar Azhikode, were at the forefront of the agitation in the interests of the restoration of the environmental balance and also to protect the workers' interests. This was also the time when studies on rayon industries worldwide were being ended prematurely as a result of widespread opposition to their continuation, as reported by Mitsubishi Rayon (1992), Anderson (1993), Carr (2001), and Noronha (1999). Having Greenpeace in Germany handholding the local struggle gave the movement a global perspective, as it identified and worked to close such industries globally, thus strengthening global epistemological convergence.

The local communities, environmentalists and other socially concerned organizations, and local body representatives began to realize that silence was dangerous in view of the procrastination tactics of Indian big capital. They spared no method in raising their voices of protest, first locally in Mavoor and then marching to the state capital of Thiruvananthapuram. The decision to close down the Mavoor factory was taken in 2001, and a gradual consensus was emerging amongst the trade unions, who were also convinced of the genuine concerns raised by the environmental groups and the local communities. An economic package was agreed upon and included measures that ensured some immediate relief to the workers who were soon to be rendered jobless. The crucial point that was missed in all the public debates in the highly literate state of Kerala was the inevitable trade-off between employment opportunity and environmental pollution, an issue that we will encounter again as we proceed to other struggles in the state.

There were two perspectives regarding the actual causes of the closure of the factory. One line of argument was that the management themselves wished to see the factory closed in the light of the lay-offs and the continuing industrial disputes in the state, the failure of the supply of raw materials as agreed at the outset, and the newly arisen opportunity to import pulp, which made the factory quite redundant. In August 1999, for instance, the Grasim management, for the first time, sought permission to shut down the pulp division and the staple fibre division. The management pointed out that the lack of quality raw material, environmental issues, workers' pressure to raise wages and salaries, high electricity rates, and the consequent economic loss sustained by the company were leading up to a situation where closure was the only viable option. However, after listening to both the management and the labour unions, the government refused the request of the company, which it then challenged through a review petition.[50] The minister for industries and social welfare, Susheela Gopalan, stressed the point in the legislative assembly that the policy of the government was to allow the factory to run on its own strength and that if the government were to take over all such companies, it would be in a difficult position.[51] She also pointed out that the management had been trying to de-merge the Mavoor unit from the larger company, which, however, fell under the jurisdiction of the High Court of Madhya Pradesh, a case in which the Kerala government also had a stake.

The second theory behind the closure of the factory was that it was due to the campaign intensified by the Chaliyar Action Committee and other organizations which declared that they would not withdraw from the struggle until the factory was closed. The environmental fallout was perhaps the most significant argument of all, and the demand for a closure of the factory gained support from the larger public, and hence the notion of a takeover by the government found little favour with environmental groups. Though the Gwalior Rayons management always maintained that the presence of mercury in the Chaliyar river – one of the most sensitive issues raised by the local communities – could not have been from the factory as none of the processes used mercury, the pollution brought about by the factory was never disputed and is clearly borne out by the rejuvenation of the Chailyar river following the closure of the factory. While the actual reason for the closure is not so much an issue, it is important to acknowledge that the action committee would have continued its struggle as a pre-figurative politics, which the company would have been unable to address. Further, at least 3–5 lakh traditionally employed people working directly in the bamboo economy were robbed of their livelihoods, whereas the industry could, in effect, give direct employment to about 2,000 only and obviously more as informal workers. And lastly, even by the most conservative appraisal, the state would be losing crores of rupees due to the stupendous subsidies it offered to the company, which otherwise would have been used towards the development of the state (see Sridhar 2000: 7).

There were issues outside of these two dominant views. First, the community that benefited from factory employment, by and large, was not the one that eventually suffered the brunt of the environmental hazards ensuing from factory operations. While the local Muslim and Dalit communities were directly affected by the adverse effects of environmental pollution caused by the factory, it was the caste Hindus and Ezhavas who took up the factory jobs. This could be viewed as a strategic error on the part of the Birlas: had it been the majority of the employees that were affected by river pollution, the struggle would have probably taken a different direction. However, when the environmental struggle against the Birlas gathered momentum, the workers and their trade unions extended their full support, says A. Vasu, the prominent and committed leader of the then GROW and a former Maoist sympathizer whose attention was initially caught by Mavoor due to the company's environmental harm, but later changed his ways and was invited to become the union's leader as the workers' continued existence was threatened by frequent lockouts of the company.[52] Further, the package offered as compensation for the closure of the factory was rather attractive, considering the fact that the factories had to close down on several occasions for want of adequate raw material.

With the closure of the first and the largest private business venture in Kerala, the entire Mavoor region of Malabar that was hitherto flourishing in terms of income flows and consumption in the town found itself on the decline. In the words of M. Dharmajan, a former *panchayat* president and union leader of CITU, 'Every month INR 92 lakh in wages used to circulate in this area and after the closure of the factory, there is a virtual collapse of the economic activities in this area spreading the crisis even to the entire Calicut city.' Although a new economy emerged with the money paid as compensation attracting various investors (Rajeev 2001), the core of the Mavoor region gradually found itself reduced to a ghost town (Ram Mohan and Raman 1988, 1989). On the other hand, the protestors who had gone on hunger strike and community mobilization for the rebirth of the Chaliyar began to celebrate the closure without hesitation.

'River biography' does not imply hydrology alone – sources, flows, and landscapes – it also encompasses the lives and livelihoods of the people who live on the banks, and their conflicts with others, narrates Peter Coates (2013) with examples of six rivers from Europe and the United States. He also explores how rivers were represented politically and culturally, and as unending trajectories. Further, Coates explains how rivers also come to be symbols of knowledge and power. Kerala in the Global South is endowed with numerous rivers, numbering over 44, that have their own river biographies not yet written, biographies of livelihood, enclosures, and liberation: hegemony and interconstitutiveness of power. Given the fact that both the workers and the local communities gained in terms of sustainable livelihood, their combined struggles encompass moral economy solutions, thanks to E.P. Thompson (1991: 188), who conceived moral economy as 'the traditional norms and mutual obligations'. When we move on to the anti-Cola struggles in Plachimada (Chapter 4), we will learn more about water struggles as well as the fact that such transverse solidarity has not been smooth and struggles may even have been in conflict with one another.

Notes

1. Jawaharlal Nehru (1889–1964) was the first prime minister of independent India until his death (1947–1964). Though the ministry was led by the Indian National Congress and Nehru was its president, he was heavily influenced by socialist ideas, often attributed to his educational exposures in Britain for graduation and law studies. Though he was socialist, his stature as the same shade dim when he abused power by dissolving the first communist government by invoking Article 356 of the Indian Constitution.
2. Having succeeded Joseph Stalin in 1956, Khrushchev began a process of 'de-Stalinization' and a foreign policy of peaceful coexistence with the United States and other countries with major implications for the Cold War. See Sleet (n.d.).
3. The agreement between the Birlas and the Forest Department, Government of Kerala (1958), p. 3.
4. Ibid.
5. Questions and answers, compensation for land acquired in Mavoor for factory site, KLA-2 (1960–1964), 21 December 1960, 5201.
6. The company appointed three executives: the technical advisor D.P. Mandeli, colonel T.P. Rajan, and the scientist V.P. Gohal who invented the production of pulp from bamboo. The Birlas began experimenting with this and also claimed to be pioneers in this venture.
7. In case the bamboo and eucalyptus were taken and weighed only after 30 days, the price was INR 2.78, and afar that it was fixed at INR 3.34. If the bamboo is collected outside the agreed places, the rate was higher, INR 18, INR 30, and INR 36, if it was weighed within a month, after a month, and still after, respectively. See KLA, 22 July 1978, as answer by the forest minister Kanthalot Kunhambu to questions raised by Aryadan Mohammed in the legislative assembly.
8. At one stage, the minister for health and sports, A.C. Shamukhadas, narrates the process of biological treatment of waste collected in lagoons; this, however, was inadequate to contain the pollution of the river.
9. Letter dated 19 July 1995, from the junior executive president of Grasim Industries to the senior environmental engineer, Kerala State Pollution Control Board (KSPCB).

10. Suit filed by Muhammedaji, brother of K.A. Rahman, former president of the Vazhakkad *panchayat* and renowned leader of the Chaliyar Action Committee, the front-line agency to spearhead the movement against the Birlas.
11. In June 1990, the Government of India commissioned a study, 'Health effects of environmental pollution caused by rayon grade pulp and fibre industry at Mavoor' with a project period of three years. The Public Accounts Committee (2000) mentions that though the Board had furnished a report on the environmental quality of area, no report had been furnished to the government.
12. See the letter dated 26 July 1995 from R.N. Saboo, president of Grasim Industries, to the senior environmental engineer, KSPCB, Calicut.
13. Though the NHRC began to engage with the concerns expressed by the local communities and their organizations, it was later decided not to take further action as the issues were taken to the level of the Supreme Court and the High Court. While the petition submitted to the High Court of Kerala by the KSSP demanded the assessment of the quantum of health hazards caused by the pollution and not to renew the agreement for supply of forest resources, individual activists argued for the application of polluter pays principle for compensation. See O.P. numbers 4633 of 1999: *KSSP vs the State of Kerala and Others*; O.P. 6653 dt. 12 March 1999, *Petition filed by Surendranath C., President, Shalimar Samara Sahaya Samithi and Jananeethi vs GoI, GoK, KSPCB and Grasim*; O.P. no. 14161 of 1997, *Chaliyar Human Rights Protection Samithi vs KSPCB and Others.*
14. Committee on Estimates (1977–1979), fifth Kerala Legislative Assembly, First Report on Prevention and Control of Water Pollution, Secretariat of the Kerala Legislature, Trivandrum, August 1977 (Chairman T.S. John), pp. 11–12.
15. Committee on Estimates (1977–1979), fifth Kerala Legislative Assembly, First Report on Prevention and Control of Water Pollution, Secretariat of the Kerala Legislature, Trivandrum, August 1977 (Chairman T.S. John), pp. 10–11.
16. Resolution passed by the Chaliyar Air and Water Purification Committee, September 1973.
17. KLA-3 (1967–1970), 29 August 1968, Proceeds of the KLA.
18. In 1978, when the factory was closed due to labour disputes, a multidisciplinary team led by K.T. Vijayamadhavan, who himself was a scientist, conducted a detailed scientific study of the pollution aspects of the factory and their impact on the people on the banks of the river. The report had a massive impact, and accelerated the protests already under way, attracting people in their thousands who then proceeded to destroy the temporary bund that had been erected by

the company in order to protect its water intake. The public took the stand that the company could be persuaded to adopt remedial measures against pollution only by being forced to consume the water it polluted. The study team further suggested that of the three main streams of effluents, the one containing residual black liquor and with a high biochemical oxygen demand (BOD), be subjected to anaerobic bacterial treatment in a closed digester, which could be implemented by modifying the existing facilities in the factory (see Damodaran 1981: 24). This was at a time when the BOD of the effluents was 133 milligrams per litre (mg/l) as against the prescribed tolerance limit of only 30 mg/l.

19. Justice K.K. Narendran, Judge, High Court of Judicature for Kerala. Judgment delivered on 30 March 1982.
20. Saboo, in his personal interview with this author (Kozhikode, 17 July 2013), continues to make the point that mercury was not used in the production process, and hence the company should not be blamed for its presence, if at all its presence is found.
21. It was in the Board meeting held on 29 January 1981 that the Pollution Control Board decided to proceed with the prosecution against the company; see KLA-6 (1980–1982), 3 March 1981.
22. See KSPCB (1992) PCB/T3110/75: Consent for discharge of effluent.
23. KLA-3 (1967–1970), Question Hour, 18 August 1969.
24. KLA-5 (1977–1979), 22 July 1977.
25. KLA-4 (1970–1977), Question Hour, 19 July 1971.
26. Warrier also mentions that it is important to have a newsprint production as it is not adequately available in India. This implies the necessity of protecting the proposed Hindustan Paper Corporation in the state.
27. KLA-4 (1970–1977), 19 February 1974.
28. The agreement to supply raw materials was ended on 31 August 1999 and 17 December 1999. No decision was taken for the renewal of agreement though it was under state consideration. The state was not supplying raw materials to the factory from 1 January 1999.
29. KLA-10 (1996–2001), 17 December 1999; this answer was given to a question raised by Elamaram Karim, who himself was a worker in the factory before becoming an MLA.
30. KLA, 11 February 1999.
31. See the letter dated 13 August 1999 from the Centre for Nature Studies, Thiruvananthapuram, to the Principal Chief Conservator of Forests, Thiruvananthapuram.
32. *Mathrubhumi*, 29 May 1999; Grasim was closed to put pressure on the state.

33. Due to the loss of bamboo and other forest resources, some of the valuable plants have been wiped out in the Western Ghats, and so also the rich biodiversity.
34. One major gherao was on 14 October 1968. When the vice-president of the factory was about to leave the office at 11 in the night, nearly 50 workers gheraoed him. The police removed them after receiving instruction from the district magistrate. KLA-3 (1967–1970), 15 November 1968.
35. KLA-5 (1977–1979), 28 June 1978. Also see Kerala High Court, *Gwalior Rayons Silk Mfg. (Wvg.) vs Government of Kerala* on 26 June, 1978; https://indiankanoon.org/doc/49304/, accessed 30 April 2023.
36. However, M.P. Gangadharan, who himself belonged to the ruling Congress party, challenged these assumptions as anti-truths. The state had failed in both providing employment to the workers and in disciplining the management; an ordinance was passed to take over the factory, which, in fact, was a facile move to appease the workers, with the company being given the opportunity to seek a stay to the ordinance prior to the official takeover. It was stayed by an advocate belonging to the party of the labour minister and the chief minister, the Indian National Congress. This was called out by Gangadharan who demanded to know what conspiracy lay behind these decisions. Oommen Chandy also reminded Gangadharan of his stance that 20,000 workers would lose their jobs, which echoed the company's stance. KLA 28 June 1978. Member of Kerala Legislative Assembly K. Avookhadarkutty Naha supported the motion and it passed in the legislative assembly.
37. N.I. Devassikkuty consistently argued that the state government had no genuine interest in passing the ordinance, as in the case of the Guruvayur devaswom; KLA, Questions and Answers, 2 August 1978.
38. T.M. Jacob was also critical of the position taken by the High Court and looked to the Supreme Court to take necessary action. He also suggested that the issues should be discussed outside the assembly with the trade union leaders and workers. There were nine trade unions in the industry in Mavoor; see (Government of Kerala/Kerala State Planning Board 1997: 1).
39. KLA, 2 August 1978.
40. Gowri Amma, KLA, 16 March 1988.
41. Gowri Amma, KLA, 29 March 1988.
42. During the freedom movement M.K. Gandhi undertook 18 hunger strikes. His longest hunger strike lasted 21 days. Here, it is worth noting that the Indian social activist Irom Sharmila participated in a 16-year hunger strike in opposition to the Armed Forces Special Powers Act (AFSPA), which grants

soldiers in Manipur the authority to make arrests without warrant and even fire fatal shots in certain circumstances. Sharmila was force-fed for more than a decade through a tube in her nose. AFSPA is in force in a number of Indian states including Manipur, Jammu and Kashmir, Nagaland, Assam, and Arunachal Pradesh to create and perpetuate a reign of terror.

43. A Maoism-sympathetic organization that was dissolved in October 1991.
44. C.P. Balan Vaidyar, 16 March 1988.
45. See the company petition nos 38 and 39 of 2000 in the Hon'ble High Court of Madhya Pradesh Bench at Indore.
46. Joint letter dated 7 January 2000, from the two organizations, namely the CSS and the CSSS, to the secretary, Labour and Rehabilitation Department, Government of Kerala.
47. KLA-12 (2006–2011), 19 June 2007. Earlier, there were discussions to start 'new generation industries' in the land.
48. For details, see *Mathrubhumi* (2001); also see Remesh (2008).
49. For details, see *Mathrubhumi* (2001).
50. See the company petition nos 38 and 39 of 2000 in the Hon'ble High Court of Madhya Pradesh Bench at Indore.
51. KLA, 19 December 2006. S. Gopalan was answering the question raised by Aryadan Muhammed who pointed out that because of the non-functioning of the factory in Mavoor, it was not only the workers in Mavoor who lost their jobs but also those in Nilambur and Wayanad.
52. This author had an opportunity to talk with A. Vasu regarding the Chaliyar protests in Calicut on 7 February 1988.

References

Administrative Report, 1958–68. Forest Department, Government of Kerala, Thiruvananthapuram.

Anderson, Patricia Ann (1993). *Environmental Impact of Agricultural Activities: Proceedings of Industrial and Agricultural Impacts on the Hydrologic Environment: The Second USA/CIS Joint Conference on Environmental Hydrology And Hydrogeology*, ed. Yoram Eckstein and Alexander Zaporosec. Washington, D.C.: USA/CIS Joint Conference on Environmental Hydrology and Hydrogeology (2nd).

Carr, Frances (2001). Indorayon's last gasp? *Inside Indonesia*: *The Environment* 65. https://www.insideindonesia.org/indorayons-last-gasp (accessed 5 May 2023).

Chaliyar Samara Samithi (2007). *Chaliyar Athijeevana Paatangal* (Chaliyar: Lessons in Survival). Vazhakkad, Malappuram: Chaliyar Samara Samithi. Chaliyar Struggle (Malayalam).

Chundamannil, M. (1986). 'Pattern of Investment in Forest and Its Implications on Sustained Yield Management in Kerala'. MPhil dissertation, Centre for Development Studies, Thiruvananthapuram

Cleghorn, H. (1860). *Forests and Gardens of South India*. London: W.H. Allen.

Coates, Peter (2013). *A Story of Six Rivers: History, Culture and Ecology*. London: Reaktion Books.

Damodaran, V.K., ed. (1981). *The Story of a Dying Village: A Case Study of Pollution Problems*. Thiruvananthapuram: Asian Science Communication Organisation.

Gadgil, M. and R. Guha. (1992). *This Fissured Land: An Ecological History of India*. Berkeley and Los Angeles, CA: University of California Press.

Gadgil, M. and S.N. Prasad. (1978). Vanishing bamboo stocks. *Commerce* 136 (3497): 1000–1004.

George, and J. Krishnan (2002). *River, People and Industry: The Politics and Pollution of River Chaliyar*. Thiruvananthapuram: Kerala Research Programme to Local Level Development, CDS.

Government of Kerala and Grasim Industries (1958). *Agreement between the Government and Grasim Industries*. Kerala Forest Department.

Government of Kerala/Kerala State Planning Board (1997). *Decentralisation in Kerala: Mavoor Gram Panchayat Comprehensive Development Document*. Thiruvananthapuram: Kerala State Planning Board, Governmet of Kerala.

Mathrubhumi (2001). Mavoor Grasim closes down: Compensation settled. 8 July.

Mavoor. http://www.mavoor.net/home/about-mavoor (accessed 4 May 2023).

Muhammed, Aryadan (2000). *Committee on Public Accounts (1998–2000)*. Thiruvananthapuram: Kerala Legislative Library.

Noronha, Frederick. 1999. India's 30-Year eco-crusade shuts rayon plant. Environment News Service, International Daily Newswire. http://www.ensnewswire.com/ens/sep1999/1999-09-15-02.asp (accessed 4 May 2023).

Rajeev, K.R. (2001). Parting time at Grasim. *The New Indian Express*, 23 July.

Ram Mohan, K.T., and K. Ravi Raman (1988). Worker rises against Indian big capital: Report on rayon's workers' struggle. *Economic and Political Weekly* 23 (27): 1359–1364.

——— (1989). Mavoor Rayons accord: Left-front government on its knees. *Economic and Political Weekly* 24, (1): 16–17.

Raman, K. Ravi (1998). Intervention in the Western Ghats: An inquiry into the historical processes of loss of biodiversity and community sources of livelihood.

In *Conservation and Economic Evaluation of Biodiversity*, ed. P. Pushpangadan, K. Ravi, and V. Santosh, pp. 525–544. New Delhi: Oxford-IBH.

——— (2010). Transverse solidarity: Water, power, and resistance. *Review of Radical Political Economics* (14 May): 251–268.

Remesh, Babu P. (2008). Mavoor: a story of corporate social 'irresponsibility' and lost livelihoods. *Labour File* 6 (5). https://www.labourfile.com/section-detail.php?aid=529 (accessed 10 October 2021).

Sivarajan (1959). *A Report on the Survey of the Bamboo Resources of the Forests of Kozhikode Circle*. Thiruvananthapuram: Kerala Forest Department, Government of Kerala.

Save Chaliyar Campaign (2011). *Plan Draft on Status Study*. Vazhakad: Save Chaliyar Campaign.

Seethi, K.M. (2000). Cleaning Chaliyar river: Pollution control or jobs? *Economic and Political Weekly* 35 (3): 97–99.

——— (2001). Kerala-Grasim: Polluter does not pay. *Economic and Political Weekly* 36 (29). https://www.epw.in/journal/2001/29/commentary/kerala-grasim-polluter-does-not-pay.html (accessed 4 May 2023).

Shaji K.A. (2008). A river reborn. Boloji. http://www.boloji.com/index.cfm?md=Content&sd=Articles&ArticleID=4790 (accessed 4 May 2023).

Sleet, Michelle Van (n.d.). Khrushchev's peaceful coexistence: The soviet perspective. *Time*, 5 May. https://blogs.bu.edu/guidedhistory/russia-and-its-empires/michelle-van-sleet/ (accessed 4 May 2023).

Society for the Protection of Environment (SPEK) (1994). *Kozhikode District Basic Ecological Status Book*. Calicut: SPEK.

Sridhar, R. (2000) Grasim: *The Burden on Our Heads*. Thiruvananthapuram: Centre for Nature Studies and Thanal Conservation Action and Information Network.

Surendranath C. (2000). Justice denied. *India Seminar*. https://www.india-seminar.com/2000/492/492%20surendranath%20c.htm (accessed 26 July 2023).

Vazhakad. http://www.vazhakkad.com/history.html (accessed 4 May 2023).

Vidhyadharan, C.N. (2009). *Oru Vyavasayabhinte Pathanam*. Aluva: Kavya Books, 2009.

Vijayamandhavan, K.T. (2011). *KA Rahman: The Valiant Warrior*. Kozhikode: Paristhithi Samrakshana Samiti, Vazhakad.

3

Occupy Muthanga

Land, Forest, and Reinventing Indigeneity and Identity

Oh Country! That Treads on Me to Reach for the Sky.

—Song heard in the refugee huts
in front of the state secretariat

Onam, the harvest festival of the Malayalis, marked the moment of departure in August 2001, when the Adivasis of Kerala planted 'refugee huts', the *kutilkettysamaram*, in front of the state secretariat in Thiruvananthapuram in protest against mass starvation deaths in their communities. The protest was historic and innovative; no other protest of this nature has ever been attempted anywhere else in India. What they sought was their right to livelihood resources – land for the landless. While there were several land struggles and movements by Adivasis in Kerala, the immediate provocation for them marching to the state capital was the report of 32 starvation deaths among Adivasis in and around Attappady and Wayanad, the tribal district in the state. They demanded a settlement outside the controversial Kerala Restriction on Transfer by and Restoration of Lands to Scheduled Tribes Bill, 1999, passed by the state legislative assembly, which repealed the original Kerala Scheduled Tribes (Restriction on Transfer of Lands and Restoration of Alienated Lands) Act, 1975. The Adivasi Dalit Samara Samithi (ADSS) argued that of the 75,000 Adivasi families in the state, 45,000 were landless, and the granting of 5 acres to each of those families would require the distribution of 2.25 lakh acres of land. The Adivasis, led by C.K. Janu – an Adiya woman who spearheaded the struggle – conducted their protest in an unprecedented manner. The struggle was considered successful by the ADSS, claiming that their demands for lands were met, at least partly, by the government. When no action was taken by the government to make the promised measures, and instead followed procrastination politics, the tribal alliance renewed their protest, now in the form of Occupy Muthanga. The indigenous people of Wayanad, under the banner of the Adivasi Gothra Maha Sabha (AGMS) – nearly 800 families – entered the Muthanga range of the Wayanad Wildlife Sanctuary (MWWS) in January 2003 and declared the area their own, a new republic. However, in two months' time, on 19 February, they were forcefully evacuated with armed police: one Adivasi and a police officer lost their lives; several Adivasis were hurt or injured in the process.[1]

Kutilkettysamaram, the origins of the historic Occupy Muthanga revolt, itself was subjected to criticisms, though the ADSS claimed it as a success. The communists, particularly the Communist Party of India (Marxist) (CPI[M]) and the Red Flag, expressed their reservations, with the CPI(M) reiterating its official position that the agitation was nothing but a state-sponsored show. The party also observed that had the present government been genuinely interested in solving the Adivasi problem, it should have persisted with the policies adopted by the former Left Democratic Front (LDF) government for the restoration of alienated lands. The Communist Party of India (Marxist–Leninist) Red Flag (CPI[ML] Red Flag), which had declared solidarity with the striking Adivasis at the outset, remained sceptical of the victory claimed by the ADSS, arguing that the ADSS has merely accepted in full that which it had previously rejected – the 1999 ordinance of the LDF government, which had promised lands in lieu of the alienated lands. The Bharatiya Janata Party (BJP), too, which had initially appeared supportive of the strike, pointed out that the final agreement between the ADSS and the state government did not refer to the restoration of alienated lands. This chapter makes an attempt to trace the truth behind all these claims and counterclaims. Before this, it is important to situate the indigenous people in the larger history of marginality in Kerala, before and after state formation.

Adivasis: The Void in Kerala

Adivasis are the only ethnic minority in the state of Kerala, constituting 1.14 per cent of its 31.8 million population. These indigenous people, belonging to different clans but of a common social origin, are spread over an Adivasi belt that straddles the highlands of Wayanad, Palakkad, and Idukki districts. While the life expectancy of an average Keralite is well above 75, and comparable with Western standards, the longevity of the Adivasis is hardly 45–50 years.

In a state that boasts 100 per cent literacy, half the tribals, until recently, remain entombed in the darkness of illiteracy. Unaware of their basic rights, they live outside the ambit of the law, harassed and beaten, and the state had to admit that the Adivasis' regions are not free from unwed mothers.[2] Yet the void remains invisible to them too. There are certain domains in the state structure in which Adivasis are heavily over-represented to a certain extent. The incidence of poverty and starvation among them is a classic case in point (IIM Kozhikode 2006; Kjosavik 1985; Kunhaman 1985, 2003). Infant deaths amongst tribal communities are uncommon. School children have comparatively high dropout ratios. By government' s own admission, even the number of unwed mothers increased to as high as 1059 among tribes.[3] While the indigenous people represent hardly 1 per cent of the population of the state, they constitute nearly one quarter of the population below the poverty line; in a travesty of the 'Kerala model', a significant size of the tribals exist in a condition of abject want and deprivation (Government of Kerala 1962, 1979, 2013).

They are over-represented with respect to landlessness and represented in those jobs that are not accumulative in terms of surplus. As far as the self-employment category – another countable category in the modern state of affairs – is concerned, the representation of the Adivasis is minimum. As I have pointed out, they are the illiterates in a state that boasts of 100 per cent literacy. They do not read; therefore, they do not exist – they form the void in the mass media. They also do not form a market for the daily newspapers, and thus they themselves are not newsworthy. There was a period in Kerala history, again in the postcolonial phase, when the officials and settlers and also the local tourists were anxiously staking claim to the bodies of tribal women; the ultimate outcome was a large number of unwed mothers in various parts of tribal regions in the state – Wayanad being the classic case (Praveen 2012). While the larger Adivasi communities form the void/'uncounted' (see Rancière 1999), the subaltern female Adivasis form the very depths of the void. Let me come to the historical roots of this marginality.

Historical Processes of Marginality

Within the larger context of the history of Kerala, various phases in the development/exclusion trajectory of the indigenous people stand out:

The first phase consists of the pre-colonial simultaneity in the existence of 'feudal' agrarian production, with tribes serving as slave labour, and that of tribes with their community ownership of resources (pre-1800) and some other communities as hunter-gatherers. Until the abolition of slavery in the mid-nineteenth century, the slave mode of production was dominant in the countryside; by and large, the uplands were no exception to this. The depressed castes such as the Paniyars, Pulayars, Cherumars, and the various tribal groups were employed as labourers but under a system of peadial/agrestic slavery: they were tied to the land and were transacted along with it; they were sold to meet arrears of land revenue and remained unfree for centuries. 'Slaves' were 'bought, and sold and hired out' both in the countryside and in the hills even after the legal abolition of slavery by the mid-nineteenth century – the distinction drawn between slavery and the actual conditions of life thus remained more academic than real in the years to come (Raman 2010a).

The second phase was the phase of colonialism and the sequestering of tribal ancestral domains. Historically, they were not even allowed to retain their own names, with the colonial authorities preferring to classify the tribes according to their own nomenclature. There was a metamorphosis of the term 'tribe' in itself. In the first census report of colonial India, 1891, the scattered 'forest tribes' were included under the subheading 'Agricultural and Pastoral Castes'. They were classified as 'Animists' in 1901 and then as 'Tribal Animists' in 1911. In the 1921 and 1931 censuses, they were described as 'Hill and Forest Tribe'. Under the Government of India Act, 1935, they were designated as 'backward tribes'.[4] Currently, they are known as Scheduled Tribes, which refers to an ethnic group geographically isolated or relatively isolated (National Tribal Policy 2004). They do not find a home among indigenous groups in international discourse. As a result, the Indian state has consistently dismissed the term 'indigenous peoples', believing their right to self-determination could fuel secessionist impulses.

In terms of sequestering of tribal ancestral domains, the massive displacement of tribals began in the early nineteenth century with the razing of forests of Malabar and Travancore, first for plantation colonialism, then for the British navy, and, by the 1850s, for the colonial railways. The process of dispossession gained momentum from the second half of the century onwards and was a result of extensive land appropriation by European and local planters (Raman 2010a).

Prior to the advent of colonialism, there had not been any official move to regulate the control of forest resources. Neither was there any need for such legislation, forests being considered public property, particularly belonging to the indigenous peoples whose rights over the resources remained uncontested for as long as anyone could remember. The creation of the Forest Department in 1865 and the implementation of the Indian Forest Act of 1878 had the specific motive of serving colonial interests: forest resources were extensively surveyed, demarcated, and reserved; grazing was prohibited; shifting cultivation was forbidden; and the most productive of tribal lands were sequestered either as 'reserved' or 'waste lands', a process of decoding the social life of the indigenous people – the beginning of the long trajectory of multiple displacements and thereby of marginality (Jacob 2006). However, from these very waste lands came the timber to build the 'wooden walls' of the British Empire (Raman 2010a: 37–39). Natural teak forests were razed to the ground, the timber being used for shipbuilding or transshipped to countries like Britain, the United States, and Germany, bringing more and more export earnings to the state. One of the most lucrative of colonial enterprises, monoculture plantations in the form of coffee and tea, also came to be nurtured in these lands.

Bourdillon, the colonial conservator of forests from England, generated the discourse to the effect that shifting cultivation was 'wasteful' and thus 'objectionable' and was to be 'condemned' (Bourdillon 1893: 11–12); Cleghorn, the conservator of forests in Dakshin Kanara, described it as 'a rude system of culture' and a 'wasteful and barbarous system' (Cleghorn 1861: 2, 68, 127–143) and continued to maintain that it had serious effects on climate and soil fertility. Shifting cultivation was also a subject of interest to the Marine Board, which in turn took the view that teak was 'devastated' on account of lands being used for shifting cultivation (cited in Pouchepadass 1995: 133). The practice of shifting cultivation was abolished, forcing the tribals to commodity themselves as wage labour under landlords or offer themselves for recruitment to plantations. The modern forestry and the planter state wields its power over the void – a void that very often proved a productive pool of labour. Adivasi labour was often treated on a par with the work done by elephants in the forests during colonial times.

Global capital continued to penetrate the traditional villages of the Adivasis, making them move out further into the periphery. In their attempts to be the world's largest integrated plantation, the big plantations like the Scotland-based global capital, James Finlay & Company, popularly known as Kanan Devan plantations, were thus built by banishing the local tribal communities. As has rightly been pointed out by the Anglican Church missionary Samuel Mateer in the 1890s, 'as soon as the planters' axe is heard, the hill kings pack their traps and desert their homes to establish themselves in another valley. In this way, they have been driven from hill to hill and from valley to valley….' (Mateer 1883: 66). As this Anglican Church missionary Samuel Mateer would have us believe, these indigenous people simply could not resist the 'onward march of a superior race' (Mateer 1883: 66).[5] Though a few of these tribes even sought employment on plantations of their own accord, they were largely disinclined to work for the Europeans (Thurston 1909: 63–64, 67).[6] Ironically, they were often labelled thieves, and planters were warned against employing them (*Planting Opinion* 1896)[7]; it was also alleged that Muslim traders coming to the hills received stolen crops from these tribes (Wilkes 1953: 274). Those who were either unwilling to work for the planters or could not be incorporated into the plantation workforce were driven further and further away. As we closely follow them, we see that the planters, backed by the state, were ultimately successful in creating a workforce out of even these groups who had been initially averse to such employment, the marginality continuously being reproduced in the highlands.

Whatever forest lands had escaped the greedy grasp of the European and local planters now became the gambling den of the settler peasants, predominantly Syrian Christians of the plains, which could be considered as the third phase of the encroachment/displacement of the tribal population, within the larger colonial conditions that were again legitimized by the state. The hardships of the capitalist depression of the 1930s and the imperialist war of the 1940s spawned the first two waves of peasant encroachments. One cannot but view the subsequent intrusions as anything but the fallout of the parliamentary politics of legitimization and procrastination. In the cases of alienation of land, the middle-class occupant farmers actively resorted to muscle power, forgery, bribery, and deceit to acquire land rights and, at times, indulged in outright violence. In legal terms, they gradually became the landlords, the ones who transferred/sold their lands to the settlers, who, in turn, suddenly became the tenants/owners. The growth rate of the population in the hill districts thus steadily progressed due to the immigration of settler cultivators. There were two waves of peasant migration: in the 1930s when the local economy was hard hit by the Great Depression and during World War II in the 1940s, an imperial war that once again brought hardships to the local people. On both occasions, poor peasants and landless labourers from the plains in Travancore migrated to the highlands of Travancore and the midlands of Malabar, while a small section moved to the highlands of Malabar itself (see Raman 2010b; Tharakan 1984; Prakash 2002). The tribals who once formed the majority in these regions fast dwindled to a minority in their own ancestral domains: their space got cramped; they become the minority; and they also become the historical agency of what Deleuze and Guattari (1987) would call minor politics.

The fourth phase begins with state formation in 1956 and the communists coming into power – the beginning of hope, but soon to realize the despair and the rise of the politics of procrastination. For the tribals in the state, history – both colonial and post-colonial – is an unbroken chain of servitude and atrocities with nary a break with the past, not even with the assumption of power by the communists in 1957. Land reforms in Kerala, where it is said to have been most effectively implemented owing to a leftist political climate, have failed to yield any benefits to the outliers such as tribals (and for Dalits and fisherfolk). When tenancy and landlordism were abolished in 1970 – which itself was partly a response to the Maoist politics in India, including Kerala – the tenants were granted occupancy rights; but in the tribal belts, things took a peculiar twist with the settler farmers acquiring the land rights in their garb of 'tenants' and the tribals losing lands from their position as 'landlords'. By the time tribals accepted the necessity of obtaining formal land titles, they had lost the opportunity to lay claim to lands that might rightfully have been considered theirs. Further, the tribals who had been displaced to the fringes of their forests were dispersed farther afield in the wake of the decision to exempt plantations from ceiling provisions of the land reforms, as executed by the left-wing governments. Equally important was the displacement of the tribal population from places like Muthanga for raising industrial plantation such as eucalyptus for the Birlas, an aspect that has been described in Chapter 2. No wonder those Adivasis staging the *kutilkettysamaram* raised the slogan in court 'for the right to live on the land where we were born'. The veracity of this historically meaningful slogans was further proven when they entered the Muthanga range of the wildlife sanctuary. The land that they have claimed in Muthanga was already cleared for the eucalyptus plantation for the Mavoor Gwalior Rayons.

This was the time when the Maoists in India were preoccupied with characterizing the Indian state. In their opinion, the Indian state was semi-feudal, and its worst form manifested in the tribal regions. This further precipitated a new series of uprisings against the landlords (see Banerjee 1980; B. Paul 2014). After the peasant uprising at Naxalbari in the Darjeeling district of West Bengal when a tribal youth, who had a judicial order to plough his land, was attacked by the local landlords in May 1967, their activities soon spread to various parts of India, including Kerala. However, with severe police repression, which led to the police killing on 17 February 1970 of young Varghese, a Naxalite who was trying to mobilize the Adivasis in the forests of Wayanad, that way of Maoism was gradually dying down, but only to rebirth as new ways of Maoist politics.[8] These were the beginnings of Naxalite days in Kerala (for details, see Bijuraj 2015, 2021: 186–192).

Yet the federal government remained under constant threat from the Maoist movements in the 1970s and was finally induced to pass Acts to restore the alienated lands of the tribals. The U.N. Dhebar Commission – who was the chairman of the Scheduled Areas and Scheduled Tribes Commission set up by the first prime minister, Jawaharlal Nehru, in 1960 – proposed restoring alienated tribal land to tribals with effect from 26 January 1950 (Dhebar 1960–1961). However, it was not until 1 April 1975 that the then prime minister, Indira Gandhi, recommended passing legislation in accordance with the Dhebar Commission. It was also part of the federal government's 20-point plan (see Prabhakaran 2003). Kerala, too, had its 1975 Act – the Kerala Scheduled Tribes Act (Restriction on Transfer of Lands and Restoration of Alienated Lands) – passed by the CPI-backed Congress-led government. However, the implementation of the legislation was jeopardized at the very outset by the settler farmers whose representatives themselves had supported the bill on the floor of the legislature. They even resorted to physical violence in their bid to stall official proceedings.

In Kerala, the state assembly, with Achutha Menon as the UDF government and EMS as the opposition leader, unanimously passed the Kerala Scheduled Tribes (Restriction on Transfer of Land and Restoration of Alienated Lands) Act, 1975, which was indeed revolutionary. The revenue minister, Baby John, even declared that the government would treat all alienated tribal lands as 'stolen property', and the government was committed to restoring the same to the indigenous owners. The Act received the President of India's mandatory assent and is also included in the Indian Constitution's 9th Schedule as unchallengeable. However, the governments that alternated power – the LDF and the UDF – took no action for over a decade, and it was only in 1986 that the rules to implement the Act were drafted (Government of Kerala 1986). That is also in response to the legal activism initiated by the Adivasi sympathizers. As part of their procrastination strategy, the UDF governments of K. Karunakaran and A.K. Antony sought multiple extensions to stall the law's implementation and even attempted to amend the 1975 Act. To quote the Committee on State Agrarian Relations and the Unfinished Task in Land Reforms constituted by the Government of India (2009: 131),

> The law of restoration was passed in 1975, made applicable in 1986, but ironically less than two decades after the law was passed, the legislature passed a law rescinding or withdrawing the law passed in 1975 on the grounds that the law cannot be implemented as eviction of the illegal encroachers on tribal land would result in law and order problems. This fact has been acknowledged by the state government. The President of India, however, rejected the law pertaining to withdrawal of the application of the Tribal Land Restoration Act of 1975. So the state of Kerala continued in

> the situation of a legal impasse till the High Court of the state directed it to implement the Act, which continues to drag its feet.

The left government's attitude towards the Act was no better. In 1996, LDF chief minister E.K. Nayanar even claimed that the Act could not be implemented due to organized opposition from powerful encroachers, which was rejected by the High Court, which firmly directed that the Act be implemented within six weeks, ending 30 September 1996. The court also directed that the revenue officers should affect the delivery of possession of alienated tribal lands to their original owners, but the officers could not do anything as there was no state support. Politicians even put pressure on bureaucrats who attempted to evict encroachers from tribal lands. What was notable was the LDF's U-turn in passing the Kerala Scheduled Tribes (Restriction on Transfer of Land and Restoration of Alinenated Lands) Amendment Bill, 1996, with the sole exception of K.R. Gowri Amma's support, in order to avoid contempt of court proceedings. The new Bill, dubbed 'the most reactionary ever introduced since the establishment of the state assembly', declared all tribal land transactions between 1960 and 24 January 1986 to be legal and valid. Furthermore, Nayanar and Antony sought Presidential assent but were denied by India's first Dalit president, K.R. Narayanan, who had to remind the chief minister and the opposition leader that an Act included in the Constitution's 9th schedule could not be amended by the state assembly.

In 1999, a second amendment was passed in the assembly (Government of Kerala 1996, 1999) to avoid presidential assent, but it was rejected by the Kerala High Court, revealing the story of how procrastination politics nearly destroyed a pro-tribal Act for social justice. The majority of the tribals in the state were landless for a significant period of time due to the Act's non-implementation, which sparked Adivasi movements and revolts. The government, both the left and the right, reacted by further procrastination in spite of repeated warnings by the judiciary. More than four decades have elapsed since the parent bill was passed, but the government has remained impotent. The settler-peasants are in a position to dictate terms: together, they constitute a significant portion of the population and are powerful in more than a dozen constituencies. The plantation-based system that they foster makes them a historically decisive force in the larger economy and society (Raman 2010a; Baak 1997). Their interests are well articulated by the Kerala Congress' with many factions, one of the factions invariably sharing in the state governance, whether the government be led by the Congress or the Marxists; so it was easy for them to quash all the proceedings against the settler lobby. The question of Adivasi land rights entails several socio-political and cultural concerns. The solution of Adivasi rehabilitation into farms thus reduces their varied worries into transferable land alone (Sreerekha 2010). The Adivasi rehabilitation experiments such as Aralam, Sugandhagiri, Pookkodu, and so on, suffer from various challenges including the absence of basic sanitary amenities, difficulty in acquiring title deeds, and also for their basic livelihoods. By this time, Adivasis themselves realized that most of the projects failed to match their political imaginations. The year 2003 saw at least 32 starvation deaths among the Adivasis, and this led to an unprecedented level of local protests by them. They waylaid the Mobile Fair Price Shop of the State Civil Supplies Corporation and distributed the spoils among the starving Adivasis in Wayanad,[9] while C.K. Janu and M. Geethanandan led a more peaceful protest that hit the epicentre of the Kerala legislature in Thiruvananthapuram on the days of Onam.[10]

First Phase of Struggle: Call to Boycott

Onam Celebrations and Refugee Huts

A few of the Adivasis who came down from the hills with their families, including children, under the direction of the ADSS made a boycott call of Onam celebrations in 2001 but were ignored by both the mainstream society and the state, the latter amid the extravagant preparations for a state-sponsored Onam celebration. On 5 September 2001, the closing ceremony and rally were staged in a tense atmosphere as the Adivasis had challenged the huge expenses incurred in the name of the celebrations even as starvation deaths were decimating Adivasi communities. The striking Adivasis repeatedly attempted to breach the police cordon protecting the Onam procession, disrupting the celebrations just as had been planned. The police attempted to take C.K. Janu into custody, but this too was foiled amid resistance by the agitating activists. To everybody's surprise, by that time hundreds of Adivasi families had joined the struggle and had started to pitch what they called *refugee huts* in front of the state secretariat, thus beginning what came to be called *kutilkettysamaram*, the most innovative struggle that has ever happened in the history of the Global South.

Almost a week after the protests, the then chief minister, A.K. Antony, finally agreed to institute talks with the ADSS leaders. The government offered 10,000 acres of land to the Adivasis, and it was decided that the tribal development programme, being funded by the general budget, would henceforth be implemented through the Tribal Department instead of the *panchayat*s. Other offers included free rations for all Adivasis for another two months, 10 kilograms of rice per month for all Adivasis with disabilities, and a restoration of full rights for the collection of minor forest produce. Ninety per cent of the jobs in the Forest Department were to be reserved for the Adivasis. It was also decided that the State Planning Board would prepare a comprehensive master plan for the development of the indigenous people in the state. It was also suggested that the chief minister would head a state-level committee to investigate all cases of exploitation, murder, and rape of Adivasis.

However, the ADSS rejected the government's offers on many counts. When asked why the Action Committee rejected the proposal, M. Geethanandan made the following arguments: First, the land offered was too meagre to be of any significance to the Adivasis, who suffered from utter deprivation and starvation. Second, the state was clearly making an attempt to appease the Supreme Court with a show of rescuing the landless Adivasis and thus giving legitimacy to the 1999 amendment. Further, the ADSS remained firm in its original demand for 5 acres of land per landless family and a settlement outside the 1999 amendment.

They also categorically stated that it was not bread and clothing that they were after; what they hungered for were basic resources – land and a source of income – which would ensure food and shelter. This, in effect, nullified the attempts made by the CPI(M) to distribute food and old clothes among the Adivasis who had been brought to this pass in part by the communists themselves. The state government then increased its offer from 10,000 to 15,000 acres of land to be distributed amongst the landless Adivasis, claiming that these lands would be identified within two months from amongst various categories of land such as those belonging to the Plantation Corporation, tribal development projects, and *poramboke* regions (land unassessed by the government). This offer also failed to win the approval of the ADSS, which now made plans to intensify the struggle. An Avakasa Sthapana Yatra – Journey for the Assertion of Rights – was commenced by C.K. Janu across the length of Kerala from Kasargode to Thiruvananthapuram. Public receptions, meetings, and rallies were organized along the way, with various solidarity groups and progressive sections of society lending their support for the strike in the capital. With the observation of Adivasi Solidarity Day on 18 September, 14 more refugee camps were opened before the secretariat, taking the number of Adivasi families participating in the strike to more than 500. They raised the slogan: 'Oh Country! That Treads on Me to Reach for the Sky.'

The Adivasi huts came up in such numbers that the authorities feared a complete blockade of the state secretariat. Practical help in terms of food, cooking, and toilet facilities (for the marching agitators) was provided by a Strike Solidarity Committee largely composed of Dalits from the capital city. An organic link was established with the slum dwellers of the city, which provided basic provisions like food grains, vegetables, and fuel wood for cooking to the Adivasis, further broadening the Dalit base of the Adivasis in the city. A Civil Forum constituted of intellectuals, poets, writers, feminists, media persons, and others also entered the arena in overt support of the Adivasis. As the plight of the landless Adivasi families caught the attention of the public, the government moved its machinery to counter mounting public opinion in favour of the ADSS. Other Adivasi organizations with obvious political affiliations were brought in to convince the public that the ADSS was not the only organization representing the Adivasi cause. The ADSS remained unmoved despite such manoeuvring by the government and firmly rejected the latter's call to them to join the 'mainstream', declaring their disinclination to become party to the corruption and cheating that has come to characterize modern society. In a sense, the protesting Adivasi communities became what Žižek has called 'part of no part' (1998: 988) within a conflicting political body.

Second Phase: The Formation of the AGMS

As the need for a stronger push became evident, the Adivasis came together to form the AGMS, the first of its kind, with 380 representatives of 31 communities from Adivasi regions all over the state. It was on 3 October 2001, after having a mass demonstration from Raj Bhavan to the city centre, that the birth of Adivasi Gothra Maha Sabha was announced. The AGMS fully backed the ADSS in its demands, and the decision to intensify the strike in each of the district headquarters followed. A mass rally of about 10,000 strong was taken out in the capital city; led by the AGMS, which was supported by a sizeable number of Dalit organizations and human rights activists.

The right-wing chief minister A.K. Antony, who seemed unmoved by the starvation deaths occurring in the most literate state in India, disapproved of the 'defiling' of the state secretariat façade by the refugee huts. He seemed more concerned about the unpleasant impact the settlers would have on tourism, fearing that they would soil the area with their open toilets – something they never did. The situation escalated with a case being filed with the Lokayukta demanding the dismantling of the refugee huts. Though the Lokayukta rejected the case, the state took up the issue. However, rather than bearing the onus for its decision, the government sought the assistance of the city corporation in the dismantling of the huts. The CPI(M) leadership, which had originally been dismissive of the Adivasi mode of struggle, calling it the 'Janu-Model', now changed sides and strongly opposed the dismantling of the Adivasi huts, in response perhaps to the rising public opinion in support of the struggle. The corporation refused to carry out the order on the grounds that this was an unprecedented situation in the history of the city corporation.

The state government then resorted to (un)constitutional means in an effort to establish that the striking Adivasis were free to put up sheds but not huts. The ADSS's rebuttal was sharp and swift: taking it as a question of discrimination against the Adivasis, they sought to raise public opinion against the move to dismantle the huts throughout the length and breadth of the country. They won the support of eminent personalities like the president of India, the former prime minister V.P. Singh, and others who supported the Adivasis in one voice. The chief minister's office was inundated with fax messages, including a few from the United States and Canada, requesting the government to retract its decision. The presence of Medha Patkar and Arundhati Roy in their midst also gave the movement greater power, as did their messages of support. Many other public intellectuals including M.T. Vasudevan Nair, Sukumar Azhikode, O.N.V Kurup, M. Mukundan, and so on, were there at the forefront of the Muthanga tribal struggle. The situation became more complex with the involvement of the police, who, however, held back from their plans to launch an attack by night for fear of trampling on the infants and children who would be asleep in the huts. They attempted to ram a jeep into the row of Adivasi huts in the dead of night in an obvious move to terrorise the Adivasis into submission. The ADSS called it a homicidal attack, with a few activists threatening self-immolation – invoking the memory of the martyrdom of Sreedharan, who waged war against the faulty developmental initiatives of the former communist government[11] – as the threat of demolition loomed close. Tension began to mount when the activists of the Civil Forum and other groups formed a human chain to keep a night-time vigil around the refugee camps. There was widespread condemnation of the government's decision, which was violative of the right to peaceful and democratic protest. The chief minister, however, denied responsibility for this misadventure, blaming it on 'overzealous' officials. In fact, the chief minister narrowly escaped legal action, which could have been instituted against him under the Scheduled Castes & Scheduled Tribes (Prevention of Atrocities) Act, 1989.

In an attempt to reinvent its image as one of a government genuinely interested in Adivasi welfare, the government increased its offer of land by 32,000 acres, and offered 42,000 acres of land to be distributed among the Adivasis – 1–5 acres of land per landless family would be distributed subject to availability in each district. Although this marked a significant shift in the government's approach and was welcomed by the leaders of the Civil Forum, the ADSS remained unimpressed, and, for the first time, there appeared to be a schism between the Civil Forum and the hardliners. The ADSS activists also began informal discussions with K.R. Gowri Amma, the veteran communist and the minister for agriculture in the state cabinet with a history of keen interest in Adivasi land struggles. More than the actual area of land to be distributed among the Adivasis, it was the constitutional protection proferred by the inclusion of Adivasi regions/hamlets as Scheduled Areas under the Vth Schedule that the ADSS requested. In a tactical move, K.R. Gowri Amma roped in support from the single largest minority community in Kerala, inviting Kunhalikkutty, the leader of the Muslim League and the second largest party in the cabinet, for informal talks.

The struggle then spread across the state, with refugee camps sprouting in Pathanamthitta, Kannur, and Thodupuzha, mostly in front of the district headquarters. The police intervened at many places, blocking the erection of thatched huts and taking many Adivasis into custody, but the camps continued to spread, at times just a cluster of roofless huts. The intense struggle of the Adivasis evoked a response in the country's capital, New Delhi, too, with around 50 public figures, including advocates, journalists, and other prominent intellectuals, gathering at Kerala House in New Delhi to request the Government of Kerala through its attaché to seek an amicable and peaceful solution to the Adivasi land question. The students of Delhi University organized a campus demonstration to proclaim solidarity with the Adivasis of Kerala.

The state cabinet took a policy decision prohibiting the erection of huts and toilets in front of the state secretariat, inconveniencing pedestrians and the travelling public. Talking to newsmen after the meeting, the chief minister asserted that the decision of the council of ministers would be implemented by relevant government agencies. The cabinet decided that all the 10 huts put up before the state secretariat and a 'tribal camp shed' functioning near the chief minister's residence would be removed. The chief minister, A.K. Antony, objected to the Adivasis using the secretariat pavement as a common kitchen and public toilet. He accused them of forcibly collecting contributions from pedestrians. He argued that the movement had inconvenienced traffic in front of the secretariat and therefore disturbed the public; he maintained that the

Adivasis could not be allowed to continue as an 'arsenal' and a 'den of antisocial elements'. What is more, even the former left-wing chief minister of the state and CPI(M) leader E.K. Nayanar made sarcastic comments, publicly questioning the highly democratic struggles staged by the Adivasis. To quote E.K. Nayanar, 'She [C.K. Janu] is a leader without any mass base. The total votes she polled in Thirunelli grama panchayat election were only seven. In the name of the stir the Adivasis converted the Secretariat premises into a toilet complex. Now the agitation is over. Will Antony and Janu come to clean the premises? When the UDF-sponsored rally marched into my official residence when I was the Chief Minister, I had sent them to prison immediately.,'[12] However, the striking Adivasis turned a deaf ear to such apolitical and immature remarks from a communist leader. As part of an intensification of their struggle, the Adivasis began to perform their traditional rituals; they also staged dramas, made speeches, and sang songs expressing their anguish and hopes. The media were soon attracted to this vortex of activity, and thus began a fast awakening of the public consciousness to the plight of these marginalized peoples.

One such ritual, called *charthu*, was intended to propitiate the gods and ensure success in any venture – in this context, their agitation for land. This was performed by the *moopan*, or the tribal leader who was making an offering to please the gods. In another context, they conducted *chaveri*, another ritual, which is thought to ensure the destruction of the enemy. When I asked C.K. Janu who the enemies were, she had no hesitation in listing them: the state, the settlers, the forest mafia, and the bureaucrats. At one stage, the agitating youth even pointed out that the state was in itself the biggest trespasser, though yet to admit it. Ritualistic performances, free of any religious fixity, act as a rallying call for those who have been practising it and also for those who seek new forms of struggle.

After the unsuccessful attempt to raze the huts pitched by the Adivasis in front of the secretariat, the government issued an order banning the setting up of huts and tents in front of the secretariat and official residences of ministers as part of the agitation. When there was a move to remove the huts by force, Janu reiterated that the Adivasis would not leave the city if the huts put up by the council before the secretariat as part of the agitation were removed forcibly. 'We will erect new camps if the existing huts are removed', she added.[13]

Until this point, the Adivasis had raised economic demands alone – land for the landless in order to ensure economic security – and, in this third phase, they added, for the first time, some political demands too, but well within their constitutional rights. This is done not to subordinate the class question as implicit in their demand for land for livelihood to ethnic otherness but by simultaneously raising both issues. It involves demanding economic rights within a territorially specific resource, the right to control over boundaries, and the limited autonomy it provides in legitimizing the ethnic other. This sort of demand does not in any sense point to an intention to progress to any kind of self-determination or separatism but a constitutionally guaranteed class plus ethnic otherness right. For them, the larger state formation of Kerala was never inclusive of them, neither has it ever taken into account their welfare desires; they thus have always remained the other. It was a democratic hope they cherished of land resources to call their own, with territorial boundaries of self-rule within constitutional provisions. In this process of struggle, they were in a position to reinvent a fresh ideological base, with a democratic generation of discourse on not only the viability of such proposals but also the necessity of guaranteeing constitutional rights to those who deserve it. This sort of territorial sovereignty does not answer the question of the extent to which capitalist expansion would subtract from their newly visualized anthropological otherness. But over the long trajectory, they found themselves far more marginalized as an outcome of larger social construction and their own inability to build up transverse solidarities and wage struggles with any degree of political meaning.

Written in 1950, three years after its liberation from colonial clutches, the Indian constitution conceived the notion of links among three critical variables relevant to the indigenous people: territory, sovereignty, and empowerment. The name of the text that emerged was in the form of a 'Schedule'. With the realization of the political, economic, and cultural implications of belonging to a scheduled area, and also with the knowledge that many other Indian states have already implemented scheduling, the AGMS began to build up their new demands on this.[14] Apart from offering autonomy, the primary goal of this constitutional clause is to impose a total prohibition on the transfer of land properties to any person other than a tribal, for peace and proven good management of a tribal area and to protect the possession, rights, titles, and interests of the indigenous peoples, an aspect we shall return to soon.

It was rather a sudden ideological intervention by the agitating Adivasis, who argued that the Adivasi areas in the state should be designated as 'Scheduled Areas'. The month-long strike reached its climax with the decision of a fast unto death by none other than the leader herself: C.K. Janu. There was no way the government could skirt the issue any longer; a day before the planned fast unto death, the state had accepted all demands, including the inclusion of the Adivasi areas under the Vth Schedule. Finally, the ADSS called off the 48-day-long agitation in front of the state capital.[15]

The Agreement and Its Implementation

The major components of the commitment made by the government are the following (Bijoy and Raman 2013; Raman 2004):

1. Five acres of land to all Adivasi families having less than 1 acre of land. To begin with, 42,000 acres of land of between 1–5 acres would be distributed while the rest would be distributed as and when lands are located and made available. This work would begin from Jan. 1 to Dec 31, 2002 giving 5 acres where possible and lesser where it is not reaching 5 acres as and when suitable lands are found.
2. A master plan would be made before December 2001, to be included in the 10th five-year plan beginning from 2002 where the focus would be to support the above beneficiaries for a maximum of 5 years until they reach self-sufficiency.
3. A cabinet decision to include Adivasi areas in the V Schedule and a proposal would be made which shall be sent to the centre for further notification by the President. Meanwhile suitable legislation would be made to protect the land being allotted under this agreement.
4. The Supreme Court judgment related to the case pending where the government has challenged the High Court judgment striking down the repeal of the Kerala Scheduled Tribes (Restoration of Alienated Lands and Restriction on Transfer) Act 1975 and alternate land up to 5 acres for alienated land in the 1999 Act and declaring contempt of court for not having implemented the High Court judgment of 1993 to implement the 1975 Act, would be abided by the Kerala Government.
5. A Tribal Mission is constituted to carry out all the above headed by a senior IAS officer.

The government agreed to provide 1 to 5 acres of cultivable land, depending on availability, to all landless Adivasi families – nearly 42,000 acres of land had been identified towards realizing this. As the largest number of landless Adivasis was in Wayanad, every attempt was to be made to identify lands from forests within that district. With the distribution of lands to be initiated from January 2002, adequate support measures would be provided for a period of five years until these lands began to yield income. The government also gave its word that it would implement the Supreme Court verdict as soon as it came.

Breaking New Ground: Reflections

Many factors set the present struggle apart from similar struggles in the past. It was for the first time in the history of Adivasi struggles in the state that demands of 'lands for the landless' and inclusion of the Adivasi regions under Schedule V were raised (Bhuria 1995). Until this point, the Adivasis and other solidarity groups had solidly focused on the sole agenda of restoring alienated lands, that too based on the Kerala Scheduled Tribes (Restriction on Transfer of Lands and Restoration of Alienated Lands) Act, 1975. Second, the mode of struggle was unique to history: while mainstream political parties mobilize paid and voluntary members to conduct their strikes or agitations, the Adivasis had only themselves to reconstruct their traditional huts in the heart of the capital city. Unlike the mainstreamed political agitations with undemocratic slogans, the Adivasis made their struggles live and imaginative with the songs of anger, peace, and love. Third, it was an anti-government struggle but one without the support or participation of the established opposition.

All these years, Adivasi organizations have been totally engaged with the issue of restoration of alienated lands as embodied in the 1975 Act. All their battles, legal or otherwise, were in direct protest against the changed character of the parent Act – a reading of the 1999 amendment and the legal tussle it has entailed is proof of this. Does the settlement arrived at between the ADSS and the government give the Adivasis an advantage superior to that inherent in the parent Act of 1975? Probably the ADSS's biggest achievement has been its ability to break free of the spectre of 'restoration', for a victory gleaned on the strength of the 1975 Act would have been quite insignificant in the final analysis. In its professed preoccupation with the applications for restoration of about 7,500 families, the 1975 Act does not consider the fundamental question of rehabilitating the 45,000 landless families as envisaged in the present agreement. C.K. Janu, the leader, and M. Geethanandan, an intensely articulate spokesman of the Dalits, elaborate on this, refuting the objections raised by the CPI(ML) Red Flag and the BJP:

> … the case for the restoration of alienated lands languishes in the Supreme Court. Both the left and the right wing parties have competed over reducing all possibility of an early High Court verdict to restore the alienated lands to us. We are only too sure that we would win in the Supreme Court too. But there is no point in waiting for the same for two reasons. Given the nature of the state, it would certainly appeal against the Supreme Court's decision,

> which we believe would go in favour of the adivasis. Secondly, the quantum of land to be considered towards the restoration of alienated land is too little, only 7500 acres as against our demand for a minimum of five acres each for landless families.[16]

These arguments of the ADSS appear to be genuine and appropriate too, considering the gravity of the situation in the high ranges. Any settlement outside the 1999 Act would provide them with a double victory, as the victory through the courts remains just a matter of time. Moreover, the assertion of the right to constitutional protection as embodied in the Vth Schedule also becomes possible outside the 1975 format. Rather than pursuing the implementation or rejection of existing legislation, the ADSS made bold to construct a fresh framework towards the protection of the entire Adivasi community. This was in the form of the protection of Schedule V, as the Indian constitution provides a greater autonomy to the Adivasis under this schedule. With this new demand, the ADSS was sharpening their strategies, which turned the negotiating table in their favour. It was indeed a war of position (Gramsci 1971),[17] on the part of Adivasis. Accusations such as these struggles were driven by Maoists or ex-Maoists in the state or even by the People's War Group (PWG) from the neighbouring states or that elements of the LTTE influenced the struggles were instantly dismissed. On the other hand, the mainstream public of Kerala, which the tribals were never part of, realized that the demands raised by Adivasis were genuine and the glorified Kerala model of development was never free from Dalit and Adivasi critiques (Steur 2010: 221).

Neither the established left forces nor the radical groups in the state seem to have recognized the political significance inherent in the agreement extracted by the Adivasis – namely the inclusion of the Adivasi areas under Schedule V of the constitution, won not by a legal battle but through a mass struggle. In fact, the process of scheduling in India began in the fifties and continued over the seventies in making the Tribal Sub-Plan and Scheduled Areas conterminous (Thakur and Thakur 1994). When the cabinet passes a resolution requesting the president of India to bring the Adivasi regions in the state under the Scheduled Areas – which the state is obliged to do as per the agreement – and the president gives his assent for the same, the Adivasi areas and hamlets in the state will have the constitutional protection to impose total prohibition of transfer of immovable property to any person other than to a tribe member, which would protect the right, title, and interests of the Adivasis. The Adivasi's self-rule could become a reality with the inclusion of Adivasi areas under Schedule V and through the provisions of the Panchayats (Extension to the Scheduled Areas) Act, 1996, which would be in conformity with the customary law, social and religious practices, and traditional management practices of the community resources.[18]

As the People's Plan Campaign has been termed a failure by the Adivasis themselves, with much of the funds from the Tribal Sub-Plans being drained by the bureaucracy and even diverted into anti-Adivasi projects like the construction of honeymoon hideaways, the empowering of the *grama sabha* and the 'ooru kootttangal' (Adivasi congregations) assumes added significance. The *grama sabha* would be thus competent to safeguard and preserve the traditions and customs of the people, their cultural identity, common property resources, and customary mode of dispute settlement, gaining further autonomy and self-rule as and when the Adivasi regions would come under the proposed legislation. The government, on the other hand, did not take any substantive steps for about a year, either on distributing the land or taking a position on Schedule V. The Rehabilitation Tribal Mission which was formed in November 2001 to implement Janu–Antony pact turned out to be a failure and the mission was redundant, as there was no concrete support from either the bureaucrats or the forest officials; the latter even raised objections. The then forest minister, K. Sudhakaran, and the SC/ST minister, M.A. Kuttappan, openly stated that they could not identify the required revenue land for redistribution. In the case of forest lands, they were of the view that if lands were given to the tribals, they would not find land for afforestation; this would also invite objections from the central government. Promises were broken from every angle, leaving the agitating Adivasis with no choice but to reinvent their struggles in new forms, giving birth to the Muthanga 'republic'.

Third Phase: Occupy Muthanga – Autonomy of the Political?

When no action was taken by the government to implement the promised measures, and instead it followed procrastination politics, the tribal alliance renewed their protest by forming a Tribal Court in August 2002 in Wayanadu, by openly even declaring that they would carry out the Janu–Antony pact on their own by entering the identified lands, in the form of Occupy Muthanga. The indigenous people of Wayanad decided to enter the forest under the banner of the AGMS. Nearly 800 families entered the MWWS and declared the area their own. They erected check posts in Ponkuzhi, Ambukuthi, and Thakarappady, with the proviso that anyone entering the area should first request an entry pass at these check posts. They started their own *grama sabha*, the village council as conceived distantly in Schedule V, as soon as they built the huts in Muthanga so that it could function independently of the rest of the community. Both rationing and a settlement were developed. Adivasis also established day care centres for their children,[19] and the landscape progressively changed into a more humane type of livelihood ecosystem – indeed, it was one of their most imaginatively imagined geographies.

On the twelfth day of the Muthanga occupation, there was a forest fire; the three forest officers and their accompanying officials, including a photographer, were detained by the activists for unlawful entry into their premises and were released the very next day. It was on the back of this incident that the forest officers planned a scheme to evacuate the occupants of the MWWS. It was reported that the Adivasis captured and assaulted a police officer and a forest official who entered the area to implement the scheme. It was in retaliation to this that the state government sent in its police force to free their officials and forcibly evacuate the illegal occupants. In the course of the events that followed, one Adivasi and a police officer lost their lives; more than 30 Adivasis were hurt or injured in the process. Although the state was not in a position to give the correct numbers, several (news) agencies, such as the United News of India (UNI), came up with their own estimates of the number of lives lost. It was also highlighted that none of the concerned ministers – the forests minister, the minister for SC and STs, or the chief minister himself – visited the affected families in this time of stress. The chief minister had promised that 5 acres of land each would be granted to each Adivasi family beginning on 1 January and by 31 December 2002. But this did not transpire, leading the Adivasis to revolt. In the question and answer session in the Kerala Legislative Assembly (KLA) on 18 June 2003, it was reported that 77 people were arrested and a police case was registered against them. They spent around 30–65 days in detention, with some of them continuing to remain behind bars; the Central Bureau of Investigation (CBI) was entrusted with the task of probing these allegations. The National Commission for Women (NCW) demanded that the government conduct an enquiry into the sexual atrocities perpetrated during this time.

To the general challenge as to why the police firing happened at all, the Congress-led chief minister of Kerala, A.K. Antony, gave this response: The police firing was made inevitable against the background of the state's attempt to evacuate the illegal occupants from the Muthanga Wayanad Wildlife Sanctuary as also the attempt to attack and abduct four policewomen. It was also alleged that the occupants of the MWWS also attempted to inflict bodily harm to and abduct the forest officers who were trying to discharge their duties. The police attacked the Adivasis mercilessly – lashing little children who had fallen to the ground and attacking women with *lathis*. The then chief minister was of the opinion that the attempt to silence the extremists led to innocent Adivasis being attacked and killed. Both the AGMS and the Adivasi Welfare Committee had encroached upon the Muthanga lands; however, it was under the umbrella of the AGMS that the various extremist organizations found a haven. It was alleged that these extremist groups came from places like Andhra Pradesh and even Sri Lanka and joined the AGMS during this period. To questions from M.V. Jayarajan, a Marxist member of the legislative assembly, regarding the number of children affected by this episode, the number admitted to hospital as a result of injuries, and also whether these children were being protected under the child protection rights, he received no clear answer from the government. The general stance taken by the government was that the CBI had been entrusted with this task, with seven of the cases of child abuse being registered with the CBI. There were threats of setting fire to the forests. There were questions relating to financial compensation for the victims and their dependants – however, the government's response was that there were no such plans at that point for any such compensation (16 July 2007). The fact that the Human Rights Commission had not recommended any such compensation was used as a justification by the government for this lack of compensation. However, the family of the deceased Adivasi Jogi was granted a sum of INR 2 lakhs from the Chief Minister's Relief Fund.

The entire case of the Muthanga firing was transferred to the CBI on 28 July 2003 and therefore the state declined to comment on any of the subsequent decisions on the matter. In a submission to the KLA (26 February 2003), V.S. Achuthanandan, the Marxist leader of the opposition, narrated the stories shared with him by the prison inmates in Kannur Central Jail. Many of them were persuaded by the organizers of the movement that a move to the Muthanga Wildlife Sanctuary would be a way to procure land for themselves, and this was what led them to move en masse with all their belongings to the sanctuary; after a month of a peaceful life in the sanctuary, they were convinced of the feasibility of the project, and the sudden attack by the state police took them completely by surprise. They reported being shocked by the sudden violence and gunfire they were subjected to by the state police. Some of them reacted in self-defence using implements at hand that they had brought along with them for purposes of cooking and cultivation – knives, axes, scythes, and so on. K.P. Rajendran, yet another left member of the assembly, stated that what happened in Muthanga was not a police operation but a merciless hunting down of the Adivasis.[20] As the government refused a judicial probe into the police firing despite repeated requests, the opposition boycotted the assembly proceedings.

V.S. Achuthananthan accused the government of going back on its promise of granting land to the Adivasis as per their previous agreement. To this the chief minister replied that although it was the left government that brought about land reforms, and promised land to the Adivasis in the districts they currently lived in, it had not succeeded in granting any lands to the Adivasis of Muthanga whereas the current government had already distributed 1,746 acres of land among 843 families as per their agreement. The plan was to continue with this programme using the 7,000 acres under the Aralam Farm in northern Kerala. The chief minister A.K. Antony went on to emphasize that the state government would do its best to complete the entire programme of land distribution to the Adivasis within its current term. The chief minister also criticized the opposition's attempt to capitalize on the issue, claiming that 14 Adivasis had lost their lives, when in reality only one person had been killed. While expressing regret at the loss of life in the police firing, he also pointed out that V.S. Achuthananthan had failed to show any compassion for the one policeman who had lost his life, who himself happened to be a Dalit. It was also alleged that the Adivasis were emboldened by the support from the government for their previous protest in front of the state secretariat in 2001. The Adivasi minister is quoted as saying that they should follow the example of Janu, the Adivasi woman leader.

According to one estimate, there were 244,000 landless people in the state when the government introduced the campaign of what is called zero landlessness. This was a project meant to distribute 3 cents of land to each of the landless households and was expected to be implemented by 2015. In the first phase, it required only 3,000 acres for the distribution of 3 cents each to the 1 lakh landless citizens. The slogan of zero landless Kerala implies the return of the real owner of the land to one's own land. This was inaugurated by Sonia Gandhi of the Indian National Congress (INC) in Thiruvananthapuram on 30 September 2015. However, this too ended as the state could not be free from its lineage of the politics of procrastination, though some changes have been made since 2016 when the left government came to power with imaginative schemes.

In Kerala, most of the public infrastructure projects hold lakhs of land under their control without any use. This includes the department of irrigation, the electricity board, the agricultural department, the Forest Development Corporation, and so on. As Geethanandan pointed out, the lands that could be acquired would form hardly even a small percentage for meeting 3 cents of land, but in implementing, the state minimizes the larger question of actual requirements of land and the availability of surplus land in the state. The district of Kannur was announced as the first zero-landless district in the state. There were several legal and procedural flaws. This was with respect to the preparation of the beneficiaries and the final selection. Those who could not find any source of living due to disease, disability, being Scheduled Castes/Tribes, and so on, were supposed to be treated as priorities but in many cases this was torpedoed. In Kannur, it was announced that 11,000 families would be given 3 cents of land each. Of this, only 795 families were Scheduled Castes and 85 were Scheduled Tribes. Many of those who got land were assigned to distant places like Thaliparambu, and it was not sure whether the fisher folk wanted to take up such an alternative. Those Adivasis listed were only 85 families as against 3,500 landless Adivasi families in the district promised 1 acre of land in Aralam Farm, a programme that was being implemented. The AGMS exposed the entire state-led campaign by pointing out the meagre number of landless Adivasis who were to be beneficiaries as per the state project.

With such a phenomenal victory in their hands, the Adivasis were probably justified in congratulating themselves. However, the victory would have been sweeter had there been a broadening of their demands to include alienated lands, particularly the hidden surplus lands owned by Indian big capital in the state. Sad to say, vast areas of confiscated lands in the hands of the government escaped the notice of the Adivasis, who had been training their attention solely on the other state-owned lands – lands currently held by certain state corporations. It is true that these corporations – the Plantation Corporation, for instance – have been running at a loss. It would still not be amiss to note here that the workers on these lands would then face the threat of displacement – something that invites counter-struggles. The ADSS's demand for the inclusion of land from Adivasi projects like the Sugandhagiri Project in the settlement might backfire with collective holdings being distributed among individual owners, which though part of the original proposal, would in all probability spark off a fresh set of agitations unless viable alternatives are worked out.

Had there been a demand for the restoration of the truly alienated lands – alienated not by peasant settlers but by the big planting companies who have vast tracts of uncultivated land tucked away out of sight – the Adivasis would have had the benefit of reclaiming lands close to their own homes and habitats. This would have also given the Adivasis the strategic advantage in avoiding direct conflict with the peasant settlers and the Christian lobby that sustains and is sustained by the Kerala Congress(es) in alternate ruling fronts; they would have even gained the support of the lowest strata of the settler community. It seems an error of judgement on the part of the ADSS that it did not choose to press for the restoration of confiscated lands that were already in the hands of the government, lands that have also outlived the lease periods for which they had been granted.[21] Had the state been pressurized to redistribute the surplus lands confiscated from Tata Tea, for instance, more than 50,000 acres would have been mobilized in addition to the area now promised by the government (at least a significant portion of the same). Had there been a focus on the vast tracks of plantation-based surplus lands owned by the pan-India corporate capital, two outcomes would have happened. First, it would have exposed the vast plantation lands and would have equipped the Adivasis to put fresh claims on these lands. Second, this would have created a wider spectrum of solidarity between the landless Adivasis and the Dalit workers in the plantation fields. Finally, this would have generated wider sympathy and affinity from the larger society. Yet another point on which the ADSS lost strategic ground was its failure to take the government up on its assurance that it would implement the Supreme Court decision without fail. The ADSS could have asked the 'generous' government to withdraw the case altogether in its generosity; this would have certainly called the government's bluff.

Concluding Remarks

As the event unfolds, it de-states the state; it de-states the state structure and distils out from it the politics of the void. In essence, this is what could be termed subtractive politics (see Badiou 2004). It was this subtractive politics that the AGMS invoked. In fact, the AGMS was a political outcome of the Adivasi struggle rather than its initiating body; it was the outcome of a renaissance movement that originated among people who are distanced and even ostracized by mainstream society. The places of resistance and the modes of resistance, that is, the setting up of refugee camps at the first site and constructing a village of their own at the second site, were unique and left no room for ambiguity: creatively constructing an ecospatiality on their own terms.

The first site of resistance they chose was the state secretariat, the symbol of state power – before which they exposed for all to see the utter failure of the state to do justice to its own people. They demanded their right to sustenance, to the land that would give them sustenance and means of livelihood. And this was a situation that could be seen anywhere in the world – among the tribals of other states in India, in Chiapas, and in the Columbian Pacific. The question of ownership rights and rights over natural resources is one that is debated the world over. The mode of struggle continued to be unparalleled in history: In beauteous contrast to the undemocratic and uncultured slogans shouted by the usual political agitator, the Adivasis swayed to the chanting of songs of anger, peace, and love. Throughout this process, one observes the Adivasis engaging and re-engaging in an articulation and re-articulation of their positioning; from time to time, they themselves either restricted or expanded their initial positioning and advanced to new notions of land claims and self-rule. This, in effect, was a renewed understanding of the Saidian notion of imagined geography (Said 1978) which is equally revealing in the case of Chengara (see Chapter 6). So if at all one were to explain this in terms of identity, it is no less what Stuart Hall calls a 'positioning' rather than an 'essence', and this positioning is forged into a political end by their transformation into political subjects. More importantly, they realize that, to quote Badiou (2003), 'a position of protest within the state sanctioned structures and rules' is only an 'oppositional' stance, a 'politically weak' position, and hence they march to Muthanga, in search of a position outside the state-sanctioned structures and rules.

Muthanga, as the second site of resistance, symbolized the anti-state, a parallel power set up by a people who were betrayed by their own government. But they were ready to take the autonomy of the political a step further (Schmitt 1996). In Muthanga, the Adivasis transformed a physical piece of land into a cultural and political landscape through a communion with nature and by resisting the state, and, in so doing, they succeeded in fashioning for themselves a new social space by humanizing an otherwise physical land – a post-eventual consequence. Moreover, in painstakingly creating a politically viable, ecologically sustainable alternative way of life, the Adivasis of Muthanga seemed to enact a universal drama of hope and change – as Žižek (1998: 988) has highlighted, a post-evental declaration for the 'whole of society, for the true universality'. No struggle or movement of any kind is ever finished; it must continue with new windows of creativity and transverse solidarities, as was the case in Chengara, to which we will turn in a moment.

Notes

1. Kerala Legislative Assembly (KLA), 20 February 2003, explanation by the chief minister.

2. KLA 11 (2001–2006), Session 12, Question Hour, dated 11 July 2005; KLA 13 (2011–2016), Session 14, Question Hour, dated 7 July 2015.
3. KLA 13 (2011–2016), Session 11, Question Hour, dated 9 July 2014; also see Cherayi, Jose, and Sudhakar (2019).
4. General Report on the Census of India, 1891; Census of India, 1901; Census of India, 1911; Census of India, 1921; Census of India 1931.
5. We do not intend to reduce the importance of the lead taken by their brethren in their struggle against the Europeans in the Wayanad forests popularly known as the Pazhassi rebellion or the Kurichiar *lahala* and other innumerable instances of tribal revolts from other regions of the world. The Kurichiars and Kurumbars (two prominent tribal communities) of Wayanad revolted against the British policy of collecting land revenue in cash instead of in kind. This was in fact the beginning of the peasant revolt in Malabar in 1812.
6. On the contrary, Mateer quotes the case of hillmen who declined to 'herd with coolies and work like common people' (1883: 66).
7. The local papers held a different view and they protested against the Coffee Stealing Bill as it led to a further victimisation of the workers and the local populace.
8. Maoist politics were brutally suppressed by the then *police raj*, particularly during the 21-month long Emergency (25 June 1975 to 20 March 77); engineering college student P. Rajan was killed by the police, as was bookshop owner Varkala Vijayan. A few Maoist sympathizers also committed suicide. Maoist politics took a different turn with the formation of Janakeeya Samskarika Samithi, which also faded quickly. For an exploration of contemporary Maoist movements in states like Bihar and Jharkhand, see Shah (2018).
9. It was orchestrated by a spontaneous regrouping of radicals led by K.M. Thampu, an Adivasi youth and four Adivasi women, two of them in their teens. There has been a renewed Adivasi–Dalit activism in Wayanad; its history could be traced back to A. Varghese who, with his Naxalite comrades, was probably the first to raise the Adivasi land question in the late 1960s.
10. The earliest response to the starvation deaths came from the worthy minister for SCs and STs, who, much to the amusement of the people of Kerala, brushed them aside as being due to the consumption of illicit liquor.
11. In spite of repeated warnings, the Kerala State Electricity Board went ahead with its plan to extend high tension electric connection that would pass over the Dalit colonies in Kurichy, Kottayam. Sreedharan resisted this move by setting himself on fire.
12. See OneIndia dated Monday, 22 October 2001, https://malayalam.oneindia.com/news/2001/10/22/ker-nayanar.html (accessed 27 July 2023).

13. Janu told this in her interview with the author in Thiruvananthapuram dated 3 October 2001.
14. The Indian constitution provides for the protection of tribal interests through Schedule V and VI of Article 244. In the mid-1800s, the British colonial government in India had designated certain areas as non-regulated areas, which were renamed scheduled areas in the post-independent phase. These areas remained outside the ambit of normal legislative and political processes; the president of India could by order declare areas to be scheduled areas on the recommendations of the state government and the governor. The Vth Schedule invests all executive and legislative power in the state governor, who could consult an appointed Tribal Advisory Council on these matters. In other words, the governor has the power to exclude scheduled areas from state legislation as well as to decree legislative provisions such as protection from outsiders. Scheduled areas have been notified in the states of Himachal Pradesh, Bihar, Orissa, Madhya Pradesh, Rajasthan, and Gujarat; but the tribal areas in Kerala, Tamil Nadu, Karnataka, and West Bengal are yet to be scheduled despite suggestions put forward by the concerned committees. The VIth Schedule allows for the formation of autonomous councils and regions, and provides for self-government. For more details, see Thakur and Thakur (1994); Government of India (2009). In an attempt at securing greater protection and as a prelude to greater autonomy, the Adivasi Gothra Maha Sabha has requested that the tribal areas in Kerala also be brought under Schedule V.
15. The Adivasis expressed their joy with traditional festivities and rites. Before dismantling the refugee camps, they assembled a thanksgiving meeting in front of the Ayyankali Square, Ayyankali being the beloved leader who helped them articulate their resistance in the early twentieth century. Prominent writers, journalists, and cultural activists including Paul Zacharia and B.R.P. Bhaskar participated in the celebrations. The Adivasis danced with burning torches, swaying to traditional drumbeats. At one stage, the chief minister joined in with the dancing, although, to prevent the Adivasi strike from becoming a precedent, he had banned the building of shacks in front of government offices. Prominent public intellectuals, including Sarah Joseph, Sugathakumari, T. Padmanabhan, and Adoor Gopalakrishnan, and others, have always provided moral supports for Adivasi rights.
16. M. Geethanandan in conversation with the author dated 1 October 2003, Thiruvananthapuram.
17. In this context, however, the Gramscian distinction between 'war of maneuver' and 'war of position' does not follow the Western Marxist approach to the

Gramscian metaphor for politics. Anderson (1979) observed that the emphasis on war of position represents a shift away from the political economy of capitalism and move towards cultural superstructures. However, the idea of the Adivasis, in this context, was to tilt the balance of power in their favour by highlighting the authority of the constitution, rather than the sub-national state. For critical studies, see Egan (2013).

18. Panchayat (Extension to Scheduled Areas) Act, 1996, p. 8.
19. In conversation with M. Geethanandan, dated 22 March 2023.
20. KLA, February 2003.
21. Under the chief ministership of C. Achuta Menon in 1971, the Kanan Devan Land Resumption Bill was introduced to acquire the uncultivated land under the company and to redistribute the same for various purposes. The KDHP possessed 1,37,606.04 acres of land, out of which the government took over 70,662 acres and the remaining 57,359 acres of land was restored to the company.

References

Baak, P.E. (1997). *Plantation, Production and Political Power: Plantation Development in South-west India in a Long Term Historical Perspective, 1743–1963*. Delhi: Oxford University Press.

Badiou, A. (2003). *Saint Paul: The Foundation of Universalism*. Translated by Ray Brassier. Stanford: Stanford University Press.

——— (2004). *Theoretical Writings*. Translated by Ray Brassier and Alberto Toscano. London: Continuum.

Banerjee, S. (1980). *In the Wake of Naxalbari: A History of the Naxalite Movement in India*. Calcutta: Subarnarekha.

Bhuria, Dileep Singh (1995). *Report of the Committee of Members of Parliament and Experts Constituted to Make Recommendations on Law Concerning Extension of Provisions of the Constitution (Seventy-third Amendment) Act, 1992 to Scheduled Areas*. New Delhi: Ministry of Rural Development, Government of India, January 1995.

Bijoy, C.R., and K.R. Raman (2003). Muthanga: The real story. *Economic and Political Weekly* 38 (17 May): 1975–1982.

Bijuraj, R.K. (2015). *Naxal Days*. Kottayam: DC Books.

——— (2021). *Keralathinte Rashtreeya Charithram*. Kottayam: DC Books.

Bourdillon, T.F. (1893). *Report on the Forests of Travancore*. Thiruvananthapuram: Government Press.

Cherayi, S., J.P. Jose, and S. Sudhakar (2019). Children of tribal unwed mothers and their non-legitimate origin: A social exclusion perspective. *Sage Open* 1 (April–June): 1–11. https://us.sagepub.com/en-us/nam/open-access-at-sage (accessed 5 May 2023).

Cleghorn, H. (1861). *Forests and Gardens of Southern India*. London: W.H. Allen Publishing Co.

Deleuze, G. and F. Guattari (1987). *A Thousand Plateaus: Capitalism and Schizophrenia*, trans. B. Massumi. Minneapolis, MN: University of Minnesota Press.

Dhebar, U.N. (1960–1961). *Report of the Scheduled Areas and Scheduled Tribes Commission*. New Delhi: Government of India.

Egan, D. (2013). Rethinking war of maneuvre/war of position: Gramsci and the military metaphor. *Critical Sociology* 40 (4): 521–538.

Government of India (2009). *Report of the Committee on State Agrarian Relations and the Unfinished Task in Land Reforms, New Delhi*. https://dolr.gov.in/en/documents/report-of-committee-on-state-agrarian-relations (accessed 14 September 2023).

Government of Kerala (1962). *The Evaluation Committee on the Welfare of the Scheduled Castes, Scheduled Tribes and other Backward Communities*. Thiruvananthapuram: Government Press.

——— (1979). *Report on Socio-economic Survey of Adivasis in Kerala*. Thiruvananthapuram: Bureau of Economics and Statistics.

——— (1986). The Kerala Scheduled Tribes (Restriction on Transfer and Restoration of Alienated Lands) Act 1975 and Kerala Gazette Extraordinary No. 89 dt. 24 January. Thiruvananthapuram: Government of Kerala.

——— (1996). *The Kerala Scheduled Tribes (Restriction on Transfer and Restoration of Alienated Lands) Amendment Bill, 1996*. Thiruvananthapuram: Government Press.

——— (1999). *The Kerala Restriction on Transfer by and Restoration of Lands to Scheduled Tribes Bill, 1999*. Thiruvananthapuram: Government Press.

Gramsci, A. (1971). *Selections from the Prison Notebooks of Antonio Gramsci*. New York: International Publishers.

IIM-Kozhikode. (2006). *Wayanadu Initiative: A Situational Study and Feasibility Report for the Comprehensive Development of Adivasi Communities of Wayanad*. Report submitted to Scheduled Caste and Scheduled Tribe Development Department, Government of Kerala. https://ethnographylab.files.wordpress.com/2016/01/wayanad-initiative-a-situational-study-andfeasilbility-report-for-the-comprehensive-development-ofadivasi-communities-of-wayanad.pdf, accessed 5 May 2023.

Jacob, T.G. (2006). *Wayanad, Misery in an Emerald Bowl*. Mumbai: Vikas Adhyayan Kendra.

Kjosavik, D.J., and N. Shanmugaratnam. (2015). *Political Economy of Development in India: Indigeneity in Transition in the State of Kerala*. New York: Routledge.

Kunhaman, M. (1985). The tribal economy of Kerala: An intra-regional analysis. *Economic and Political Weekly* 20 (11): 466–474.

——— (2003). Tribesmen being cheated out of their lands. *Indian Express*, 22 December.

Mateer, Rev. Samuel (1883). *Native Life in Travancore*. London: W.H. Allen.

National Tribal Policy (2004). *The National Tribal Policy: A Policy for the Scheduled Tribes of India*. New Delhi: Ministry of Tribal Affairs, Government of India.

Paul, B. (2014). *The First Naxal: An Authorised Biography of Kanu Sanyal*. New Delhi: Sage Publications.

Planting Opinion (1896). Thieving tribes as coffee labourers. 9 May.

Pouchepadass, Jacques (1995). British attitudes towards shifting cultivation in colonial south India: A case study of south Canara district, 1800–1920. In *Nature, Culture and Imperialism*, ed. David Arnold and Ramachandra Guha, pp. 123–151. Delhi: Oxford University Press.

Prakash, P.K. (2002). *Anyadheenappedunna Bhoomi Adivasi Bhoomi rasnattinte Charithravum Rashtriyavum*. Kozhikkode: Pappiyon.

Prabhakaran, G. (2003). Road to Muthanga: Sabotaging the Tribal Act. *The Hindu*, 4 February. Countercurrents.org.

Praveen, C.S. (2012). 'Factors Influencing Quality of Life of Tribal Unwed Mothers: A Study in Wayanad District Kerala'. Doctoral Thesis, Pondicherry University, Pondicherry, India, 2012.

Raman, K. Ravi (2004). Muthanga A spark of hope. In *State, Sovereignty, War: Civil Violence in Emerging Global Realities*, ed. B. Kapferer, Vol. 5, pp. 107–124. New York: Berghahn Books.

——— (2010a). *Global Capital and Peripheral Labour: The History and Political Economy of Plantation Workers in India*. London: Routledge.

——— (2010b). In-migration vs. out-migration. In *Mass Migration in the World System*, ed. T.-A. Jones and E. Mielants, pp. 122–143. Milton Park: Routledge.

Rancière, Jacques (1999). *Disagreement: Politics and Philosophy*. Minnesota: University of Minnesota Press.

Said, Edward W. (1978). *Orientalism*. New York: Pantheon (New York: Vintage, 1994, with new Afterword; New Delhi: Penguin Books India, 2001).

Schmitt, C. (1996). *The Concept of the Political*. Chicago: The University of Chicago Press.

Shah, A. (2018). *Nightmarch: A Journey into India's Naxal Heartlands*. New Delhi: HarperCollins.

Sreerekha, M.S. (2010). Challenges before Kerala's landless: The story of Aralam Farm. *Economic and Political Weekly* 45 (21): 55–62.

Steur, Luisa (2010). Adivasi workers' struggles and the Kerala model: Interpreting the past, confronting the present. In *Development, Democracy and the State: Critiquing the Kerala Model of Development*, ed. Ravi Raman, 221–236. London: Routledge.

Thakur, Devendra, and K.N. Thakur (1994). *Tribal Life in India, Vol. 7: Tribal Law and Administration*. New Delhi: Deep & Deep.

Tharakan, M. (1984). *Intra-regional Differences in Agrarian Systems and Internal Migration: A Case study of the Migration of Farmers from Travancore to Malabar 1930–1950*. Thiruvananthapuram: Centre for Development Studies.

Thurston, Edgar (1909). *Castes and Tribes of Southern India*. Vol. 7. Madras: Government Press.

Wilkes, J.H. (1953). The Nilagiri–Wayanad. In *UPASI 1893–1953*, ed. S.G. Speer, pp. 263–278. Coonoor: UPASI.

Žižek, S. (1998). A leftist plea for 'Eurocentrism'. *Critial Enquiry* 24 (4): 988–1009.

4

Dalits and the Global Cola

Water, Power, and Resistance

Mayilamma – the Dalit woman leader of the anti-Cola water movement in Plachimada – explicitly told this author: 'I do not know whether it was due to globalization or not, what I know is that our wells are getting dried up; whatever little water left was polluted.'1 This political statement came at a time when water has rapidly become a contested commodity worldwide, with local communities in many parts of the world suffering the threat of multinationals working in collusion with the state apparatus to usurp their precious natural resources, including in Plachimada.

There has been a recent proliferation of scholarship on water conflict and governance, both within and outside political landscapes, attempting to address the various nuances of global and local governance strategies. Increasing concern has been expressed regarding the widespread social and political-ecological implications of current and potential 'water wars' and water conflicts. Water supply, once considered a public utility or a service, is now fast becoming a marketable commodity, one that is to be sold on a full cost-recovery basis, an approach that is vehemently opposed by social agencies, which fight back, often as part of a wider struggle, but also within specific locales. Such movements throw into stark relief the ironies inherent in the discourse–counter-discourse (Grillo and Stirrat 1997; Terdiman 1985; Ashcroft 2001; Daudi 1983; Escobar 1985; Byrant and Baily 1997) generated as part of the process of conflict resolution. And now 'governance' as a conflict-resolution strategy wrought through the multiple agencies of a legislative, institutional, and regulatory framework promoting equitable access to and ecologically sustainable management of water resources appears to be the new polemics.[2] This chapter critically engages with the multiple knowledge conflicts and the multiple agencies involved in the vexed question of water access, power, and community rights in Plachimada, a small hamlet in the Palakkad district of the south Indian state of Kerala.

Social movements by themselves are not merely sensitizers of the public, but have an important role to play in exposing the ever-increasing threats to marginalized communities in terms of their livelihood, culture, and ecology. The social agencies involved in these movements are also credited with exposing the untruth in claims made by scientific and expert knowledge in their reproduction of hegemonic power relations that gnaw away at the roots of community existence and the right to live. Perhaps their greatest contribution is that they expose for all to see the utter lack of ethics in water use, thus lending credence to the resistance against such unethical practices, and earning for themselves the title of what this author prefers to qualify as 'post development social movement' (Raman 2007).[3] The present chapter, however, neither addresses the 'cycles' of any particular movement nor the challenges that it faces, but rather unravels the complex and multiple issues involved in a social struggle over water use and its pollution, largely rendered visible as part of a post-development social movement, in this case, the anti-Cola movement in Plachimada. It examines the claims made by the hegemonic structures – both the dominant scientific body and the state legal apparatus – which in turn prepares the ground for a perpetuation of the hegemony of global capital over local resources with far-reaching consequences. Further, it also attempts to provide a brief sketch of an alternative mode of governance – which could be termed 'governance from below'[4] – incorporating the twin priorities of local control over resources and socio-ecological sustainability aided by community wisdom and socially informed inferences, which together form 'knowledge as emancipation' (see Santos 2007, 2009). This is a counter-discourse – as narrated in the rest of the book – that effectively questions the deployment of knowledge production for a perpetuation of hegemonic power relations (see Foucault 1980, 1997).

Second Coming: Cola Arrives in Plachimada

Coca-Cola dates back to 1886 when production began in Atlanta, Georgia, in the United States. It then gradually spread to the rest of the world with factories in around 119 countries; the company has grown to become the largest multinational soft-drink company in the world. The Hindustan Coca-Cola Company Pvt. Ltd. (hereafter Coca-Cola), an Indian subsidiary of the multinational Coca-Cola, was forced out of India in 1977 when the then ruling

Janata government decreed that foreign firms could own no more than two-fifths of their Indian subsidiaries' shares. Further, it was also insisted that every foreign company, including Coca-Cola, should disclose the ingredients used in their products. Coca-Cola was wary of disclosing its ingredients, on the one hand, and disinvesting its equity in favour of Indian shareholders, on the other. After India changed its laws regarding trademarks, which had previously required that trade secret information be disclosed, the multinational was allowed re-entry in 1993, provided it divested 49 per cent to Indian shareholders by 2002. In the end, Coca-Cola issued shares to those who had no voting rights and, therefore, had no voice in policymaking.

The very fact that the multinational Coca-Cola successfully negotiated a re-entry into the Indian market is testimony to the neoliberal complexion acquired by the Indian state in the 1990s. Coca-Cola proceeded to acquire assets in the country on an unprecedented scale, buying up the Indian soft-drink company Parle, and establishing its monopoly over the soft-drink industry in India. No less than 61 per cent of the market was captured by Coca-Cola, with its closest competitor, PepsiCo, lagging far behind with a share of 36 per cent. As Coca-Cola steadily expanded its market, it was inevitable that it gravitated towards the lush green landscape of south India, where land and water resources were aplenty and labour cheap.

The Plachimada hamlet in the Palakkad district of Kerala was situated in a prime location in Perumatty *panchayat,* and it was clearly chosen by the multinational for just such an abundance of resources. This agricultural hinterland lies in close proximity to the main irrigation canal from the Moolathara barrage and is just 3 kilometres from the Meenkara dam reservoir, a little to the west of Kambalathara and Vengalakkayam storage reservoirs and the Chitturpuzha stream, a major tributary of the Bharathapuzha river. Though the average rainfall in this area is low (around 2,425.8 millimetres in 1998) in comparison with the other regions of the state (2,513.1 millimetres), it has a greater potential for groundwater recharge on account of the gently undulating nature of the terrain and the numerous surface water reservoirs and dam irrigation canals. In Plachimada village, most of the population lived as farmers on a 2,350-hectare area of rice fields. Those living near the factory were mostly Adivasis and Dalits – landless workers and migrant families who came from neighboring Tamil Nadu and settled there decades ago. As has always been their lot, they were the outliers of society, the perpetually disadvantaged who stood to lose even more when dealing with multinationals. Furthermore, Coca-Cola set up the plant with the provisions of the Kerala Panchyat Act, 1994, and with the assurance that all infrastructure facilities would be provided by the state under the original agreement. This also included water supplies from the Moolathara dam, which was a few kilometres away. However, this did not happen, and the company had to seek out other sources of water.

Overmining of Groundwater Resources

Scientific Knowledge vis-à-vis Liberatory Knowledge

Coca-Cola commissioned its factory in March 2000, riding on the wave of state-led/sanctioned developmentalism of the neoliberal era, with the state sanguine in the expectation of an investment of around INR 80 crores. However, the purchase of the 34-acre marshy land for the factory was in itself in violation of the Kerala Land Utilisation Act, 1967, which had till then been the only solace for the landless labouring Dalits trapped within the degenerating rice economy of the state, prohibiting as it did the conversion of areas under food crops to non-food crops or any other purposes. With the beginning of its operations in Plachimada, the multinational giant began drawing water for its factory at a rate that far outstripped the regeneration capacity of the local water bodies. Though the company has its own facts and figures to justify its rate of extraction of groundwater, local experience and community-centred knowledge gathered by the anti-Cola movement clearly prove the environmental unsustainability of Coca-Cola's scale of operations. In this process, various scientific bodies successively brought out volumes of information that were completely at odds with their own previous findings. And what is more, the hegemonic structures often paid scant regard to the ethics of environmental protection, dumping toxic waste in neighbouring lands that ultimately leached into the drinking water sources of the village, causing diseases and illnesses that were unheard of in Plachimada until then. The peaceful village of Plachimada thus became witness to scenes of protests and violence as the Dalits and Adivasis joined hands with socially concerned activists to constitute the Coca-Cola Virudha Janakeeya Samara Samithi (Anti-Cola People's Struggle Committee).

What precipitated the movement, however, was neither the low employment generated – 150 permanent workers and 250 casual workers,[5] despite promises to the contrary – nor the discrimination in the very meagre employment it offered for the local people or even the low wages paid to the workers, but the excess mining of groundwater, pollution of whatever little was left, and the wrecking of the entire local community life, all amounting to an outright violation of community livelihood and human rights. Eventually, villagers began to develop a protest consensus on traditional rights to natural resources, the ethics that must be observed when using land and water, and how to prioritize and allot competing traditional resources. Consequently, a multitude of issues were raised, opening up a plethora of inherent knowledge conflicts, the details of which we will explore soon.

The 22nd of April 2002 ushered in the beginning of a long-drawn-out fight of peoples' power against global capital, which resulted in the joining of forces moderate and radical. Together with the Peoples' Struggle Committee, other NGOs and social organizations formed the Plachimada Solidarity Committee. This group represented a melting pot of individuals and groups, united by their call for an outright closure of the Coca-Cola factory. As the protests gained momentum, successive groups of activists joined in, and the local government was forced to admit its naivety in assuming that the multinational would follow through on all environmental promises. In addition to acknowledging the unexpected environmental impact of the entire project, the *panchayat* also denounced its arbitrary approach to digging wells, sinking boreholes, and installing electric pumps, none of which were part of the original agreement.

Having realized its folly in permitting access to its precious resources, the local *panchayat* stood firm in its decision to cancel the licence granted to the factory – and eventually cancelled the licence in April 2003, but the company continued its operation.[6] Three things were clear: first, despite the prospect of major losses in terms of jobs and revenue, the *panchayat* was ready to cancel the licence. This was a rare but equally crucial exception to the norm of deliberate evasion of responsibility practised by the ruling hegemonic class. Second, the company's continuing operation, despite the cancellation of the licence, was a violation of laws, but no such question was raised in public at the moment. Third, this only showed the government's lackadaisical attitude towards the multinational as it was not clear whether it wanted to support the Cola Quit Campaign or the local *panchayat* or simply to bear the loss of employment and income. While the company appealed against the decision to the government and the High Court, the state refused to intervene in the local government activities.[7] And the linkage effects of this fundamental move of the local government against global capital were apparent soon enough with the other multinational operating in a nearby *panchayat*, namely PepsiCo in the Perumatty *panchayat*, beginning to face threats of eviction. It was also at this juncture that an awareness of the subliminal war being waged between truth and untruth began to dawn on the Malayali psyche. A slow mobilization of public opinion thus followed, gathering momentum as the strategies to counter Coca-Cola adopted by both the Anti-Cola Peoples' Struggle Committee and the Perumatty *panchayat* mutually reinforced one another, taking the movement to a different realm altogether. Perhaps the first major victory won by the movement was that it succeeded in convincing the *panchayat*, in which it had no significant stake in terms of membership, of the authenticity of its allegations against the multinational. After a much more protracted and tortuous struggle, the anti-Cola struggle also succeeded in tilting state-level opinion in its favour, with the succeeding Marxist-led government too backing it up, in turn leading to a closure of the factory, which still remains in force.

However, this is not to discount the numerous knowledge conflicts generated at every step of the fight between the multinational and the villagers of Plachimada. The authorities diligently churned out their own version of scientific knowledge, often going to great lengths to exonerate Coca-Cola of all blame with regard to the environmental disaster in Plachimada. The legal apparatus, in its turn, proved quite erratic, with its inconsistent rulings further aggravating the war between the knowledge systems (Raman 2005; Parmar 2015). Even as the *panchayat* issued orders to cancel the factory licence, it met with opposition from the local self-government department, forcing it to turn to the Kerala High Court, which completed the circle with a decision in support of the *panchayat* ruling. The Single Bench of the Kerala High Court thus declared in December 2003 that the company would have to seek alternative sources of water for its bottling plant in Plachimada. The Kerala High Court maintained that groundwater belonged to the people and that neither the company had any 'claim [to] a huge share of it' nor the government had any power to allow a private party to extract it in such huge quantities, it being 'a property held by it in trust'. To quote:

> If there is artificial interference with the ground water collection by excessive extraction, it is sure to create ecological imbalance. No great knowledge of Science or Ecology is necessary to infer this inevitable result.... If (the company) is permitted to drain away this much of water, every land owner in the area can also do that and if all of them start extracting huge quantities of ground water, in no time, the entire Panchayat will turn a desert.[8]

The knowledge at this level of the legal hierarchy thus stipulated that the company restrict its water consumption to the quantity used by a landowner with

34 acres of land, the size of the land owned by the company to be ascertained by the *panchayat*. However, the multinational did not capitulate to the CSE report and consumer backlash; Sushma Swaraj, the BJP's central minister for health, family welfare, and parliamentary affairs, actually helped save the company. The minister stated in the Lok Sabha (the lower house of the Indian parliament) on 22 August 2003 that neither of the brands tested at the Mysore-based Central Food Technological Research Institute (CFTRI) nor the Kolkata-based Central Food Laboratory showed high levels of pesticide residue. There was an uproar in the Parliament. A 15-member Joint Parliamentary-Chemical Expert Committee (JPC) was constituted to assess the CSE findings and suggest criteria for establishing safety standards for soft drinks, fruit juices, and other beverages containing water.

It is to the credit of the CSE that the JPC report, which was presented to the Indian parliament on 5 February 2004, confirmed its allegations regarding pesticide residues within the carbonated waters of 12 brands of PepsiCo and Coca-Cola. It basically affirmed the Kerala High Court's Single Bench ruling that groundwater is a public resource and may only be used domestically and agriculturally. In line with the National Water Policy, drinking water must come first, followed by irrigation, and only surplus water be assigned exclusively to commercial use; however, the current proposal would leave no scope for commercial activity, an argument that actually originated with the movement itself. An updated study in 2006 found that pesticides were present in all samples of Coca-Cola and PepsiCo carbonated products across the state tested by the CSE.

Two immediate effects resulted from the findings of the CSE and the JPC: Coca-Cola products were immediately forbidden in the parliamentary complex in India. Other institutions, including the Defence Ministry, followed suit, and a partial ban was imposed in half a dozen states, especially in educational institutions. Based on the CSE report and the direction from the Union Ministry of Health and Family Welfare, a total ban was imposed in Kerala on 10 August 2006 wherein the left government took the initiative for such a bold move. For the state to become an active participant in the transverse solidarity (TS), this was also a transformational moment for society as a whole. It is reasonable to claim that this was a triumph for the campaign and other solidarity organizations, which originally began in the fight against drinking water shortages and pollution. However, they now encompassed many facets, including the consumer market and the broader civil society. Later, the ban was lifted in the state as the High Court of Kerala ruled that the state government did not possess the authority to impose any such restrictions, as the multinational had argued.

Additionally, the Rajasthan High Court also ruled that manufacturers of carbonated beverages and soft drinks must delineate the composition and contents of the products and, if applicable, they should also list the pesticides and chemicals on the bottle.[9] The soft drink giant(s) refused to comply with the verdict again here, but, as far as Coca-Cola is concerned, this refusal continues in its trade war with the United States (see Clairmonte and Cavanagh 1988). Laws and regulations are frequently tailored to suit the interests of multinational corporations, either to justify their appropriation of common water resources, to win trade wars, or to justify human rights violations. Coca-Cola sees no contradiction between its marketing of bottled products and its brand of corporate social responsibility (Raman 2005, 2007). In varying contexts, the multinational denied all charges, claiming that these were 'wrong, frivolous, baseless, and malafide'.[10] The company claimed that it had marked out a 71,760 square metre stretch of the 35 acres of its premises for the purpose of rainwater harvesting, but this did little to convince the villagers who carried on with their protests with undiminished vigour (Prabhakaran 2003).

Problematizing the 'Scientific Knowledge'

Quite predictably, this knowledge version that abided by the historical and cultural experiences of the social-ecological community was challenged by Coca-Cola, upon which the matter was referred to the Government of India–owned Centre for Water Resources Development and Management (CWRDM), Kozhikode, for expert scientific opinion. Meanwhile, other official studies too were underway on related issues, such as groundwater pollution, mostly sponsored by state-led institutions like the Kerala Ground Water Department and the State Pollution Control Board, which appeared to arrive at quite contradictory conclusions. The net effect of all this discourse–counter-discourse was the verdict of the Division Bench of the Kerala High Court on 7 April 2005, which annulled the decision of the Single Bench and virtually entitled Coca-Cola to resume operations in its factory in Plachimada. This decision drew much criticism from the public as it was evident that the Kerala High Court had been swayed by the rhetoric of global capital; the court had obviously not probed enough into the matter, be it with regard to the scientific facts or the ethical issues involved (Raman 2005).

The CWRDM report, on which the Division Bench of the Kerala High Court based its verdict in favour of the company, is a prime example of the manner in which scientific knowledge could be fragmented, vitiated, and completely misrepresented. The CWRDM version maintained that 'under normal rainfall conditions, the planned groundwater withdrawal of 5 lakh liters per day by the Coca-Cola factory will not adversely affect the availability of groundwater in and around the factory complex' (CWRDM 2004). This position was sufficient enough to generate knowledge controversies with respect to water resources and its extraction by the company. Though it is true that deep aquifers are also replenished by rainfall in nearby areas, what is significant is that Plachimada lies in a rain shadow area and, more importantly, the extraction of groundwater for cola production far exceeds the amount of recharge that may occur in that area. This has been partly established by a study of the Central Ground Water Board (CGWB) – 'Dynamic Groundwater Resource of Kerala, 2004' – which found eastern Palakkad, where the Coca-Cola factory is situated, to have a significant decline of water level in both dry and wet seasons (CGWB 2006: Appendix V, 85). Further, the entire Chittur block in which the factory is located has been categorized as 'overexploited' by none other than the CGWB.

What all this means is that the amount of withdrawal of water is always in excess of the recharge component from rainfall, and it was predicted that this would ultimately lead to the downward – vertical component – percolation of groundwater from the top zone, or phreatic zone. Hence any extraction through bore wells and dug wells as practised by the factory would ultimately result in the drying up of dug wells in the nearby areas, and that is precisely what has transpired in the case of Plachimada, and it is against this that the local community launched the anti-Cola movement. It implies that though aquifers are replenished by rainfall in both nearby and faraway places, it is the excessive groundwater mining from a 'rain shadow' and 'overexploited' (groundwater depleted) region that is the issue in Plachimada.[11] The CWRDM had also committed a gross overestimation of rainfall infiltration in the factory premises, which obviously went in favour of the company: while the percentage of rainfall infiltration factor in the Chittur block has been considered to be 5 to 8 per cent based on the joint study of CGWB and the Kerala government, the CWRDM fixed it at 11 per cent in the Plachimada watershed.[12]

It is also a telling commentary on the sanitization of facts that both the CWRDM and the CGWB, using different units of assessment, provide us with pure base statistics with no attempt at all at an analysis or interpretation. This is totally unacceptable on two counts. First, the task that the CWRDM had been assigned was to conduct a scientific investigation into the allegation that the functioning of Coca-Cola has resulted in shortage and scarcity of drinking water in the neighbouring areas. Second, it is obvious that if they had attempted a sincere interpretation of data, they would have had to take a totally different stand, particularly on certain undisputed facts. For instance, the Expert Committee Report acknowledges that within the 1 square kilometre area, there are 42 dug wells, 2 bore wells with hand pumps, and 7 bore wells with energized pumps. Of the 7 bore wells with energized pumps, all but 1 were operated by the company and, considering the fact that all other bore wells and dug wells being used were either for domestic purposes or livelihood utilization, the amount of water extraction would be quite low as against the water extraction by the company, the quantity of which is itself a matter of debate.

The annual requirement of water for the company was worked out at 0.183 million cubic metres based on the figure supplied by the company of 5 lakh litres of water per day. Considering the fact that the annual installed capacity of the factory would require 15 lakh litres of water per day, and given the fact that until the intervention made by the Kerala High Court, there was no attempt on the part of the company or from other state agencies either to meter the draft of the factory or to monitor the actual extraction, how could the company's claim of 5 lakh litres per day be accepted? As the Delhi-based Centre for Science and Environment (CSE), a leading public interest research and advocacy group in India, pointed out, the CWRDM, first of all, had overestimated the groundwater availability in the area and, second, it had underreported the daily consumption of water by Coca-Cola. With Plachimada being an area of a high-density population largely constituted of colonies of depressed communities – 1,500 population in 1 square kilometre, almost double that of Kerala as a whole, which stands at 819 – the impact of such over-extraction was all the more severely felt and hence quite devastating.[13] In the legislative assembly, the government admitted that there was a drastic reduction of water in the nearby wells, attributing the same to the operation of the cola factory and claimed that the company's extraction was reduced by the state from its original 5 litres to 2 litres; the issue of hazardous waste was also admitted in the house.

But the more interesting issue by far is whether the factory has been mining surplus water or not, since the 'truth effect' is that local residents have been experiencing a water shortage, both for drinking and agriculture, ever since the factory started operating. The *panchayat* and the Cola Quit Campaign have allied to challenge the claims made by the company, a successful victory that has marked the beginning of a new approach which is based on not just discursive but also non-discourse strategies. Having failed to obtain a truly just ruling, the *panchayat* and the campaign groups have petitioned the Supreme Court of India, which at a later stage directed the State Pollution Control Boards in 2003 to issue closure directions to all manufacturing units in the country that were operating in violation of the Hazardous Wastes (Management and Handling) Rules, 1989, which also helped reveal yet another dimension of the campaign.

Water Pollution: Hidden Truths

Plachimada's environmental debacle was arguably characterized by the gross pollution of the remaining groundwater by effluent discharged by the cola factory: if the Chaliyar river was polluted by the Birlas' rayon factory, now it was the entire groundwater of Plachimada by a multinational company. As already mentioned, this was a complete violation of the company's assurance that all chemical waste would be handled and disposed of properly. The factory wastes, which contained pollutants like hydrochloric acid and alkali compounds, were being partially treated as 'irrigation' for the company's premises; much of it had been dumped in nearby lands and even given to local farmers as fertilizer. The chemicals gradually seeped into the groundwater table, polluting the already depleted precious drinking water, resulting in skin and stomach disorders among the villagers.

However, just as with the conflicting streams of knowledge regarding the volume of groundwater extraction, the quality of surface water and the probable pollution of groundwater in the nearby wells and other water reservoirs have also come to be much debated. There has been precious little in terms of consistency or validity with regard to the knowledge on pollution, with the self-same scientific bodies repudiating their own 'regimes of truth' as and when the situation arose. It is interesting to note that the Ground Water Department of the Government of Kerala in its study in November 2002, as per directions from the Kerala Pollution Control Board, arrived at the conclusion that the pollution of surface water, if any, could not be attributed to the discharge from the factory. The CGWB too was of the view that only 24 per cent of the wells had total dissolved solid (TDS) values higher than that considered normal. This claim, however, was baseless considering the fact that the wells with excess TDS were actually those that were in close proximity to the factory, an incriminating piece of evidence that Coca-Cola had deliberately concealed.

In the case of the analysis of sludge samples collected from Plachimada too, the state-led institutions tried to build up their own edifices of truth behind which the multinational took cover. This is thrown into sharp relief by the results of a study on sludge from the farms surrounding the factory and those on drinking water from the surrounding wells carried out by David Santillo, of the University of Exeter.[14] He reported in *Face the Facts* on British Broadcasting Corporation (BBC) Radio on 25 July 2003 that

> of the three solid wastes analyzed, one showed relatively high levels of two toxic metals, namely cadmium and lead. Some other heavy metals including nickel, chromium and zinc were also present at levels significantly above those expected for uncontaminated soils and sludges. The presence of high levels of lead and cadmium is of particular concern. Lead is a developmental toxin in humans, particularly noted for its ability to damage the nervous system. Cadmium is especially toxic to the kidney, but also to the liver – it is classified as a known human carcinogen.

The BBC too confirmed that sludge material was useless as a fertilizer and that it contained a number of toxic metals in quantities that were well above the permissible limit set by the World Health Organization.

In fact, the multinational had completely concealed the fact that the sludge that they had been distributing as fertilizer contained toxic chemicals harmful to humans and the environment, an almost criminal error of omission. It is worth noting that the local communities themselves had many a time voiced their concerns regarding the health problems attendant upon the usage of polluted water and indeed living in the area. It shows that in addition to the denial of the right to water by excess use of it and the corresponding depletion of groundwater, the multinational had, in effect, polluted the precious little that remained of the drinking water, caused damage to village life, and exposed the local populace to disease and health hazards.[15] It was in spite of such clear evidence that the upper echelons of the legal apparatus persisted in its support of global capital, which, in effect, proved to be a culmination of hegemonic knowledge.

This pollution of well water around the company could have been (mostly) due to three reasons, working either independently or in unison. First and foremost, it could have been due to the spreading of leachate to the surface water from the liquid and solid wastes of the company produced in the process of washing, production of syrup, bottling, and cooling of water. Second, it could have been (partly) due to the increasing concentration of minerals due to the shrinking water table, the latter a direct consequence of groundwater mining by the company itself. Third, the pollution could also have been due to the sludge discharged by the factory. Following the studies conducted by the Chennai-based Sargam Metals Ltd, in 2002, an institute recognized by the Department of Science and Technology, Government of India, and local pressure from the *panchayat* and the Cola Quit Campaign, the local level primary health centre was forced to conduct a chemical test of the water from within a close radius of the factory. The result found the water to be highly alkaline, with a high chloride content and hence 'unfit for human consumption'[16]; the study was analysed at the state-owned Medical Laboratory, Kozhikode. The study conducted by the Integrated Rural Technology Centre in June 2002 too revealed high levels of hardness, salinity, and alkalinity, with the presence of chemical components such as chlorides and sulfides, which rendered water unfit for domestic purposes.

Faced with irrefutable evidence of such high quality, which, it must be noted, originated from within institutes that functioned outside the purview of the state construct, the KSPCB was forced to retract its own knowledge base, admitting to the presence of high values of 201.8 milligrams per kilogram of cadmium in the sludge samples collected from Plachimada; it went even as far as to indicate that the toxic content in the waste actually exceeded the levels reported by the BBC. As the sludge supplied by the company to the farmers as fertilizers[17] contained dangerous levels of cadmium and lead, it proceeded to direct the company to set up hazardous waste management measures,[18] and further instructed the company not to let the sludge out of the factory premises and to desist from supplying it as fertilizer. Further, when the Central Pollution Control Board decided to make public its arrival at the truth that the cadmium content in the polluted waters of Plachimada was as high as 328.8 milligrams, the Government of Kerala finally capitulated and withdrew 'its' own earlier verdict in August 2003.

Interestingly, when the left-wing opposition member pointed out that the company should be closed due to its pollution and its health consequences, the then industries and social welfare minister, P.K. Kunhalikutty, agreed to look into the matter; yet he mentioned that there were four to five such companies in West Bengal and why only in Kerala were the problems being analysed. Further, the initial report of the State Pollution Control Board did not express alarming concerns; only after the newspaper reports did the Board want to go for new enquires.[19] Meanwhile, the Supreme Court of India directed the State Pollution Control Boards in October 2003 to issue closure directions within three weeks to all manufacturing units in the country that were operating without authorization or in violation of the Hazardous Wastes (Management and Handling) Rules, 1989, as amended up to 2003. This direction was true to the spirit of the Basel Convention, which was ratified by India in June 1992, and which, in turn, effectuates the fundamental rights guaranteed under Article 21 of the Indian constitution.

As the Coca-Cola factory came under the purview of the Hazardous Waste (HW) Rules and as the company had no 'satisfactory facility for the disposal of hazardous waste generated' in the factory, authorization was refused to the multinational by the KSPCB. In its report (2004), the Supreme Court Monitoring Committee that visited the factory site in Plachimada, read the evidence available and confirmed the damages caused by the company, directing the Company (*a*) to provide piped water to the households free of cost and (*b*) to enforce the Supreme Court order on Hazardous Waters regulations. Additionally, the committee criticized the KSPCB for laxity in enforcing the Supreme Court rules and orders. This, in conjunction with the decision of the local *panchayat*, which refused to renew its licence, has ensured that the factory remained closed to date. Ironically, the very same governmental body had released a report earlier in September 2002 revealing that the water in the wells located around the company was free of heavy metals like cadmium, lead, and chromium; the credibility of the state machinery has thus come under severe strain. Evidence after evidence suggested that Coca-Cola's stand that wastewater generated was being adequately treated in the effluent treatment plant (ETP), in which the company had invested millions of rupees, and that it could not pollute nearby wells as it was being recycled for their own use for gardening and other domestic purposes, thus remained exposed. Because Coca-Cola generates hazardous waste, approval was refused to the multinational by the KSPCB, leading to an effective closure notice that was issued only in August 2005; the closure order had been preceded by the state declaring the area drought-stricken earlier in March 2004. Thus, Coca-Cola had no choice but to close the factory.

Coca-Cola employees, who had now lost their jobs, formed a union after being tossed from their jobs, which spoke out about their concerns. The union built a shed right across the street from the one built by the Cola Quit Campaign, which demanded that factory operations be resumed. Their argument was that the state government's negative attitude towards even the most limited kind of industrialization is largely responsible for the persistent unemployment problem in the state. The voices of the workers carried little weight, as virtually all of them came from outside Plachimada and were not representative of the villagers' livelihood concerns. In the minds of the locals, the very depletion and pollution of groundwater resources, as well as its ecological damages, threatened their everyday strategies of livelihood. Furthermore, in the course of the movement, questions arose regarding custodial rights over common resources, such as water, and whether villagers were allowed to use these resources, thus opening up an entirely new chapter in the anti-Cola movement.

There was a clash between the two parties within the ruling coalition – the Janata Dal alleged that while the CPI(M) was working against the production of Coca-Cola for various reasons, it did not pay attention to the neighbouring village of Puthusseri where the Pepsi factory was functioning unhindered (Chandrasekharan 2003). It is important to understand that it was the Congress-led government that had sanctioned the Pepsi Company in Perumatty *Panchaya*t, but the final licence was issued by the left government on 22 November 2000 for a period of five years. There was also an argument that the depletion of the water table in the region could not be exclusively attributed to Coca-Cola as there were other factories functioning in the vicinity. For instance, there are around 200 bore wells within a 6-kilometre radius of the Coca-Cola factory. This too could have contributed to the depletion of the water table in the area. The CPI(M) maintained that the PepsiCo factories were located on an industrial estate and therefore did not have an impact on human activities or health; therefore, there were no protests against the PepsiCo factories until the issues of Coca-Cola were contested.

In the Chittur *taluk* (block), where the Coca-Cola factory is located, the entire area is prone to drought and is supplied with water through the Parambikulam–Aliyar project. However, the state failed to secure its fair share of water resources from this project, which exacerbated the problem. Although both companies were American-owned, the CPI(M) seemed to take a different approach to the two. Even the CPI(M)'s youth wing, the Democratic Youth Federation of India (DYFI), applied a different approach to the two companies, and this was viewed as double standards. The CPI's youth wing, which was active in the protests against Coca-Cola, also objected to Pepsi factories' operations and demanded their closure as well. Since the clash between the parties was seen as election propaganda, the strike committee ignored these exchanges and continued with their own protest. Vijayan, one of the local leaders of the movement, said, 'We are not affiliated with any established political party. The local people are with us and we join in the struggle for global water justice as well.'[20] The late CPI leader Ardhendu Bhushan Bardhan argued that Coca-Cola and Pepsi licences should be revoked not only in Kerala but also in other states (*Indian Express* 2003b). When Coca-Cola's licence for the production of Coke was supposed to be renewed, the opposition leader V.S. Achuthanandan and Janata Dal state president Veerendrakumar intervened in order to block the renewal. As a result, the licence was declined; with the help of the Janata Dal leadership, the *panchayat* asserted that since the company refused to comply with the renewal terms, it stood void from April 2003.

Additionally, the state government was asked to explain by the legal institutions how it could intervene in a situation in which the local self-government had decided to cancel the company's licence. *Panchayat*s are responsible for taking care of such matters, as they are local self-governments. The state government does not have the right to intervene in the day-to-day functioning of the local government. However, the state government has the right to intervene if the local *panchayat* acts against the spirit of the Panchayat Raj Act or if the latter is unable to effectively implement any part of the Act. Neither of these situations applies in the case of the state's intervention in the Coca-Cola debate. This in itself is probably an indicator of the success of the Panchayati Raj and the way in which decentralization was implemented in the state. The opposition Congress leaders even went to the extent of observing that the state could not acquiesce to every move made by the *panchayat* (Mattancherry 2003).

A month after Coca-Cola's licence was revoked by the Perumatty *panchayat*, the Puthusseri *panchayat* also revoked Pepsi's licence. Pepsi argued that it did not contribute to the water shortage because they were not located in an area that had a water shortage, and it harvested rainwater. In addition, the plant, built with an investment of INR 50 crores, provides employment to 2,000 people (*Mathrubhumi* 2003). A defence was advanced that it would be unjust to cancel the licence after it had been active for two and a half years. Pepsi purchased 50 acres from the government-owned WISE park in 2000 for INR 2.75 crores (*Indian Express* 2003a). The local Perumatty *panchayat* cancelled Coca-Cola's licence, but Pepsi in Puthusseri in Permatty *panchayat* continued to operate. Maybe this was due to the absence of local protests against Pepsi, which was not surprising as the company was located on an industrial estate with no local residents who would be affected by it (Chandrasekharan 2003).

Capitalism, Nature, and Governance: Political-Ecological Concerns

Despite there being a considerable degree of decentralization in Kerala,[21] the fact that new social movements become imperative to air the concerns of the local people is a pointer to the failure of the way in which the former has been effected; what has obviously been missed is the fact that decentralization takes on full meaning only when the local community enjoys complete command over its own resources and is free to design its own forms of development in keeping with its needs and aspirations. In this sense, the Perumatty *panchayat* and the people it governs have placed an example before the rest of the country as to how a local community could assert its rights and resist the onslaught of corporate giants: a prime example of governance from below. This was despite the fact that the *panchayat* was getting INR 9.5 lakhs a year as professional and building tax from the company, apart from the employment it generated.[22]

Throughout the struggle, state-led institutions like the KSPCB, the Kerala Ground Water Department, and the judiciary have been found wanting on political, ecological, and ethical grounds. In a sense, the new social movements have helped focus attention on 'scientific knowledge and its social roles and functions, reconnecting to earlier challenges to the hegemony of science and technology' (Eyerman and Jamison 1991). The success in Plachimada has generated a wave of knowledge that liberation is possible through socially concerned bodies and locally specific movements in various parts of the country – Shiva Ganga (Tamil Nadu), Hajipur and Patna (Bihar), Varanasi, Ballia, Dasna, Hathras, and Bijnor (Uttar Pradesh), Panipat (Haryana), Mandideep (Madhya Pradesh), Ahmedabad and Khera (Gujarat), Thane (Maharashtra) – where Coca-Cola or PepsiCo had begun to threaten the local livelihoods, like in Plachimada.

The Cola Quit India Movement grew from an initial group of individuals into a nationwide TS that transcended boundaries. Medha Patkar, the leader of the Narmada Bachao Andolan, led the National Alliance for People's Movement towards Plachimada on 26 January 2003, in an act of solidarity with those who had been displaced and encroached upon at different times. In its support of the movement in Mumbai, the World Social Forum was announced on 18 January 2004. There were numerous organizations, literary figures, and activists present at the World Water Conference that same year, including José Bové, Vandana Shiva, Sukumar Azhikode, Maude Barlow, and M.P. Veerendrakumar, who signed a declaration stating that water resources could not be stolen by multinational corporations. Documentaries and countless writings, messages, and features showed the struggle outside the borders of Plachimada to a global audience. After 1,000 days of agitation (15 January 2005), protesters from India and around the globe and campaigners from other areas in India who wereaffected by the pollution joined forces at Plachimada, where a resolution was adopted to continue the agitation until the plant was shut down.

In Plachimada, the post-development social movement has succeeded in securing a temporary closure of the Coca-Cola factory. Campaigners have developed a Janakeeya Jaladhikara Yathra (People's Water Assertion March) – calling on Hindustan Coca-Cola Beverages Private Ltd to permanently close its factory in Plachimada and to take steps not to repeat the tragedy in any other country. It also demands the initiation of criminal proceedings against the company rendering the company culpable and, therefore, liable to pay for damages owing to the ill effects of the functioning of its plant in the locality. The march presses for demands that the company be directed to pay compensation on the basis of the 'polluter pays' principle for the rapid depletion of groundwater, the pollution of water in the wells and bore wells that have rendered them unfit and harmful for drinking, washing, and cooking within a radius of 1.5 to 2 kilometres, for causing pollution of the land by dumping waste sludge and slurry extensively on the land, for causing health problems to the people in the vicinity, for destroying agriculture, and for leaving large numbers of agricultural labourers unemployed, especially the Scheduled Tribes. The demands also include the institution of measures to ensure the availability of safe water until such time that the surface and groundwater levels in Plachimada are back to the safe limit, the provision of free health care for all those affected by disease, and the guarantee of potable water in all the affected areas. Amendments to the Panchayat Raj laws are also being demanded to bring groundwater under the authority of the local governing body.

In essence, governance involves a constant engagement with power relations. Any governance strategy should therefore begin by addressing the hegemonic achievements of the structure authorities, which operate either alone or in conjunction with the state. Rather than simply reflexing its opposition to corporate capital, the Plachimada struggle represents the cry of a beleaguered community against the deterioration and destruction of its very fabric of life, which has become a chaotic, contested land. Throughout the agitation in Plachimada, the demand that rings loudest is the one for an immediate closure of the plant or, what one could convincingly argue, undoing the development process (Escobar, 1995: 217; also see Ferguson 1990), for, as the villagers (Mayilamma) constantly remind us, water shortage and pollution were terms that migrated into Plachimada along with Coke. 'We,' Mayilamma stated in an interview, 'are the victims. We are not the only ones fighting against Cola. Even though we are not educated, the educated are also with us (in our struggle), which indicates that it is a struggle of major importance.'[23] In the long struggle for retribution for the usurpation of their traditional means of livelihood, the Adivasis of Plachimada proved that they were far more erudite than the guardians of modern science and knowledge. Despite the multinational agreeing to build a facility for waste disposal and to follow revised standards for soft drinks, achieving a permanent closure of Plachimada's factory has served their residents perfectly until such time that the precarious water situation in the area has been addressed and autonomy over local resources has been re-established.

A High Power Committee was formed in April 2009 by the Kerala government to study the impact of the bottling plant on the local environment and community,[24] and it found that the Coca-Cola plant caused damages worth INR 216.26 crores to the local people.[25] Following the suggestions made by the High Power Committee, the left government and the opposition unanimously passed the Plachimada Coca-Cola Victims' Relief and Compensation Claims Special Tribunal Bill, 2011, in February 2011[26] to adjudicate disputes related to compensation but was rejected by the Indian parliament by accepting the version of the company that it was unlawful. The company was of the view that the bill was devoid of facts, scientific data, or any input from or consideration given to Hindustan Coca-Cola Beverages Pvt Ltd (HCCB). Within no time was HCCB offered an opportunity to present facts, engage in dialogue around the issue, or share independent data before the bill was tabled or approved. Coca-Cola made a submission to the Supreme Court in July 2017 regarding compensation, saying it did not intend to resume operations at its Plachimada plant, which, however, could not be considered an excuse for not paying compensation.

Although there were a lot of discussions in the assembly highlighting the importance of the bill and by and large the members were in favour of the bill, the delay in passing the same is puzzling. The prominent Marxist leader Kodiyeri Balakrishnan cited this as evidence of how much influence the company had that even after four years the bill was not passed.[27] The former chief minister of Kerala and opposition leader V.S Achuthanandan reacted sharply to the news. To quote: 'This is a planned conspiracy of the Centre against the bill. This is an anti-people decision and the Centre is trying to sabotage it … the Central government is playing the role of Coca-Cola's postman' (Misra 2011; see also Narendran 2010). The government's idea was to create a tribunal to determine individual losses and pay compensation, as it was convinced that the company had violated a number of laws. There were violations of the Water (Prevention and Control of Pollution) Act, 1974, the Environmental (Protection) Act, 1986, the Factories Act, 1948, the Hazardous Waste (Management and Handling Rules), 1989, the Scheduled Caste and Scheduled Tribe (Prevention of Atrocities) Act, 1989, the Indian Penal Code, the Land Utilization Order, 1967, the Kerala Ground Water (Control and Regulations) Act, 2002, and the Indian Easement Act, 1882, making ecospatial scars, temporary and permanent, across regions.[28] The earlier minister for water and irrigation, N.K. Premachandran, was highly vocal about the damages caused by the company in the assembly, but neither he nor those assembly members who on varying occasions earlier raised the issues – including Binoy Viswam – nor any other political leaders paid any significant attention to making it a reality; nor did the victims receive any financial compensation until today. Local people should receive compensation for their losses, though no further steps have been taken at the government level.

As recently as 2020, when the Kerala government proposed the conversion of the abandoned plant area into a Covid-19 centre, some of these issues came up (Thomas 2021). The Coca-Cola struggle has suddenly become a tussle between the centre and the state, throwing the local communities in the lurch.[29] The company has agreed to return the land to the government for the establishment of farmer producer organizations (FPOs). Nevertheless, it seems that the anti-Coco-Cola committees have continued with their demand that the government should compensate the local communities to the tune of INR 216.26 crores, which was decided by none other than the erstwhile left government appointed a High Power Committee more than a decade ago. The bill failed to get the assent of the President and it was irresponsibly returned by the BJP-led NDA government in December 2014, terming it as unconstitutional.

No wonder the struggle continues to this day, with no forms and demands, despite the movement's frail power.

Concluding Remarks

The Plachimada struggle began 30 years after the Chaliyar struggle. If the Birla family was invited to Kerala to build a rayon factory at the cost of natural resources and river ecology, Coca-Cola was invited at the cost of adverse effects on water scarcity and pollution. Both firms – Indian big capital and global capital – were invited by the then leftist governments. It would be too simplistic to consider the closure of a factory in any particular locale as sufficient in itself as one finds that, as part of global capitalism, the devastation of Plachimada and the resistance it put up could take place anywhere and at any time in the world – as has happened in Chiapas (Harvey 1998) in Mexico, Cochabamba in Bolivia, and, most recently, in Muthanga and Nandigram in India.

Plachimada stands as a metaphor for post-development social movements (Raman 2007) in the world. As long as market-driven forces dictate the management of commons – particularly land and water – such natural wealth will remain beyond the reach of the very people who are historically entitled to it as part of their right to livelihood, which is a basic human right. Interestingly, if it was caste status that determined access to land and water resources in historical phases (Roy 2022), it is the corporate capital with and without the state that executes the grand schema of enclosure projects in present times, all in the name of development. The fight against such a sequestering of livelihood resources and the human rights violation therein cannot be viewed as a mere tussle for ownership over material resources or as a victory over the domain of materiality involved in political-ecological questions, but rather as a backlash against the denial and deprival of the basic social and democratic right to live. Further, it is also a protest against state-led, corporate-driven developmentalism of the times, which is aimed at further global accumulation. For this reason, any social movement, either within or outside fixed ideological and political boundaries, would be directed against the neoliberal version of global capitalism, which views nature as just another business asset to be packaged and commoditized. Given the fact that neither the state has succeeded in passing the Relief Bill nor the centre wanted to approve it is a reminder that the state must articulate its social democratic power to the centre to become more autonomous.[30]

A reclaiming of the state, which is gradually withdrawing from the welfare sphere at one level, and a re-educating of the newly commoditized/consumerized civil society at another level, are essentially part of the solution. However, the culmination of this process of political rejuvenation would be the ethics of resistance against world colonization by corporate life. A movement's real value comes not only from addressing the immediate concerns of the people but also from maintaining its momentum and addressing a wider egalitarian and emancipatory politics of universal significance. The author is of the view that only through this profound alchemy do simple social movements become post-development social movements with system-wide implications, within a territorially defined state and beyond. Like the Chipko movement, which eventually evolved into the Save Himalaya movement, the Plachimada movement also evolved into an anti-Cola movement throughout Kerala, and even outside to a certain extent, and mutually intelligible struggles were taking place abroad as in the case of Cochabamba – Bolivia's urban resistance against water colonization – helping us imagine new ecospatial futures.

Notes

1. Interviewed on 23 April 2023 in Plachimada.
2. Major transboundary conflicts (see Ravnborg 2004) are associated with river basins that span international boundaries, such as those of the Nile and the Tigris, and interstate boundaries such as the Mullaperiyar in the Indian south. On the other hand, local water conflicts continue to occur in various countries like India, China, Pakistan, and Latin America; Cochabamba in Bolivia is a classic case. New governance approaches have been developed towards the creation of institutions such as the Integrated Water Resource Management that are being increasingly recognized as one of the possible solutions for the widespread water conflicts (see Mollinga et al. 2006). Yet many of the governance agencies such as Water Boards fail to address the preexisting hegemonic structures and thus only serve to reinforce and legitimize existing power relations.
3. The post-development perspective aims at an eschewal of established scientific discourse and instead lay emphasis on alternatives to the mainstream thinking on development. Overall, it favours local culture, social autonomy, and cultural identity in preference to the Eurocentric enlightenment project of modernity; see Escobar (1999, 1995, 1985); Ferguson (1995); Rahnema (1992); Ziai (2004); Levine (2001); Nustad (2001); (Raman 2007).
4. For a parallel argument, see Meinzen-Dick (2003).
5. 19 June 2003, Session 6, KLA-11 (2001–2006).
6. 30 July 2003, Session 6, KLA-11 (2001–2006).
7. Legislative Proceedings (LP), 13 August 2003, Session 6, KLA-11 (2001–2006); In his submission to the legislative assembly, Neelalohithadas Nadar raised the issues from the left bench, but the local self-government (LSG) minister, Cherkalam Abdulla, reiterated that it was the LDF that sanctioned the licence and it should have been careful before doing this. Further, he also alleged that K. Krishnankutty was the one who traded water with the company; there were nine such companies in the country, of which four were in left-ruled West Bengal; see 4 August 2003, Session 6, KLA-11 (2000–2006); 28 February 2003, KLA-11 (2001–2006). When contacted, Krishnankutty, who is currently the minister for electricity in the state in the current Pinarayi Vijayan led LDF government, on 28 July 2023, he responded by saying that the company was invited after E.K. Nayanar and Susheela Gopalan, the then chief minister and industrial minister respectively, had an initial discussion with the authorities. He further stated,

> [T]his was a continuation of the left consensus on inviting industrialists as part of advancing the manufacture base of Kerala. However, when we all realized that the company was not complying with the pollution rules and damaging the environment and the livelihood of the local people too, we ourselves took a stand against it and eventually the factory was closed. People like M.P. Veerendrakumar took an initiative for the same. Now the government has succeeded in getting the land back from the company; steps are in progress.

8. *Perumatty Gram Panchayat vs State of Kerala* WPC 34292, Kerala High Court, 27–28, dated 16 December 2003.
9. *Santhosh Mittal vs State of Rajasthan* RLW 2005(1) Raj 486, dated 8 October 2004.
10. Letter dated 29 March 2004; From the legal regional manager, Hindustan Coca-Cola Beverages Private Limited (HCCB), to the special grade secretary, Perumatty *grama panchayat.*
11. The silence of Saleem Romani, the chairman of CWGB, on this particular point appears quite inexplicable; see *R*omani (2005). Romani was responding to the author's paper in the same journal (see Raman 2005).
12. I am thankful to Romani for having pointed out this fact.
13. See 14 August 2003, Session 6, KLA-11 (2001–2006); 21 January 2004, KLA-11 (2001–2006), 7; 6 February 2004, KLA-11 (2001–2006), 7. 28 July 2006, KLA-11 (2001–2006); several of the political and representative leaders including Binoy Viswam, Thomas Isaac, and Neelalohithadasan Nadar participated in the discussion.
14. When the BBC anchor John Wait presented the results of the study from Exeter University, and also quoted the comments of Dr John Henry from St Mary's Hospital, London, all to the effect of confirming the ill effects of the pollution caused by the accumulation of wastes from the Cola plant, the general public began to take note and widespread protests began.
15. For more political-ecological expositions in varying contexts, see Escobar (1999); Roger, Bell, Penz, and Fawcett (1998); Susan, Gezon, and Watts (2003); Peet and Watts (1996); Barlow (2002); Greenough and Tsing (2004); Guha and Martinez-Alier (1997); Porta and Diana (1999). While there were scientific studies exposing the ill effects of the pollution, such an intervention by international experts helped generate a global epistemology ('International Report Challenges to Coke: Coca Cola Group Visits Plachimada', *Madhyamam* 30 July 2003); also see *Deshabhimani* (2003); *Malayala Manorama* (2003).

16. The alkaline and chloride contents of the water were 352/396 and 364 parts per million and 770/910 and 860 parts per million respectively, both far above the normal level.
17. Also see the answers to the questions raised by Kovur Kunhimon on hazardous wastes generated due to the operation of the plant; PCB's initial findings of excess of cadmium and so on. 11 August 2003, Session 6, KLA-11 (2001–2006).
18. See Letter dated 7 August 2003 from the KSPCB, Government of Kerala, Thiruvananthapuram.
19. See the discussion, 31 July 2003, Session 6, KLA-11 (2001–2006).
20. Interviewed on 24 April 2003 at Plachimada.
21. Through the provisions of the Panchayats (Extension to the Scheduled Areas) Act, 1996 (PESA), *panchayat*s have been extended to the tribal areas as well in an attempt to enable tribal societies to assume control over their own future and to preserve and conserve their traditional rights over natural resources. The Act came into force on 24 December 1996, with the notification of scheduled areas in many states like Himachal Pradesh, Bihar, Orissa, Madhya Pradesh, Rajasthan, and Gujarat but remains unimplemented in Kerala, as it would first of all require the bringing of areas under Schedule V, which has not been done yet in the state. Perhaps one politically meaningful way of bringing resources such as land and water under the control of local communities is to fortify the decentralization process in Kerala, with the strategic empowering of *grama sabha*s (see Bijoy 2006).
22. Interview with the *panchayat* president A. Krishnan of the Janata Dal; he pointed out that it was the very left government that allowed Coca-Cola to come and run the factory. 13 August 2003, KLA-11 (2001–2006).
23. Interviewed on 23 April 2023 in Plachimada.
24. The committee was headed by K. Jayakumar with other members; see Jayakumar (2010).
25. For a discussion related with the High Power Committee in the KLA, see 11 March 2015, KLA-13 (2011–2016).
26. Plachimada Coca-Cola Victims Relief and Compensation Claims Special Tribunal Bill, 2011, as passed by the KLA, KLA-12 (2006–2011).
27. V.K. Vijayadas, V. Chenthamarakshan, P.J. Joseph, and others participated in the discussion. K. Radhakrishan even cited that the company owes more than 5 crores of sales tax to the state, which was stayed through the High Court; see 10 July 2014, KLA-13 (2011–2016), (11).
28. Legislative proceedings (LP), 22 February 2011.

29. V. Surendran Pillai (2010) Water scarcity and environmental pollutions caused by Plachimada Coca-Cola Company, KLA-12 (2006–2011), (2009–2011), (11), KLA; also see 24 February 2011, Session 17, KLA-12 (2006–2011); on compensation issues, see LA discussions, 3 December 2008, (9), KLA-12 (2006–2011).
30. Ever since N.K. Premachandran suggested the KLA to take up the issue of the bill and the then finance minister Thomas Isaac supported it, KLA-12 (2006–2011), no further steps have been taken. It implies that the discussions in the KLA for more than four years continuously, say from February 2011 to 2015, did not bring fruit.

References

Ashcroft, Bill (2001). *Post-Colonial Transformation*. London: Routledge.

Barlow, Maude, and Tony Clark (2002). *Blue Gold: The Fight to Stop the Corporate Theft of the World's Water*. New York: The New Press.

Bijoy, C.R. (2006). Kerala's Plachimada struggle: A narrative on water and governance rights. *Economic and Political Weekly* 41 (41): 4332–4339.

Bryant, R., and S. Bailey. (1997). *Third World Political Ecology*. London: Routledge.

Central Ground Water Board (CGWB) (2006). *Dynamic Ground Water Resources of India*. New Delhi: Government of India.

Centre for Water Resources Development and Management (CWRDM) (2004). *Interim Report: Investigations on the Extraction of Groundwater by M/s Hindustan Coca-Cola Beverages Private Limited at Plachimada*. Filed before the HC of Kerala, 14 May. Kozhikode: CWRDM.

Chandrasekharan, T.V. (2003). Cola factory: CPM in a fix owing to Dal's stance. *Madhyamam*, 30 April.

Clairmonte, Frederick, and John Cavanagh (1988). *Merchants of Drink: Transnational Control of World Beverages*. Penang: Third World Network.

Daudi, Philippe (1983). The discourse of power or the power of discourse. *Alternatives* 9 (2): 275–283.

Deshabhimani (2003). Disaster awaits Plachimada. Editorial, 30 July.

Escobar, Arturo. (1995). *Encountering Development: The Making and Unmaking of the Third World*. Princeton: Princeton University Press.

——— (1999). After nature. *Current Anthropology* 40 (1): 1–30.

Eyerman, Ron and Andrew Jamison (1991). *Social Movements: A Cognitive Approach*. London, Polity Press.

Ferguson, J. (1990). *The Anti-Politics Machine: 'Development', Depoliticization, and Bureaucratic Power in Lesotho*. Cambridge: Cambridge University Press.

Foucault, Michael (1980). *Power/Knowledge: Selected Interviews and Other Writings*. New York: Pantheon.

Greenough, Paul, and Anna Lowenhaupt Tsing, eds. (2004). *Nature in the Global South*. New Delhi: Orient Longman.

Grillo, R.D., and R.L. Stirrat, eds. (1997). *Discourses of Development: Anthropological Perspectives*. Oxford: Berg.

Guha, R., and J. Martinez-Alier (1997). *Varieties of Environmentalism: Essays North and South*. London: Earthscan.

Harvey, Neil (1998). *The Chiapas Rebellion: The Struggle for Land and Democracy*. Durham: Duke University Press.

Indian Express (2003a). Overexploitation of water resources alleged. 16 May.

——— (2003b). Revoke licences given to Coke, Pepsi: Bardhan. 10 April.

Jayakumar, K. (2010). *Report of the High Power Committee to Assess the Extent of Damages Caused by the Coca Cola Plant at Plachimada and Claiming Compensation*. Thiruvananthapuram: Kerala Legislative Assembly.

Malayala Manorama (2003). The low tide in Kanchikode. 3 September.

Mathrubhumi (2003). Decision to cancel Pepsi's license. 16 May.

Mattancherry, Abdullah (2003). Plachimada: Conflict between local self government and the department of industries. *Madhyamam*, 30 July.

Misra, Savvy S. (2011). Centre returns Plachimada tribunal bill, seeks explanation from Kerala government after Coca-Cola questions validity of the bill under its consideration. *Down to Earth*, 17 September. https://www.downtoearth.org.in/news/centre-returns-plachimada-tribunal-bill---34039 (accessed 6 May 2023).

Mollinga, Peter P., Ajaya Dixit, and Kusum Athukorala, eds. (2006). *Integrated Water Resources Management : Global Theory, Emerging Practice and Local Needs*. Delhi: Sage.

Narendran, Aromal (2010). Coca-Cola asked to pay Rs 216 crore. *Down To Earth*, 15 April.

Nustad, K.G. (2001). Development the devil we know. *Third World Quarterly* 22 (4): 479–489.

Parmar, Pooja (2015). *Indigeneity and Legal Pluralism in India: Claims, Histories, Meanings*. New Delhi: Cambridge University Press.

Peet, R., and M. Watts, eds. (1996). *Liberation Ecologies: Environment, Development, Social Movement*. London: Routledge.

Porta, della Donatella, and Mario Diana (1999). *Social Movements*. Oxford: Blackwell.

Prabhakaran, G. (2003). Soft drink giant caught in political crossfire. *The Hindu*, 25 April.

Rahnema, M. (1992). Introduction. In *The Post-development Reader*, ed. M. Rahnema and V. Bawtree, pp. ix–xix. London: Zed.

Raman, K. Ravi. (2005). Corporate violence, legal nuances and political ecology: The cola war in Plachimada. *Economic and Political Weekly* 40 (25): 2481–2486.

——— (2007). 'Plachimada resistance: A post-developmental social movement metaphor. In *Exploring Post-Development: Theory and Practice, Problems and Perspectives*, ed. Aram Zai, pp. 163–180. London: Routledge.

Ravnborg, H.M.E., ed. (2004). *Water and Conflict: Conflict Prevention and Mitigation in Water Resources Management*. Copenhagen: Danish Institute for International Studies. .

Romani, Salim (2005). Plachimada water. Letter. *Economic and Political Weekly* 40 (49): 5134–5211.

Santos, B. de S., ed. (2007). *Another World Is Possible: Beyond Northern Epistemologies*. London: Verso.

——— (2009). A non-occidental west? Learned ignorance and ecology of knowledge. *Theory, Culture and Society* 26 (7–8): 103–125.

Terdiman, Richard (1985). *Discourse/Counter Discourse: The Theory and Practice of Symbolic Resistance in Nineteenth-Century*, Ithaca and London: Cornell University Press.

Thomas, Rosanna (2021). Don't accept charity from Coca Cola, take over plant, Ecologist Faizi writes to Kerala CM. Coutercurrents.org, 13 May. https://countercurrents.org/2021/05/dont-accept-charity-from-coca-cola-take-over-plant-ecologist-faizi-writes-to-kerala-cm/ (accessed 6 May 2023).

Ziai, Aram (2004). The ambivalence of post-development: Between reactionary populism and radical democracy. *Third World Quarterly* 25 (6): 1045–1060.

5

Politics, Epistemology, and Environmental Modernity

Anti-endosulfan as Ethical Practice

This chapter addresses how politics, epistemology, and modernity are co-produced, and, in this process, how the pre-defined notions of politics, epistemology, and modernity themselves are transformed and reconstructed. The emergent theoretical framing is empirically informed by the place-specific campaign against the aerial spraying of endosulfan pesticide wherein 'life is cheaper than cashew'.[1] The chapter highlights the structural connections between global capitalism and state-driven developmentalism but also how the very state was conscientized by the transverse solidarity of the 'constituent power', including the victims and the larger civil society as agents of modernity, the latter understood as resistance for egalitarianism. However, it does not stop there. We shall also touch upon the 'epistemological break' (Bachelard 1938; Althusser 1969) that has occurred in the larger context of knowledge controversies and conflicts (see Whatmore 2009).

In May 2010, the left-front government in the Indian state of Kerala took the historic decision to ban more than a dozen toxic pesticides in the state.[2] This was the culmination of over a decade and a half of struggle and movements in protest against the aerial spraying of endosulfan on the state-owned cashew plantation in the northernmost district of Kasaragod. This chapter follows the prolonged struggle led by the victims of the deadly pesticide, the awakening of a general consciousness among the public, the building up of transverse politics and solidarity, and, finally, the persuasion of the state to ban the pesticide, along with other toxic wastes. The chapter is situated in the larger context of what Beck (1986), Habermas (1987), and Gaonkar (2001) would call risk society, a society in which modernity has become 'a theme and a problem for itself', and thus the crisis inherent in it is to be managed through a reinvention of politics.

The chapter suggests that the concept of risk society and reflexive modernity as the outcome of a series of struggles and movements demanding the ban on endosulfan in the state offers fresh insights into the power of the people and the civil society in joining the victims. Further, going beyond Beck and Giddens (Beck 1986; also see Beck and Grande 2010; Sørensen and Christiensen 2012; Giddens 1990; Beck, Giddens, and Lash 1994; Raman 2020), I would suggest that managing the crisis in modernity also implies a mobilization of victims, and those around them, and thereby complicates the understanding of 'reinvention of politics' through the generation of a transverse politics and solidarity (Raman 2010) and thereby a subaltern modernity. The process of conscientization of the state is a complex one and takes place at multiple levels.

While acknowledging the significance of the reinvention of politics to 'prevent, minimise, dramatise, or channel' the risks in modernity, Beck seems to undermine the role of the state in transforming into an agent of deliverance, joining hands with the victims and thereby reshaping its own vision of development. More importantly, the risk society and the reinvention of politics in both Beck (1994) and Giddens (1994) do not have much to say about the risklessness as articulated by the dominant institutions, both within and outside of the state. I would argue that risklessness can equally be the outcome of a manufactured consent, and should be given equal weight to that of risk, and it is for the people who are subject to these risks to try and distinguish the external or actual risk from the manufactured risk. The quantifiability and narration of such risks are important, and the point of conflation between risk and uncertainty is explored at three levels, the spatial, temporal, and agential levels, while the gravity of the narrative is brought out in the form of scientific reports, though they remained contested. The scalar is, by and large, an account of the published material on scientific research which recognizes and proves the potential dangers of exposure through lab experiments, field studies, and so on. Risk as social and cultural constructs, not confined to scientific experiments and statistical calculations alone, would also form a powerful source of argument.

I shall elaborate on the nature of endosulfan and the historical context in which it became an acceptable pesticide for farmers and public sector undertakings, all of which helped commercialize cashew production in the state. I shall trace the links between the acceptance of endosulfan as part of a global commercialization of agriculture and the resulting increase in the competitiveness of cashew from India in the global market. However, the human impact of the aerial spraying of endosulfan was unforeseen; I shall first explore the nature of this impact and then go on to examine how the constituent power – the victims and the larger civil society, and also the state – responded to this situation and thereby generated a new epistemology and politics but not free from knowledge controversies. In fact, my idea is to uncover the process by which a co-production of politics, epistemology, and modernity helped reconstruct the predefined notions of the same in an attempt to create a new ethical practice in the state of Kerala.

Emergence of Endosulfan

Like any other plantation crop in Kerala, the origin of cashew too could be traced to colonial times. With the formation of the Plantation Corporation of Kerala (PCK) by the state in 1962, it became one of the largest cashew plantations in India, with more than 6,000 hectares, mostly in the Kasaragod district.[3] PCK also grows rubber, oil palm, cinnamon, areaca nuts, coconuts, pepper, teak, and other crops, but cashew gained prominence in the operations of PCK. Like many other sources of urban food – particularly those like cashew, which is a rich man's item – cashew too comes from the rural Global South. The cashew supply chain is extensive, connecting countries, people, and markets in the Global South (see Kannan 1983; Nair and Sreedharan 2004). There are three major social classes who are directly involved in the cashew industry: the cashew planters, who are basically the large farmers; the large number of workers employed by the cashew-processing factories; and the locals employed on the plantations, whose number is rather minuscule. The cashew coming from this plantation feeds a large number of workers who are employed in the processing factories, which are not in the nearby regions but in the southern part of Kerala. Yet they have never been free from poverty or deprivation, by any standard. However, it is the local community that fails to directly benefit from the plantations other than those who are employed as endosulfan sprayers and attendants, who, in turn, become the victims of the spraying. The local communities were hard hit, and that became a major tragedy in Kerala, with its effects far-reaching even after years of banning endosulfan.

It was no surprise that the very production and patenting of endosulfan coincided with the emerging green revolution across the world. By the year 1954, the US-based Hoechst introduced endosulfan into the world market, meeting the demand for increased production of certain agricultural crops to make them more competitive in the world market. With the first wave of the Green Revolution in India in the 1960s, endosulfan became a natural ally as it assured high productivity through effective insect control. Responding to the cry for higher and higher levels of productivity, the Government of India started a new firm with the prime aim of manufacturing pesticides, one of which was endosulfan. India eventually grew to be one of the largest producers of pesticides in the world and remains, to this day, the largest producer and user of endosulfan; until recently, there were more than 60 manufacturers and formulators involved in the production and sale of endosulfan in India. In fact, the pesticide lobby in India carries a lot of weight, with frequent allegations by NGOs and others about government agencies and regulatory bodies heavily favouring pesticide manufacturers and their business interests.

To put things in perspective, three of India's top manufacturers – one of which is the government-owned Hindustan Insecticides Ltd (HIL), Kochi – together produced 9,500 tonnes of endosulfan between 2007 and 2008, 5,500 tonnes of which was used within the country. HIL, the Government of India enterprise, is situated on the banks of the Periyar river in central Kerala, which is home to some of the most polluting industries in the state. HIL is one of the largest producers of endosulfan in India, manufacturing 1,500 tonnes of endosulfan (technical grade) and 1,900 kilolitres of liquid endosulfan a year, both for use within India and for export. The other two units of the company are located in Raigad, Maharashtra, and Bathinda, Punjab. The private sector too has some big manufacturers of crop protection chemicals, such as Excel Industries Ltd (Mumbai, Maharashtra), Murugappa Group of EID Parry (India) Ltd, and Coromandel Fertilizers Ltd, both in Chennai, Tamil Nadu. Until recently, in India, endosulfan is reported to be one of the most commonly used pesticides in the cultivation of almost all major crops. It is widely used on rice, cotton, soy, coffee, tea, vegetables, and cashew crops. However, it was its application on cashew plantations in Kerala that led to most of its disastrous effects, leading to a historic mobilization of public and scientific opinion against its use. With thousands of residents in nearly a dozen villages, it is argued that the use of endosulfan is directly to blame for the physical and mental disabilities affecting both adults and children in the region. These villages, situated in between the cashew plantations, have been systematically sprayed three times every year in order to protect the cashew trees from the tea mosquito and to maintain high levels of productivity (see Prabhakaran 2012), particularly aerially, again in the name of increasing productivity and profit.

'Life Cheaper than Cashew': Reports to the World[4]

The Department of Agriculture of the Government of Kerala began planting cashew on the hills of Kasaragod in 1963–1964. A decade and a half later, the cashew plantation was taken over by PCK, a newly formed government establishment for the growth and development of plantations in the state. As the tea mosquito affected the cashew plantations, PCK applied endosulfan as an antidote. Within no time, PCK shifted to aerial spraying of endosulfan to save none other than the labour cost of manual spraying. As three times a year of manual spraying was considered labour costly, PCK found it all the more rational to go for aerial spraying and improve its revenue-raising strategies, which, in fact, was materialized – while the profit of the corporation declined from 1997–1998 to 2001–2002, it increased with aerial spraying, from INR 6 crores to INR 11.4 crores in 2007–2008 (PCK Kasaragod). Though PCK managed to increase its profit, it could not forestall the tragedy of the local communities that followed, at least in the adjacent *panchayats* of Enmakaje, Mulyar, and Karalka. While focusing on the revenue mode, what PCK ignored was the houses within the plantation, around 300, and adjacent to it, which were around 2,026. It implies that a significant number of people – women and children – were exposed to aerial spraying, which essentially depends on the direction and speed of wind and the duration of aerial spraying. A planned erasure of multicrops and the introduction of mass cultivation of cashew has significantly altered the lives and livelihoods of the people in Kasaragod. The state has punished its people without the proper removal of endosulfan residue in the region (Rahman 2011; Satheesh 2017).

Regular aerial spraying started in 1981 onwards: two–three times a year by helicopters and small planes. PCK ignored stipulations with regard to aerial spraying of pesticides. First of all, endosulfan should not have been applied very close to the canopy level, which was ignored. In trying to avoid electricity cable lines, helicopters flew higher than the stipulated 3 metres above the cashew trees. The same pesticide should not be used continuously for long periods of time in an area. PCK also ignored the risk of the bugs acquiring immunity due to long-term exposure. Further, all the warning signals went unheeded – dead birds, frogs, and fish in the streams and rivulets were found, and cattle and wildlife were found dead in the plantation areas, but spraying continued. Local people began experiencing acute endosulfan toxicity symptoms after the spraying sorties over their villages. It has been suggested that the toxicity may enter the human body in several ways. It could be from the mother's body to the foetus via the placenta or the mother's milk to the baby. It could be from locally grown plant and animal foods, namely food-borne exposure. People may get exposed through water and air, the latter through breathing and stress chemicals – that are generated by the living systems in response to the exposure. Cattle with congenital anomalies and cancers are more likely to be sold for slaughter. Chronic exposure through contaminated water and food was found to be the major pathway for the deleterious effects caused by endosulfan.

The first reported major complaint against the aerial spraying of pesticides in Kerala was voiced in 1979 when a small farmer in Padre village found that three of the calves born on his farm had limb deformities and stunted growth. Refusing to accept this as divine retribution, he instead reported this to a local journalist, pointing out that he had read that pesticides like endosulfan could cause such problems. The paper report, titled 'Aerial spray of pesticides makes life cheaper than cashew' (Padre 1981), brought the matter to the attention of the public. The local *panchayat* councils, the decentralized units of administration in the state, were quick to respond and began gathering details of similar incidents, which were found to be not uncommon. Two of the village *panchayat*s passed a resolution demanding that the state desist from its aerial spraying of the pesticide, and the government of Kerala ordered the suspension of the aerial spraying, which remained in effect for two years. However, these protests did not grow into a full-fledged campaign because of the contrasting claims on the cause and effect of endosulfan spraying. The local *panchayat*s, nevertheless, persisted in highlighting the negative consequences of spraying, on the strength of the right guaranteed by the Indian constitution to speak on behalf of the local communities. Overall, the *panchayat*-led mobilization against endosulfan drew the attention of various agencies and organizations to the seriousness of the case as a public issue in the state. An anti-endosulfan campaign began to emerge in the state. First, a large number of environmental and civil society organizations were drawn into the campaign. Second, the issue was taken up at the level of the judiciary against the spraying of the pesticide by PCK.[5] Third, the media, which normally was loathe to intervene in such issues as they feared the consequences, joined the protest and began serializing the everyday developments in terms of not only the activities of the state but also the ailments of the victims. Fourth, the state was forced to enter into the debate, not only because the cashew plantations were state-owned but also because a left-wing government was back in power. The main concerns raised by the public were the health disorders of the local communities and how PCK ignored the health hazards of aerial spraying, including cerebral palsy, mental retardation, skin disorders, and so on, but also raised the question of violation of the protocols as the per the Insecticides Act, 1968.[6]

This, in turn, aroused the interest of various scientific and non-scientific bodies, which tried to establish whether a link existed between the aerial spraying of pesticides and the kind of diseases found in the region. This also opened up fresh debates on the causalities and the claims and counterclaims on the possible effects of aerial spraying, followed by a massive mobilization of the local people, in alliance with a large number of civil society organizations in the state. This movement expanded to such an extent that its echoes were heard in Stockholm amid the resolution demanding that endosulfan be listed as a major cause of concern; this also followed the near ban on almost all the pesticides in the state in May 2011. It was essentially the delegate-activists from Kerala, who were directly involved in the struggle against the spraying of pesticide on cashew plantations, who raised the issue at the Stockholm conference. This was yet another addition to transverse solidarity making a new politics possible in the international domain of resistance politics.

Expert Knowledge, Arguments, and Counterarguments

Seven years later, after aerial spraying was made a continuous practice, in 1988, PCK was advised by the National Research Centre for Cashew (NRCC) to use endosulfan only at a concentration of 0.05 per cent; however, this dosage was not adhered to by PCK on the grounds that it was ineffective at such low strengths. Further, even the scientists from the Kerala Agricultural University (KAU) (2001) were not fully cognizant of the potential impacts of the residues. There were instances where the KAU supported the claims made by PCK that endosulfan use was not harmful but took a position that what is required is 'need based spraying', which, in effect, supported the claims of PCK. However, this was not the case with the large number of studies done at various levels.

The Government of Kerala had formed two committees on endosulfan: one committee formed by the Kerala State Council for Science, Technology and Environment (KSCSTE) to study the health impacts of endosulfan in Kasaragod district and the other committee comprising members from civil society organizations, agriculture universities, and the Health Department to study the impact of pesticides in the state. The level of endosulfan residues in the water samples was found to be within the permissible limits as per the World

Health Organization (WHO) standards (20 μg/litre; WHO 2003). However, the study informs the government and the larger public that the impact of endosulfan spraying was evident and measurable in all aspects of life of the people in the area; the adverse effects on environment were very pronounced. The impact of health-related problems and the increase in expenditure for the treatment of affected persons had led to financial difficulties for the families around; the study also pointed out that women and children, students, and the tribal communities – the Kodagas – were the worst affected as they are more vulnerable to exposure (KSCSTE 2011: 24). While the KSCSTE study did not suggest the banning of endosulfan, the studies that followed recommended the ban at any cost.

Two major conclusions of the National Institute of Occupational Health (NIOH) (under the Indian Council of Medical Research, or ICMR) in 2002 were significant: First, there is a significantly higher prevalence of neuro-behavioural disorders, congenital malformations in female subjects, and abnormalities related to the male reproductive system in the study group (Padre village, Enmakaje *panchayat*) as compared to the reference group (Miyapavadu village of Meenja *panchayat*).[7] Second, regarding the aetiological factors responsible for these health problems, various factors were compared, and it was found that the two groups differed mainly with respect to exposure to endosulfan. Studies done by institutions such as the Calicut Medical College (December 2010–January 2011) also brought forward the harmful effects of the aerial spraying of endosulfan (see Prabhakaran 2012). The final report of NIOH recommends a 'ban [on] aerial spraying of pesticides in all the cashew plantations of PCK Ltd in Kasaragod district' (2002: 95).

In 1991, the Central Insecticides Bureau, the agency mandated to regulate pesticide use in India, appointed a High Power Committee under the chairmanship of Dr S.N. Banerjee to review the continued use of some pesticides, including endosulfan. The committee, though not blocking the continued use of endosulfan, recommended that authorities must not allow the use of endosulfan in land adjoining rivers, ponds, lakes and sea. This was upon the recognition that endosulfan was a chemical of high aquatic toxicity, but the committee's recommendations were not implemented or practised as mentioned by another committee led by R.B. Singh (1999), which also, while allowing continued use, suggested that endosulfan should not be sold in small packets and the minimum container size must be 1 kilogram, so as to avoid misuse. Despite the fact that the same recommendations were made by the Registration Committee (195th) and the Inter-ministerial Committee

(10th) to review the use of insecticides and hazardous chemicals, none was implemented, and had there been a diligent response on the part of the authorities, a significant improvement in the life of the communities would have been possible (Jayakumar 2011).

In some cases, endosulfan was not even declared as harmful as it was highlighted. Committees such as the O.P. Dubey (2003) committee and the C.D. Mayee Committee (2006) had declared endosulfan safe to use; yet the latter pointed out that endosulfan spraying should be withheld in Kerala, considering the concerns expressed by the local communities. Both the reports were challenged by the local communities, NGOs, and environmental activists and also later by scientists as a manipulation of the truth in order to favour the endosulfan lobby. It cannot be argued that the state or the public corporation was unaware of the harmful effects of endosulfan. Ironically, India argued against a ban on the pesticide at the Stockholm Convention on Persistent Organic Pollutants, guided by the above reports, and also due to the pressure from endosulfan manufacturing companies. Despite India's opposition, the convention (a global treaty to protect public health and the environment from persistent organic pollutants) recommended a ban; however, the Indian government managed to avail a remission for 10 years with a gradual phasing out with respect to certain crops (Kumar and Jayakumar 2019). In his study on mental retardation and physical deformities in Kasaragode, Sukumaran (2005) found that endosulfan spraying had affected the local population and women were at a higher risk of adverse impact of pesticides, with many cases of abortions and stillbirths. This report says that these effects were due to chronic exposure to persistent organic pollutants. Similar studies have previously been conducted in Maharashtra in the 1980s and also in the cashew plantations in Odisha. L.K. Advani, a BJP member of parliament (MP), had called for an enquiry into the scientific consequences of the spraying of endosulfan. This was periodically echoed by numerous NGOs across the country. The subsequent studies and movements against the pesticide in Kerala must be evaluated against the backdrop of these investigations.

The environmentalist A. Achuthan has unequivocally stated that the only abnormal activity in the area of high morbidity in the study area of endosulfan spraying, which has no causes of industrial or other pollutions, was aerial spraying of endosulfan. Though it is difficult to prove the cause–effect relationship of chronic low-dose environmental poisons and miseries of living beings, the Achuthan Committee clearly opined that the absence of proof could not be considered as proof of absence. In any case, as the Achuthan

Committee said: '[T]he onus of responsibility to prove or disprove the cause effect relationship should be that of the polluter and not of the general public who are the victims of the pollution' (Achuthan Committee 2001: 50)[8] This was the first major committee that suggested a 'ban [on] aerial spraying of pesticides in all the cashew plantations of PCK Ltd' and a five-year pesticide holiday in the Kasaragod plantation area. However, the committee neither conducted any comparative studies of the villages that were exposed to endosulfan and that were not nor grouped the diseases to evaluate the cause–effect relationship. Although the committee recommends an epidemiological study in the area, that has not been carried out (Sreekumar and Prathapan 2013). This was followed by the report of the Fact Finding Committee titled '*Endosulfan Poisoning in Kasaragod, Kerala, India*, undertaken by the Pesticide Action Network Asia and Pacific (PANAP) (Quijano 2002), which also suggested that the 'use of endosulfan should be permanently banned' (p. 7) and a comprehensive environmental survey be undertaken to understand the extent of adverse health and environmental damages.

The report of NIOH, Ahmedabad, on endosulfan exposure in Padre village found endosulfan residues present in 85 per cent and 75 per cent of female and male subjects and highlighted the health effects of endosulfan spraying (NIOH 2002). With the report of the Sivaraman High Power Committee (2003), set up by the Government of Kerala, too concluding that endosulfan was the cause of the health problems in Kasaragod district, it became prominent that there was no further space for any debate other than to accept its adverse effects. Though the committee did not suggest banning endosulfan, it recommended that health facilities be provided to the victims. As a follow-up, the Kerala State Pollution Control Board (KSPCB) banned the use of endosulfan in the state on December 2004 until a final decision was taken on the matter. The study done by the Indian Medical Association (IMA 2003) heavily criticised the aerial spraying of endosulfan: 'Padre is a village with very high morbidity.... Not only should the profession join in the activism to scientifically evaluate the role of Endosulfan into the causation of the tragedy in Padre but also should join ranks to fetch them medical help, social and economic support and rehabilitative avenues.' However, there are concerns over the nature of the studies that were conducted by the Sivaraman Committee. Instead of a detailed scientific study, the committee conducted medical camps and sourced the data from the camp attendees. The report suffers from research design and methodological issues wherein the study loses its credibility due to its subjective nature. In addition, they critique the absence of any studies that evaluate the cause–effect relationship between the pesticide and diseases. This has, to an extent, led to the attribution of endosulfan as the reason for hundreds of types of diseases present in the region, which is unusual in the medical history.[9] An overwhelming popular notion about endosulfan should not be a reason to discourage evidence-based scientific studies and the consequent policy formulations.

Solidarity Groups Gathering

While the experts and study groups continue to highlight the health effects of endosulfan, at times contradictory to each other, the local communities were increasingly mobilized by environmentalists and social activists. The first major credit for mobilizing the local communities and organizing protests against aerial spraying goes to the local club, Punchiri Sports and Arts Club, Muliyar. This was followed by the formation of the Endosulfan Spray Protest Action Committee (ESPAC) that mobilized the rural people in December 2000; a few urban NGOs, civil society activists, and individual activists, including medical doctors, joined the struggle.[10] Media and civil society activists too took a particular interest in this issue and helped mobilize mainstream political parties and their representatives in their movement against the use of the pesticide. The District Environmental Committee was also formed in order to look into the wider issues involved in this case. The Kerala Shastra Sahitya Parishad (the Kerala People's Science Movement), which had a long history of protecting the environment and leading struggles, as in the case of the Save Silent Valley Campaign of the 1960s and 1970s, was also actively involved. Thanal, a non-profit NGO with committed scholars and scientists, began to take particular interest in articulating the arguments against the use of endosulfan, providing literature to back their arguments and representing various official and non-official agencies on behalf of the local protesting organizations and their people. This formed a major source of inspiration for other neighbouring *panchayats* and communities, which soon followed suit, drawing the attention of the state in the process.

However, the protests were also coloured by a degree of uncertainty, as the extent to which the reported maladies could be directly attributed to the aerial spraying of endosulfan was still debatable. Local agencies such as cultural clubs, community organizations, agricultural scientists, medical doctors, and various environmental groups, such as the Society for Environmental Education in Kerala (SEEK), soon began rallying behind the *panchayats* to push for a complete ban on the use of pesticides and for a total discontinuation of spraying and its ban. The combined action group also released the document *The Chemical Free Century: Declaring a Toxic Free Future*, elucidating the concerns expressed by Our Common Future. As scientific studies also began to support their cause (CSE 2001; Achuthan Committee 2001; Quijano 2002; Thanal 2001; KSSP 2001; NIOH 2002; Sivaraman 2003; Prabhakaran 2012), the local communities and activists derived more confidence in their mobilization and protest. As in the case of Chengara, there was a protest from the cashew plantation workers, as they were concerned about the loss of their livelihoods. A few of the workers organized themselves as the Plantation Samrakhana Samiti (Plantation Protection Committee) and opposed the demand for closing down the plantation. Within the larger context of the anti-endosulfan ecospatial movement, though, their voice became insignificant (Satheesh 2013). However, PCK failed to be persuaded and persisted in its practice of aerial spraying, earning for itself the title of the worst polluter in the state on the 15th anniversary of the Bhopal disaster.

The study done by the CSE, which found alarming levels of endosulfan in all the samples collected from the village, was a major intervention that forced the wider public to take note of the events in Kasaragod.[11] More importantly, the Cashew Export Promotion Council, in consultation with the NRCC, suggested that PCK refrain from aerial spraying. The NRCC further suggested that cashew growers in the country withdraw the recommendation of endosulfan application for cashew in the knowledge that a market once lost is lost forever. This is particularly relevant in the context of post-World Trade Organization phytosanitary measures, which are being enforced in the downstream European market in which the NRCC already has a stake. The endosulfan victims of Kasaragod have caught the attention of the media once again, and along with this, there is pressure from international NGOs, academics, and experts on India to rethink its opposition to the proposal for a global ban at the Stockholm Convention under the pretext of lack of concrete evidence to prove the health and environmental impact of the pesticide.[12]

In general, successive governments have either actively denied the connection between the use of the pesticide and its deleterious effects or have taken an ambivalent stance with respect to a total ban on its use. This may owe largely to the fact that an open acknowledgement of the situation in Kasaragod would have led to an immediate demand for compensation on the basis of the 'polluter pays' principle, in addition to a call for fitting judicial action against those found guilty of such an appalling practice.

Pesticides are considered harmful at three levels: First, while they increase productivity, they simultaneously deprive the soil of fertility in the long run. Second, its application is harmful, both for those who actually spray the chemicals and also for those who live in the vicinity through the residues in food and water. This was admitted by PCK itself, as has been clear from their instructions to be followed by the local people when spraying is done.[13] It is this negative externality that has surpassed the benefits of boosting productivity, which, in turn, led to the consolidation of those victims, joined by the civil society organizations in the state, who suspected endosulfan spraying for more than two decades as the causative factor for their ill health.

The debate regarding the possible link between the actual spraying of endosulfan and various health effects continues, while evidence is being accumulated to support the belief that the incidence of such diseases and disorders is particularly marked within the areas in which these state-owned plantations lie.[14] While the struggle against PCK was for its continued spraying of endosulfan, there were sections who spoke to this author that PCK has never been socially responsive in other matters as well. For instance, when PCK wanted to extract a toll from the Adivasis using the Rajapuram-Thottodi checkpost of the plantation border, the local Adivasis strongly protested against this, and the State Human Rights Commission was forced to intervene. PCK was thus forced to stop this practice altogether. Further, PCK declined a popular request for the allotment of land to start a local university; however, it did not hesitate to agree when a similar request was put in to start a petrochemical factory. Nevertheless, a sustained protest by the local populace resulted in the awarding of land for the university.

Legal Activism Combined with Local Protests

A significant turning point in the anti-endosulfan protest movement was legal intervention initiated by a woman agricultural assistant, Leela Kumari Amma, of the state Agriculture Department. When her request to PCK to stop spraying at least near the houses in the locality was refused by the authorities, she had no option other than legal suits. To quote Leela Kumari Amma, as said to this author:

> I have approached several departments and authorities, including the Principal Agriculture Officer, the State Pollution Control Board and so on

> but nobody was ready to come forward and ask the PCK to stop spraying. I began my fight owing to my own experience as my son developed some health problems; I also understood that the neighbours also have health problems. Finally, I had to approach the court with the limited resources I have ... but I won [the] heart of the local communities.[15]

Leela Kumari Amma filed a suit in the Hosdurg Munsiff Court against PCK, asking for a stay on the spray and related operations under Article 21 of the Indian constitution, and the court stayed the spraying operations in the area. Instead of accepting the court order, PCK went to the District Court, which, however, upheld the judgment of the Munsiff Court. Leela Kumari Amma continues, '[A] part from physical threatening to me, the PCK even asked compensation from me; paradoxically, instead of compensating the communities, they asked the victims to pay the polluter.' She had to approach a lower court (Munsiff Court, Hosdurg), and the court temporarily stayed the aerial spraying of endosulfan in cashew plantations. Following complaints from various quarters, the local court in Hosdurg ordered the permanent prohibition of the use of any insecticide by air. This restriction, however, was valid only for one of the plantation areas, Periya, leaving the other two areas unprotected; aerial spraying continued in these other areas, thus stoking the anger of the local people and their agencies. The state government extended the ban on the sale, distribution, and use of endosulfan in the state when the initial ban of 60 days ended on 1 May 2001. The state was compelled to extend the ban again when the legal action on one hand and local protests by various groups on the other gained momentum. As a follow-up, the Kerala High Court banned the use of endosulfan in the state[16] in response to two public interest litigations filed by the Thiruvamkulam Nature Lovers Movement, the People's Council for Social Justice, and the Samatha Law Society.[17] The High Court banned the pesticide, pending a decision from the Central Insecticides Board (CIB) of the union government, making it clear that endosulfan cannot be used in any of its formulations or under any of its brand names. Since then, the Government of Kerala imposed a ban on the use of endosulfan, the outcome of a combined battle on two domains, civil and legal.

The first political expression of support came from the then opposition leader, V.S. Achuthanandan, of the Communist Marxist Party of India in the state. The local people invited the leader to a public meeting in 2004 when he made his opinions known. When he subsequently came to power in 2006, his ministry took a particular interest in investigating the health consequences of endosulfan use. This also led to the announcement of relief measures, largely in terms of financial compensations paid to the affected families. While the debate regarding cause and effect rages on, the question as to who it is that possesses the right to protest against a violation of their very livelihood remains unanswered. The state, on its part, has had the advantage of a cumulative political-ecospatial consciousness and the prior experience with regard to the effectiveness of transverse solidarity. The case of the Birla-owned Mavoor rayon company comes to mind in this instance (Chapter 2), in which the absence of any method for discharging waste led to the pollution of the Chaliyar river. The resulting ecological destruction and threat to human security prompted a mass mobilization of the local populace, resulting in the closure of the factory. The second case was in Plachimada (Chapter 4). In both cases, while the local community struggled to give voice to their subjugated knowledge, in an expression of the notion of environmentalism from below, they were aided in their efforts by numerous agencies that came together to form a transverse solidarity.

The National Human Rights Commission (NHRC) visited the endosulfan-affected areas in December 2010 and recommended that the Government of India take administrative and legislative action to ban the use of endosulfan. The commission also suggested conducting a nationwide survey of populations that have been affected by the use of endosulfan, particularly sprayed from the air, to determine the scope of relief and rehabilitation that may be needed. On 18 November 2011, the NHRC issued a notice to the central and state governments seeking clarification regarding media reports linking the disease patterns in the Kasaragod region to the aerial spraying of endosulfan in the district. This elicited a prompt response from the KSPCB, which issued a notification reintroducing a state-wide ban on the pesticide under pollution control laws the very next day.

With the KSPCB banning the use of endosulfan in the state in December 2004, a new chapter opened up in the state: the KSPCB first suspended the aerial spraying of endosulfan, by and large based on its own investigations, confirming that aerial spraying has far-reaching health consequences. By December 2005, the union ministry had issued a gazette notification notification and withheld the sale and use of endosulfan in Kerala. This was the first official decision from the highest authority in India. However, it was only in November 2010 that the KSPCB went for the final notification of banning endosulfan in the state, this time under provisions of the Water (Prevention and Control of Pollution) Act, 1974, and the Air (Prevention and Control of Pollution) Act, 1981. The KSPCB itself found in its studies the presence of endosulfan in water and sediment even after the initial ban, and thus more diligent implementation of the ban was executed as any violation of the ban under the aforesaid Acts would lead to imprisonment of up to six years and a fine.

Widening the Protests: Second Phase

It was not sufficient that the state banned endosulfan in the state; it was equally important for the state to offer an adequate rehabilitation policy for the victims. By the year 2000, the number of endosulfan victims was pegged at 4,182. Another 1,318 were added in 2011 and 349 in 2013. The victims began to hold several rounds of agitations, sit-ins, and hunger strikes in front of PCK, district headquarters, Kasaragod, and, more importantly, the state capital in 2012, 2013, 2014, 2016, and 2018, demanding adequate financial compensation, free medical facilities, and sources of livelihood for the future. In 2012, the victims, women and children, staged a 128-day strike in front of the state secretariat in Thiruvananthapuram. It was called off after the government agreed to all their demands, including financial aid and setting up of treatment facilities. A year later, when the government failed to deliver, the women and children resumed their agitation, which lasted 36 days and was called off after another set of assurances from the government. In 2014, the women and children again began an indefinite strike in Thiruvananthapuram, now in front of the chief minister's home, then ruled by the Congress-led United Democratic Front (UDF). This was also called off after two days as they were assured of financial aid and free medical facilities, all those recommended by the NHRC much earlier, including the upgradation of healthcare facilities and rehabilitation projects. As the government again failed to meet the promises and continued to play the classic form of procrastination politics, they restarted their agitation in January 2016, which lasted for about a week.

The Left Democratic Front (LDF) was in power in 2016; a year later, the Supreme Court intervened and directed the state to provide financial assistance and free medical facilities. The Indian Law Conference also demanded the same. Responding favourably, the state government assured as much as INR 4.63 crore for writing off loans up to INR 3 lakh of endosulfan victims. This was in addition to loan waivers of up to INR 50,000, with an outlay of around INR 2.67 crores. The state would also expect the centre to provide the INR 483 crore sought by the state, and the victims would be identified by the Health

Department based on the norms fixed by the High Court in 2013. Kerala had earmarked over INR 180 crores as compensation to victims, cash compensations ranging from INR 2 to 5 lakhs. The rehabilitation programme continues even today. The government continued to provide financial aid and medical facilities to the endosulfan victims. The other recommendations of the NHRC, such as the establishment of a central institute for the rehabilitation of the victims, were also considered favourably by the left government.

In responding to the memoranda and the struggles led by victims, the NHRC had suggested to the state government in December 2010 to disburse INR 5 lakhs to seriously ill and bedridden victims and INR 3 lakhs for other victims within eight months. The state failed to comply with the same. It was at this time that the Supreme Court had to intervene in January 2017, directing the state government to disburse INR 500 crores to over 5,000 victims within three months. The state also granted compensation worth INR 50,000 (USD 1,075) to families affected by fatalities from the aerial spraying of the poisonous pesticide. A welfare package was also later outlined following the intervention of the NHRC, which visited the region in 2010. A special purpose cell has started functioning in the *panchayats*, and special programmes have begun to emerge under the authority of various *panchayats*.[18]

However, reducing the rehabilitation question to funding and compensation would obviously be too narrow an approach as the complexities involved are equally a question of epistemological break.[19] The challenging studies conducted by Sreekumar and Prathapan (2013) revealed that 17 different types of diseases found in nearby 48 wards were the same as found in other 115 wards away from the cashew plantations, demonstrating that no cause–effect relationship could be established between endosulfan and disabilities (also see Dubey 2003; Mayee 2006). Furthermore, no systematic epidemiological studies were conducted by those who attempted to establish cause–effect relations as mentioned earlier. Any conclusion at this stage which states endosulfan spraying is to blame for the disabilities is problematic; while this revelation may be part of an epistemological break, the findings are worth investigating by the state's scientific institutions. Even though science is frequently an approximation of a situation's reality, the status of 'knowledge controversies' (Whatmore 2009: 587–598; Harding 2008) and the question of 'does scientific knowledge accurately represent an independently existing reality' (Barad 2003: 804) have not yet been addressed in the endosulfan debate. Science engagement is crucial because it is the best move a society can make towards reason: a logical approach to comprehending reality.

Rehabilitation of Endosulfan Victims and Concluding Remarks

Endosulfan pesticide was used widely on crops like cashew, cotton, tea, paddy, fruits, and others until 2011, when the Supreme Court banned its production and distribution. This was in the context of the larger struggle that was happening wherein the youth wing of the CPI(M), the Democratic Youth Federation of India (DYFI), had filed a public interest litigation. The Supreme Court invoked article 21 of the constitution of India within the backdrop of the precautionary principles as well as the harmful effects of the pesticides, the latter as highlighted by the protesting communities and DYFI.[20] The health effects of the chemical include neurotoxicity, late sexual maturity, physical deformities, and poisoning, among others. People, especially newborns, have suffered deformities, health complications, and loss of family members due to exposure to the agrochemical. Civil society was also involved in discussing the question of the disposal of obsolete stock of endosulfan after the ban. Though it was temporarily kept in the warehouses of PCK, causing a public threat due to leakage, it was finally resolved by following the leakage standards set by the United Nations (UN) at all stages of operation. The rehabilitation measures are being continued by the state, following the suggestions of several committees (Prabhakaran 2012).

The use of the pesticide endosulfan has been widely banned across the world owing to its high toxicity and its persistence in the environment, with residual contamination of food and water bodies and risks from occupational exposure. A report by the International Programme of Chemical Safety shows the persistence of endosulfan on the hands of pest-control operators for about a month after exposure, resulting in bio-accumulation. The US Environmental Protection Agency (EPA) too reported in 2002 on the acute and chronic effects of endosulfan exposure on the environment. It is mandatory that the product labels in the United States specify: 'Do not allow spray to drift from the application site and contact people, structures people occupy at any time and the associated property, parts and recreation areas, no target crops, aquatic and wetland areas, woodlands, pastures, rangelands or animals.' Further, in 2007, the US EPA reiterated its warning on the ill effects of endosulfan use, including short- and intermediate-term risks for mixers, loaders, and applicators, despite the use of maximum personal protective equipment and engineering controls. It pointed out the potential threat to indigenous populations based on the fact that endosulfan has been detected in areas far removed from the point of use, such as the Arctic, thus proving its potential to bio-accumulate and, furthermore, to bio-magnify in certain terrestrial food-webs. This is attributed to the ability of endosulfan residues to volatilize and redeposit ion in the atmosphere. Although more reports of endosulfan poisoning have come from the South, it has been a global problem with instances of congenital deformities, male and female hormonal disorders, cerebral palsy, and other neurological disorders, as well as skin conditions being reported in association with its use.

The issue of endosulfan use that was brought up at the Stockholm Conference too was the result of decades of resistance against its use. It was the WHO that requested the UN to impose restrictions on the use of persistent organic pollutants (POPs) owing to the manifest health issues accruing from their use. The member countries of the UN requested the United Nations Environment Programme (UNEP) to explore this issue in depth, and a draft agreement accepted by the member nations was ratified at the Stockholm Conference (POPs Convention) in May 2001. It took another six years to bring endosulfan into the purview of the agreement – at the 2007 Stockholm Convention. A POP Review Committee Meeting in 2010 established a definite link between the use of endosulfan and the many health issues that were surfacing. However, India was one of the five nations that opposed the ban on endosulfan. India participated in the 2011 April Stockholm Conference. Against the expectation of legislatively banning endosulfan, a number of pesticide manufacturers joined the Indian contingent. However, they had to accept the general consensus regarding the banning of endosulfan but managed to negotiate an 11-year exemption of its use in relation to 23 crops.

The Endosulfan Victims Relief and Remediation (R&R) Cell is the outcome of the consultative workshop held in 2005 between the Kasaragod district *panchayat*, *grama panchayat*s of the affected villages, health, social, and agriculture departments of the Government of Kerala, and civil society groups like Thanal and ESPAC. The cell was initiated formally in 2007 and is located in the district headquarters of the Kasaragod district *panchayat*. It is a government-approved body and has 34 members – 10 members from the government, including the *district panchayat*, 11 members from the *grama panchayat*s of the affected villages, and 13 members from civil society. Meetings are held almost every two or three months to discuss the issues related to the remediation measures for the victims and the future activities of the cell. The initial amount that was allocated by the state government for the relief and remediation measures was INR 50 lakhs. It was decided by the cell that the allocated amount should be used as follows: INR 37 lakhs for compensation (medical and other) of affected families, INR 6 lakhs for research work in the affected area, and INR 7 lakhs for aids like wheelchairs and spectacles.

The state is driven to an ecospatial positionality, first, by banning the use of endosulfan and, second, by taking steps to rehabilitate the victims as a humanitarian project. It is worth noting that the obligations and responsibilities of the state need to be well integrated and embedded in any sustainable policies towards rehabilitation and beyond (see Gilligan 1982). It is the self-critical awareness of the hazardous effects of endosulfan spraying that made the state more obligatory and responsible towards human rehabilitation programmes. The struggles that began with the locally concerned individuals and 'affected' communities grew to a collective form of power of what Sundar calls 'law-struggles' (2011; Parmar 2015) in neoliberal India, which also helps rally other social groups and activists beyond the land and water struggles, which we found in the case of Muthanga and Plachimada. We will return to these aspects in the concluding chapter, as the landscape of knowledge controversies and the conflicts that emerged are not yet settled; so also the ecospatial struggles.

Notes

1. An article titled 'Aerial spray of pesticide makes life cheaper than cashew' was published by Shree Padre in *The Evidence*, in December 1981 (pp. 25–31). Padre ends his eye-opening report by stating, 'And the plantation corporation has no right to endanger villager's health and rural economy in order to supply cashew to rich foreigners, just because the poor Kerala villager cannot complain' (Padre 1981: 31).
2. This must be seen as a highly delayed outcome as more than half a century has passed since the *Silent Spring* (Rachel Carson 1962/2000) first approached the public to conscientize with regard to the toxic effects of chemicals and pesticides that put the lives of humans and non-humans at risk.
3. There are four cashew estates: Kasaragod, Cheemeni, and Rajapuram Estates in Kasaragod district and the Mannarghat Estate in Palakkad district. Out of these four estates, Rajapuram and Mannarghat Estates are raised in leased-out forest lands. The Cheemeni Estate is surplus revenue land. The Kasaragod Estate is fully owned by PCK Ltd.
4. See Padre (1981).

5. For details, see the court orders including the papers related to the district court of the Munsiff of Hosdurg, dated 31 October 2000; also see the rejection of petition moved by the civil revision petition filed under section 115 of the code of civil procedure, before the High Court of Kerala, dated 27 January 1999. The legal fight between PCK and the respondents including M.K. Leela Kumari Amma, original suit no. 579/1998, 7 February 2000; Original suit no 579 of 1998 in which the management sought permission for aerial spraying of endosulfan, see High Court of Kerala at Ernakukulam, dated 13 January 2000. 579/1998 of the Munsiff's Court, Hosdurg between Leela Kumari Amma and others and PCK, dt Na. 579 of 1998 in the court of Munsiff of Hosdurg; Objections to be reconsidered filed on behalf of the defendant to the report of the commissioner dated 11 October 2000 with respect to 579 of 1998.
6. Individual scholars such as Sunita Narain of CSE, M.K. Prasad of the Kerala Sastra Sahithya Parishad (KSSP), and V.R. Raghunandananof the Integrated Rural Technology Centre (IRTC) were active in collecting evidence for the studies in this series.
7. Mohan Kumar, a medical doctor who started his clinic in Vaninagar in 1982, was intrigued by the damage done by endosulfan spraying on the patients who came with unusual illnesses from the adjacent villages of the plantations of PCK; he was also responsible for bringing national attention to the health hazards of the endosulfan victims.
8. There are other scientists who have warned that the Achuthan Committee did not conduct a detailed epidemiology study and did not provide accurate evidence on the matter assigned to them (see Sreekumar and Prathapan 2021). They also criticize the NGOs, including Thanal, for igniting the issue without carefully understanding the situation and for taking advantage of it.
9. Telephonic conversation with K.M. Sreekumar dated 10 May 2023.
10. Two medical doctors who were active in the movement are Y.S. Mohan Kumar and Sripathy Kajampady and given the fact that rural communities heavily rely on doctors, it was easier for the environmental and social activists to mobilize people against the common threat.
11. In February 2001, *Down To Earth* broke the story and continued to report the plight of the victims for close to two decades; see the back volumes of *Down To Earth*.
12. The author's discussions with a local doctor confirms that there were 51 cancer deaths within just 126 households near the Kodenkeri stream in Enmakaje *panchayat*; many of these deaths were due to liver and blood cancer. The high incidence of diseases and deaths were also reported by other agencies.

13. See the circular to the public, PCK, Cashew Project signed by the Manager, PCK 1999; S. Usha, Endosulfan, problems and facts, Thanal, January 2001; Endosulfan rehabilitation discussions and decisions at the level of Health and Family Welfare Department Government Order (GO). No 113/2013 Health and Family Welfare Department (H&FWD) dated 18 October 2014, 26 March 2013; complains for those not included in the rehabilitation project queries done by Krishnan, dated 16 January 2013; project proposal for rehabilitation village in Kasaragod district, sub collector, Kasaragod, 2015; for financial support, letter from Justice K.G. Balakrishnan, NHRC to the chief minister, V.S. Achuthanandan, dated 13 August 2012; rehabilitation projects submitted by the Society for Nursing, Education and Habitation for Mentally Ill (Sneham, Kanhangad, Kasaragod). Organic village project document; NHRC recommendations on endosulfan, NHRC case no. 477/11/6/2010 dated 31 December 2010, Justice K.G. Balakrishan, Justice B.C. Patel, and Shri Satyabrata Pal. Report of the committee constituted by the government to recommend on the constitution of tribunal and sources of fund for the endosulfan victims of Kasaragod district, submitted to Government of Kerala, by Justice (retd.) C.N. Ramachandran Nair and others.
14. The virtual role played by NGOs such as Thiruvananthapuram-based Thanal stands against the usual criticisms lodged against NGOs. The above information is heavily drawn from the publications of Thanal, and I particularly thank the activists, including S. Usha and Jayakumar, for their help.
15. Interviewed on 19 July 2013 in Kasaragod.
16. A Division Bench comprising Chief Justice B.N. Srikrishna and Justice G. Sivarajan.
17. *Thiruvamkulam Nature Lovers Movement vs Plantation Corporation of Kerala* (2002) 20716/2002, 17026/2002, 16300/2002 and 29371/2001, http://elaw.in/public/insecti/endosulfan.htm (accessed 11 May 2023).
18. In August 2006, the district *panchayat*, under the leadership of the *panchayat* president Smt. Padmavathi, developed a Comprehensive Relief and Remediation Plan with technical support from Thanal and with expert advice from medical doctors. The current *panchayat* president Balakrishnan is now leading the implementation of the plan.
19. *Democratic Youth Federation of India vs Union of India and Others* (2011) Supreme Court of India (civ) 213.
20. 'Epistemological break', or a period when ideological concepts are replaced by scientific ones, was first developed by French philosopher Gaston Bachelard (1938), later developed by the Marxist philosopher Louis Althusser (1969).

References

Achuthan Committee (2001). *Report of the Committee to Study and Analyze the Effects of Aerial Spray of Endosulfan in the Cashew Plantations of PCK LTD. in Kasaragod District*. Thiruvananthapuram: Government of Kerala.

Althusser, L. (1969). *For Marx*, trans. Ben Brewster. London: Penguin.

Bachelard, G. (1938). *The Formation of the Scientific Mind*. Paris: J. VRIN.

Beck, U. (1986). *Risk Society: Towards A New Modernity*. London: Sage.

——— (1994). The reinvention of politics: Towards a theory of reflexive modernization. In *Reflexive Modernization: Politics, Tradition and Aesthetics in the Modern Social Order*, ed. U. Beck, A. Giddens, and S. Lash, pp. 1–55. Cambridge: Polity Press.

Beck, U., A. Giddens, and S. Lash, eds. (1994). *Reflexive Modernization*. Cambridge: Polity Press.

Beck, Ulrich, and Edgar Grande (2010). Varieties of second modernity: The cosmopolitan turn in social and political theory and research. *British Journal of Sociology* 61 (3): 409–443.

Carson, R. (1962/2000). *Silent Spring*. London: Penguin.

Centre for Science and Environment (CSE) (2001). A *Centre for Science and Environment Report on the Contamination of Endosulfan in the Villagers*. New Delhi: Centre for Science and Environment.

Giddens, A. (1990). *The Consequences of Modernity*. Stanford: Stanford University Press.

——— (1994). Living in a post-traditional society. In *Reflexive Modernization: Politics, Tradition and Aesthetics in the Modern Social Order*, ed. U. Beck, A. Giddens, and S. Lash, pp. 56–109. Cambridge, UK: Polity.

Gaonkar, K. (2001). *Alternative Modernities*. Durham, NC: Duke University Press.

Gilligan, Carol (1982). *In a Different Voice: Psychological Theory and Women's Development*. Cambridge, MA: Harvard University Press.

Habermas, J. (1987). *The Philosophical Discourse of Modernity: Twelve Lectures*. Trans. Frederick Lawrence. Cambridge: Polity.

Harding, Sandra G. (2008). *Sciences from Below: Feminisms, Postcolonial Ties, and Modernities*. Next Wave. Durham: Duke University Press

Jayakumar. (2011). Status of the endosulfan disaster. Annex III in Kerala State Council for Science, Technology and Environment, *Report on Monitoring of Endosulfan Residues in the 11 Panchayaths of Kasaragod District, Kerala*. Thiruvananthapuram: KSCSTE.

Kannan, K.P. (1983). *Cashew Development in India: Potentialities and Constraints*. New Delhi: Agricole Publishing Academy.

Kerala Sastra Sahithya Parishad (KSSP) (2001). *Household Survey to Assess the Health and Environmental Impact of Aerial Spraying of Endosulfan in PCK Cashew Plantation of Kasaragod District*. Kasaragod District Committee, KSSP.

Kumar, A.D. and C. Jayakumar (2019). From precautionary principle to nationwide ban on endosulfan in India. *Business and Human Rights Journal* 4 (2): 1–7.

Mayee, C.D. (2006). *Report of the Expert Group For Pesticides Reviewed for Their Continued Use or Otherwise in the Country*. New Delhi: Ministry of Agriculture.

Nair, Radhakrishnan K.R., and C.S. Sreedharan (2004). *Study of Policy on Cashew Industry in Kerala*. Thiruvananthapuram: State Planning Board, Government of Kerala.

National Institute of Occupational Health (NIOH). (2002). *Final Report of the Investigation of Unusual Illnesses Allegedly Produced by Endosulfan Exposure in Padre Village of Kasargod District (N.Kerala)*. Ahmedabad: National Institute of Occupational Health.

Padre, S. (1981). Aerial spray of pesticide makes life cheaper than cashew. *The Evidence*, December.

Prabhakaran, P. (2012). *Report on the Development of Kasaragod District*. Thiruvananthapuram: Government of Kerala.

Quijano, R.F. (2002). *Endosulfan Poisoning in Kasaragod, Kerala, India*. Penang: Pesticide Action Network Asia and the Pacific.

Rahman, M.A. (2011). Kasargode janithakabheekaratha. In *Endosulfan Naragathilekku Thurakkunna Vaathil*, ed. S. Pooppalam, pp. 28–39. Kozhikkode: Solidarity Youth Movement.

Raman, K. Ravi (2010). Transverse solidarity: Water, power and resistance. *Review of Radical Political Economics* 42 (2): 251–268.

——— (2020). Ecospatiality: Transforming Kerala's post-flood riskscapes. *Cambridge Journal of Regions, Economy and Society* 13 (2): 319–341.

Satheesh, S. (2013). *Environment, Development and New Social Movements: The Political Ecology of Endosulphan in Kasargod, Kerala*. New Delhi: Jawaharlal Nehru University.

——— (2017). Development as recolonization: The political ecology of the Endosulphan disaster in Kasargod, India. *Critical Asian Studies* 49 (4): 587–596.

Sivaraman, P.K. (2003). *Health Hazards of Aerial Spraying of Endosulphan in Kasaragod District, Kerala*. Thiruvananthapuram: Government of Kerala.

Sørensen, Mads Peter, and Allan Christiensen. (2012). *Ulrich Beck: An Introduction to the Theory of Second Modernity and the Risk Society*. New York: Routledge.

Sreekumar, K., and K. Prathapan (2013). A critique of the epidemiological studies on health in allegedly endosulfan-affected areas in Kasaragod, Kerala. *Current Sciences* 104 (January): 16–21.

Sukumaran, A. (2005). *Geographical Mapping of Mental Retardation and Physical Deformities and A Case Control Study of Mental Retardation in Kasaragode District of Kerala State, India*. Thiruvananthapuram: SCTIMST. http://dspace.sctimst.ac.in/jspui/handle/123456789/2102 (accessed 11 May 2005).

Sundar, N. (2011). The Rule of law and citizenship in central India: Post-colonial dilemmas. *Citizenship Studies* 15 (3–4): 419–432.

Thanal (2001). *Preliminary Findings of A Survey on the Impact of Aerial Spraying on the People and Ecosystem*. Thiruvananthapuram: Thanal Conservation Action and Information Network.

Whatmore, S. (2009). Mapping knowledge controversies: Science, democracy and the redistribution of expertise. *Progress of Human Geography* 33 (5): 587–598.

World Health Organization (WHO) (2003). *Pesticide Residues in Food–2003: Toxicological Evaluations*. Geneva: World Health Organization.

6

Caste, Land, and the State

What If Chengara Took the Place of Muthanga?

Edward Said (1978) introduced the notion of *imaginative geography*: Groups with a hunger for land essentially reimagine the landscapes they desire, elevating the notion of themselves as the owners of the land they seek, a process of reinventing the meaning of territorial landscapes as 'imagined geography'. This would help them frame arguments justifying why they are entitled to take possession of the landscapes they desire. Before the actors themselves see and conquer the land, they entertain themselves under a discursive understanding that they are the owners of the landscapes that they covet. Hence, this imaginative geography is a theory of human action deriving from the interplay of material impulses and human consciousness (Gregory 1999); it is 'performative'. Reimagining landscapes is the first step to acting upon them and creating the very outcomes on the land being imagined (Gregory 2004: 17–20). In this process, hegemonic forces with territorial ambitions refashion themselves as owners of the territory they desire by asserting themselves as masters and sovereign of the land.

Here, one wonders, what is the landscape that has emerged as part of the subaltern project of the imagined geographies? This entails the counter-imagination and a contra-discourse of the imaginative geographies by the oppressed, intertwined with the notion of egalitarianism and justice, which could be realized through ecospatial struggles. If this imagined landscape and the struggle for the same is for livelihood and basic human and 'post-human' survival, the struggling poor would be forced to follow the logic of their own 'moral economy' that historically protected their rights to subsistence (Thompson 1991). The large number of 'land-wars' (Levien 2013) that have been taking place in Latin America and Asia, particularly in India, offers how the subalterns imagine their struggles as part of their livelihood and citizenship rights. If it was Muthanga in Kerala in 2003, it was Chengara in 2007. If Muthanga was occupied by the Adivasis, it was the Dalits – formerly the agrestic slaves and the most marginalized of all the outcastes of the Hindus – that occupied the Chengara part of the colonially evolved Harrisons Malayalam plantations. Even after three and a half decades of land reform experimentation how does one explain the Dalit land struggles in Kerala? Can Chengara replace Occupy Muthanga in terms of strategies, struggles, and outcomes? How far did the state succeed or fail in addressing the Dalit land question, their resource endowments, and livelihood? How far have the subaltern power succeeded in ecospatializing the otherwise enclosed monocultures?

Communism, Caste Bias, and Land Reforms

Dominant narratives take the land reforms in Kerala to be some of the most 'radical' initiatives ever implemented of all the Indian states (see Franke and Chasin 1992; Heller 1995, 2000). It is true that the legislation initiated in 1957 and promoted and implemented by the communist alliance in 1969 with the abolition of landlordism were indeed landmark events in the post-state-formation phase, though reforms altering property relations had their origins in the colonial period itself. However, it was the communists who spearheaded the tenant–worker alliance that fought to abolish the tenurial relations that existed then. But while the landlords were well compensated for their losses, and the direct tenants conferred full ownership rights, the reforms provided practically nothing for the vast body of landless agricultural workers who were the actual tillers of the soil (see Krishnaji 1979, 2007; Sreekumar 2009; Omvedt 1993; Rammohan 2008; Ajith 2003; Herring 1983; Kapikkad 2008). The Kerala Agrarian Relations Bill (KARB) was passed by the first communist ministry in July 1959; though protective of tribal lands and of the assignment of lands to them, no substantive effort was taken. It also exempted plantations and private forests from the ceiling provisions (Raj and Tharakan 1983; also see Radhakrishnan 1981; Isaac 2008). The possibility of release of any surplus land in the high ranges, which would have brought some relief to the landless Adivasis and the plantation workers, was forestalled (Raman 2010). Subsequent reforms benefited the tenants but put the Dalits and Adivasis at a further disadvantage; by conferring tenant status to settler farmers who had either encroached on or acquired tribal lands, the Kerala Reforms (Amendment) Act of 1969 marginalized the Adivasis and Dalits further as their cultural ethics did not conceive of legal documentary support of any sort (Bijoy and Raman 2003). In the case of Dalits, all studies uniformly show that they are at the bottom of land ownership, and not much has changed even after the land reforms were ushered in. The share of the land they owned in relation to their share in the samples was extremely low. In an earlier survey (Varghese 1970), Dalits in total constituted 19.43 per cent of the sample, while their share in total landholdings stood at a meagre 0.9 per cent. Those with lower-value land holdings will fall behind, and, of course, those without land will fall even further behind in their income-generating capacity and so in social status (Varghese 1970: 86–87).

Two major schemes that would have radicalized democracy in Kerala were the application of ceilings on holdings, at least with respect to foreign-owned plantations, and the acquisition and redistribution of surplus land. However, both these schemes met with failure (see Rammohan 1991). Though the surplus land was originally estimated in 1957 at around 17.5 lakh acres, it declined to 1.15 lakh acres in 1964, and further down to less than 1 lakh acres after 1970 (see Radhakrishnan 1981). No single mainstream political party in the state has ever raised the question of how this surplus land has virtually 'disappeared', nor of who actually benefited from this. Marxist scholars predicted that a fragmentation of the estates would be an economically counterproductive move and that it would be practically impossible to induce the peasants in the lowlands to move up to the highlands; however, this too can be seen as nothing but a weak justification for avoiding the class question in the state.

The Marxist scholar E.M.S. Namboodirippad (1981) rightly termed this system as *jati–janmi–naduvazhi medhavitvam*, which means upper caste–landlord–chieftain hegemony. However, both in Travancore and Cochin, landlordism was abolished, and tenants were put in direct relationship with the state, and peasant proprietorship was also created. But the lower ranks in the agrarian hierarchy, the Dalit workers and households, remained untouched by the reforms, and they continued as workers without land. In Malabar, the *janmi*s continued to control the land and hence both the intermediate castes, such as Ezhavas, and Dalit workers remained landless; the former, however, enjoyed the status of tenancy. But not all the Ezhavas were tenants; there were also agricultural workers among them, as in the case of Dalits. The land reforms of 1970 did not recognize them as the tillers of the soil. Today, Dalits are unable to participate in the land market, resulting in their exclusion from land ownership. During an era of skyrocketing land prices, they found it very difficult to acquire land (Tharakan 2002).

The land refroms in Kerala were evaluated at three levels. First, the abolition of tenancy; second, provision of hutment land to agricultural workers; and, third, imposition of ceilings. So the tenants got the ownership rights, and most of the tenants were Thiyyas and Ezhavas – outcastes. They gained. The workers also got dwelling rights and a few cents of adjacent land – 5 or 10 cents. Most of them were those in the lowest rung in the agrarian hierarchy, the Dalits. In both cases, the communist party played a critical role, in the passing of both the initial Agrarian Relations Act of 1959 and the Kerala Land Reform Act of 1969 and 1970, yet these were only partially successful. The third provision, the ceiling provision, was rather a failure, which was one of the reasons behind the failure of the second provision. First of all, the big plantations remained exempt from land ceilings. Second, the party failed to stop the bogus transfers of land from the previous landlords, including the plantation companies,[1] which effectively reduced the lands available for distribution. It is true that there is a drastic decline in rural landless households in Kerala since the Land Reforms Act. It declined from 15.7 per cent in 1971–1972 to 12.8 per cent in 1982 and 8.4 per cent in 1992. Within another decade it went down to 4.8 per cent. However, of the landless households in terms of social group, highest landless was among Dalit households at 8 and 12 per cent in rural and urban areas respectively. The corresponding figures for ST communities is 5.5 per cent and 59.4 per cent for rural and urban respectively.

In an important study on the land–caste nexus and how the Dalits are deprived of land resources, Yadu and Vijaysurya (2016) reveal the following: The Christian community has disproportionate access to both land owned and cultivated. Their index values are 1.82 and 2.19, respectively. Hindu upper castes have index values greater than 1, indicating a higher proportion of land vis-à-vis their population. In both land owned and land cultivated, other backward classes (OBCs) have higher index values than Muslims. For Scheduled Castes (SCs), the index of access is the lowest. Their index of access to land owned stands at 0.34, and their index of access to land cultivated stands at 0.22. According to this study, the pathetic state of land ownership for Dalits in Kerala is due to the 'triple exclusion'. The land-based caste system has systematically deprived Dalits of land ownership rights. Land reform policies have failed to address this issue (see Mohanty 2001; Omvedt 2006; Sreerekha 2010).[2]

This was the background in which the Dalits and other marginalized communities in the state felt they had no option other than to occupy the Chengara part of the colonially evolved Malayalam Plantations. The company began as a trading company in Liverpool in 1907 and merged with the existing tea plantations in Kerala to form Harrisons Malayalam Ltd (HML) (HML 2017). In 1921, the sterling company bought the assets of a large number of smaller companies producing both tea and rubber in Thiruvithamkur and Wayanad; the Mooply Valley Tea Co. Ltd, the Wallardie Tea Estates Ltd, the Wynad Tea Co. Ltd, and the Malayalam Rubber & Produce Co. Ltd were some of the estates acquired by the UK-incorporated Malayalam Plantations Ltd. In Wayanad, even big firms such as Parry & Co. sold their estates to the East India Tea Produce Company, which finally went into the hands of Malayalam Plantations. With the amalgamation of these estates along with Harrisons & Crosfield properties in Kochi, the Malayalam Plantations Ltd became one of the leading plantation companies to be quoted in the London Stock Exchange (Langely 1962: 63–64; also see Ganapathy 1978).

In 1973, following the Foreign Exchanges Regulation Act (FERA), which limited foreign share of capital to 74 per cent, the company was sold to RPG enterprises and listed in the capital market. In 1984, it became a fully owned Indian company called HML. Today, HML is the largest integrated rubber plantation company in India, employing more than 10,000 workers over its 26 plantations, 12 tea factories, and many blending and processing units, and is as diversified as to include tissue culture, engineering and services, private labelling, trading and exports, and clearing and shipping, with an annual turnover of USD 83 million (HML 2017). This unrestricted entry of colonial forces upon the nation's land is only a part of the larger imperialist project which extracts the lives and livelihoods of the conquered (see Said 1978; Ajith 2003; Sunil 2019).

It has been observed throughout colonial plantation economies that vast tracts of land were generally acquired at low prices, far in excess of the required minimum for viable plantations. In certain cases, the planters acquired more land than they had the capital to invest in. In both cases, what prompted the planters to acquire more than the minimum required could possibly be the desire to maintain the plantation as a single contiguous unit, to have additional land for speculative businesses, to control the right of way to other nearby areas, and/or to keep prospective competitors out of the enterprise. All these factors, either singly or in combination, led to over-acquisition and thus the under-utilization of plantation land in India as in other colonies the world over[3] and the HML was a classic example of the same.

We do not intend to overlook the fact that the very nature of the plantations, which were built on a large scale, necessitated the acquisition of land for factory sites, labour lines, quarters, and bungalows, land for forests to make firewood for factories, and land for gardens and pastures for cattle. But the fact remains that the land actually required for these 'ancillaries' formed only an insignificant proportion of the total area leased. Imperial reply, routed through the Government of India, was to the effect that Europeans would be placed under 'no restrictions to acquire lands for plantations'.[4] It was also specified that persons whose residence in the state was authorized should not be subjected to formalities in matters other than those imposed by the general law of the country, thus removing all hurdles in the planters' way. The development of plantations is often explained in terms of the favourable land policies followed by the respective local states or the better transport facilities that were set up by the same (Varghese 1970). Whenever the local authorities refused to comply with the wishes of the planters, the former were badly dealt with.[5] Over-acquisition of land was at times indulged in by the planters without a thought towards the means at their disposal. And when government rules were modified to the effect that the planters could acquire land without declaring their means for investment, business forces centred in London began to enter Kerala frequently. Upon implementation of FERA and the purchase of the plantation by RPG Enterprises, the plantation came under the protection of the Indian government; with the exemption of the Kerala Land Reforms Act's ceiling provisions – the details of which we will explain soon – the plantation became even more protected from any land reform.

Birth of Chengara

On 4 August 2007 – after four years of Occupy Muthanga – hundreds of landless Dalit families, including women and children, began the process of reimagining the colonially evolved landscapes of Chengara hills of the Harrisons Malayalam, owned by an Indian big capital, the Goenkas (RPG Enterprises). They virtually occupied around 350 acres a couple of hours before midnight. They pitched huts here and there and started cooking and dining with whatever little foodstuff they carried and those procured from the surrounding areas. They raised huts with the help of plastic sheets, bamboo, and whatever material was available around; the huts were in continuity with what Kerala had observed in the case of *kutilkettysamaram* (sit-in strike) in front of the secretariat (see Chapter 3) as a non-prefigured Muthanga revolt, but the nature and form of protest and occupation were different from that of Muthanga (Bhaskar 2008). Within no time those who occupied the plantation area started cultivating the nearby plots mostly with tapioca, the age-old food of the Dalits and the least expensive and fast growing; banana was equally emphasized, followed by tuber crops, all meant for basic social reproduction and sustenance.

The protest site was divided into divisions and counters for better coordination and management of the families. Most of the protesting families were suffering from starvation such that the adults were only having rice boiled water while the kids were given *petharu*, the residue rice in which water was added and boiled, when it was required (Prakkanam 2013: 56–57). The sympathisers of the protest, especially the solidarity workers, tried to supply food and other essentials to the starving protestors. However, this was blocked by the plantation workers who were opposing the protest by all means. There was hardly anyone who had sufficient monetary resources to survive, but the new source of solidarity brought them together and helped them form the *chain of equivalence* (Laclau and Mouffe 1985; also see Raman 2008). They constituted themselves as the Sadhujana Vimochana Samyukta Vedi (SVSV: People's Liberation Committee), primarily from two Dalit castes – Dalit Christians and Pulayas – but also the other backward communities, the Ezhavas, the Muslims, and so on, broadly Dalit *bahujan*s (backward classes) (Ilaiah 1996), to form *transverse solidarity* (Raman 2008) in the process of producing greater *political ecospatiality*. The movement was led by *avarna* leaders such as Laha Gopalan, Saleena Prakkanam, and Thattayil Saraswati.[6] Fearing that *savarna* (caste Hindu) leaders would appropriate and hijack their movement, they were alert to not entertain any intrusion of *savarna* activists in the protest site (see Prakkanam 2013). Given the hisotircal dimension of caste Hindu leaders entering the subaltern struggles in varying sectors (see Raman 2010: 135–145), their fear seems not to be misplaced.

Neither protests nor struggles are tolerable to any state forms, so too in the case of Chengara. The state also seeks legal help when it fails to counter the struggles. In early February – after around six months of distant observation of what was going on in Chengara – the state, for instance, sought the help of the High Court to evict the 'encroachers', in which the court supported the state but with a different legality. The court allowed the state to evict the occupants but without any violence, that is, the eviction should be done peacefully. The government admitted in the assembly that when it started to de-occupy the area in a peaceful manner, the 'encroachers', obviously in the state's language, attempted suicide and hence the eviction could not be done effectively[7]: The SVSV activists climbed up the rubber trees threatening to burn themselves alive if they were evicted from their occupied lands. The Dalit *bahujan* families defeated the orchestrated move of the state and corporate capital to drive them out of the land they had occupied for a means of livelihood. The subaltern war of position thus yielded benefits.

Several such imaginative and strategic forms of protests emerged in Chengara ever since they occupied the plantation demanding the confiscation of the land and the redistribution of the same to the Dalits. In fact, the Dalit families, with women and children, first commenced their struggle on 21 June 2006, erecting refugee huts in the Elappovar region of the Chemmanapally division of the state-owned Plantation Corporation of Kerala (PCK). The promises made by the district collector in this regard to the effect that they would be given lands did not materialize for over a year. Having tasted procrastination politics, this community decided to occupy Harrisons Malayalam, a privately owned plantation, opening up a new chapter in Kerala's subaltern modernity struggle.

A retrospective of the past 10 years since Occupy Chengara became an inspiration for the Dalits to search for an identity, which would have to acknowledge that Dalit as an identity has been integral in the developmental thinking of the state. It is the Dalits and the Adivasis who are enclosed in a poverty trap, with neither access to land nor any entry into accumulation domains. If identity has been invoked as an instrument of liberation, it is jubilant for the marginalized, given the fact that the class question did not help them much. This is an idea that many Marxists in the state do not want to acknowledge. Overlapping caste and class – and also gendered intersectionality – is an issue expressed in the form of resistance identities, which is a variant of exclusion, disempowerment, and poverty (see Raman 2020). More importantly, the birth of Chengara was also the outcome of what I have termed the *procrastination politics* of the state, similar to that of the attitude towards Adivasi lands struggles in the state. To know more about this, we need to situate the struggle in the historical context of Kerala land reforms, the plantation enclosures, and Dalit precarity.

Procrastination Politics and the Struggles

As early as October 2001, the SVSV submitted a memorandum to the government for assuring equal rights for Dalit Christians; there were meetings, gatherings, and discussions on how to move forward. The Independence Day in 2005 witnessed a hunger strike by the SVSV members, which extended until January 2006 – for about 150 days – in front of the mini civil station, Pathanamthitta. The strike began with hardly 30 persons, who were the only members of the organization then. However, the situation drastically changed.

On 2 January 2006, the blockade of the mini civil station in which nearly 4,000 people participated made the SVSV an organization that could not be ignored either by the closely related Dalit organizations and intellectuals or the state. The SVSV withdrew the strike when the then Congress-led United Democratic Fund (UDF) chief minister, Oommen Chandy, agreed to most of the demands raised, including the land question. However, until June 2006, no promise was met.

By that time, the UDF had been replaced by the Left Democratic Front (LDF), offering fresh hopes. However it did not change the prevailing condition of Dalits until they asserted themselves politically. It was this procrastination politics that led them to occupy the state-owned Kodumon plantation/Chandanappalli estate on 21 June 2006, when thousands of Dalits families first pitched their huts. The estate was managed by the PCK in the state, the corporation that was responsible for endosulfan spraying on cashew plantations. The then revenue ministry was under the portfolio of the Communist Party of India (CPI), and the minister, Rajendran K.P., promised them an acre of land, which may even stretch to a hectare. The protesters left Kodumon and awaited the promised land. A year went by without any progress; the SVSV announced a hunger strike until death in front of the collectorate from 19 September 2006. However, this was withdrawn owing to the revenue minister's assurance of settling the issue at the meeting scheduled on 27 September. The state agreed to meet most of the demands, and the festive gathering in front of the Ayyankali statue in Vellyambalam infused fresh hope into those who participated in the struggle. It was agreed that most of the demands, such as land distribution, access to education to the most marginalized communities, and the implementation of SC/ST (Scheduled Caste/Scheduled Tribe) laws, were all said to be implemented before 1 August 2007, thus giving one full year to the state to implement the agreement. This also turned out to be part of the procrastination politics, and it was then that the protesters entered the corporate-led HML plantation on 4 August 2007. It was in the form of a mass movement that nearly 30,000 persons from 7,000 families occupied the Chengara part of the plantation empire. More than 90 per cent of them belonged to the converted Dalit Christians; the rest were from other Dalits and backward communities, including Muslims. They named it the Ambedkar Memorial Model Colony. The colony is now functioning as five *sakha*s (wings) in the name of Dalit icons: Ambedkar Nagar, Ayyankali Nagar, Panchami Nagar, Kallara Sukumaran Nagar, and Sribudha Nagar. Each *sakha* has an 11-member committee to discuss issues, tactics, and strategies, including financial matters.

The original idea of the SVSV was to occupy undisputed state-owned lands. However, they have had different experiences from land struggles such as Muthanga. There were discussions about which land and where to occupy the lands. The case of Chandanappalli was first selected as it was again state-owned land. The protesters initially announced that they would occupy the forest land on the easternside, which was later dropped. Accordaning to the SVSV, Chengara in the Kumbazha division belongs to the government rather than the private company because the lease period had already expired. The agitators reinforced the argument that it is only reasonable that the government distribute the land to the landless, including those who occupied Chengara, as it is now government property. As a precaution, the HML authorities set up security in places like Konni, Chengara, Perubetti, Kalleli, and Laha. Consequently, when a few jeeps full of activists entered Kalleli forest lands, they were arrested by the police, and it was on this occasion that nearly 1,000 people entered the Chandanappalli estate. This occupied struggle lasted for about four days, and following an agreement with the PCK authorities that the state would resolve the issues, the struggle was suspended. When this was not done, the strikers had no choice but to begin the historic Occupy Chengara movement. The particular geography of Chengara was also favourable for the occupiers. On two sides of the estate was the River Kallar, another side had a small *thodu* (water trench), and the remaining part was forested. As Kallar assured water, and so also the small *water trenches*, the forests and other plantation areas offered geographic protection from outsiders.

Yet Occupy Chengara was not an easy task for the protesting Dalits, as this invited stiff resistance, interestingly not from the owner-planter, but from the plantation workers, who are also landless Dalits. Stiff resistance also came from the CPI(M) trade unions, both within the estate and outside of it, thus leading even to the blocking of the entry of outsiders to the estate. On 4 August 2008, the first anniversary of Occupy Chengara, the trade unions erected a road blockade against the 'illegal occupants'. It was a human blockade of about 60 to 70 workers, isolating the workers inside the estate. Consequently, the company's goons turned the site into a violent one: they blocked women and men from going out for work; food and medical supplies were halted; and women were threatened with violence.[8] As the government, the trade unions, and the estate owner all formed hegemonic opposition to the struggling community, the police was also trying to enter the estate, which was blocked by the community. They stood with ropes and kerosene bottles in their hands and climbed up the rubber trees, warning loudly that if the police entered the site of struggle, they would burn themselves. Kerosene bottles were carried by protesters of all ages, including children, serving as powerful symbols of the struggles of the underclass. The police and neighborhood anti-social elements repeatedly threatened to evict the protesters. Saleena Prakkanam, a fierce protestor of the Chengara movement, lists several of these occurrences in her biography. In one instance, she describes how activist Omana Sunil poured kerosene on herself to prevent the police from entering the area and arresting the activists. Saleena herself stated that she was directed by Laha Gopalan to pour kersoine over herself (Bijuraj 2021: 762; see Prakkanam 2013). Asked about Prakkanam's statement and the widespread anxiety over the violent means of protesting, Gopalan told the author that these means consitited the strategies and tactics of politics, to jolt the state.[9]

On seeking judicial advice, the left government was granted permission to evacuate the Dalits but without bloodshed. However, the resisting communities, often with the support of social and political groups, such as the Socialist Unity Centre of India (SUCI), Solidarity, and so on, continued to negotiate with the trade unions, which lasted for about two years, and made the left government direct the trade unions to lift the blockade. The estate management did not waste time in attacking and disrupting the occupation, even with the help of goons. The police presence literally cordoned off the occupied Dalits, pressuring them to vacate the land. The SVSV, however, was adamant about not vacating the occupied land, as they visualized it as an abrogated promised land. On the petition filed by the HML, the High Court, however, ordered the eviction but with stipulations. As the state failed to do so, they went for yet another agreement and package, which, according to SVSV, was only an eyewash to meet the requirements of the High Court order. The demands of Occupy Chengara, by June 2008, were as follows:[10] Families belonging to the SC and ST communities and backward Christian communities to be awarded an acre each of land per family; financial assistance for the cultivation of land and food supplies for one year; and 5 acres of land to be awarded to the Kalleley Appooppan Kaavu (local temple), which was brought back to life by the occupants. The SVSV also suggested that reasonable consideration be given to the landless forward castes who participated in the struggle.

The Chengara Package

On 5 October 2009, the government and SVSV finally came to an agreement (see Suchitra 2011; Sreerekha 2012; Iyer 2018), though Laha Gopalan, at a later stage, stated that he had been forced to make this compromise (Suchitra 2011). As per the agreement, it was stipulated that 1,495 of the 1,738 families occupying the estate land in Chengara would be given land elsewhere in the state and assistance for building houses. At the beginning of the implementation, it was decided to distribute 831 acres of land among 1,495 persons. The settlement formula was to allot 1 acre of land to ST families, half an acre each to SC families, and 25 cents each to other categories. As per the agreement, 27 landless Adivasi families were to be given 1 acre of land and INR 1.25 lakh each to build a house. A total of 832 landless Dalit families were to receive 75 cents of land and INR 1 lakh each. Other 48 families would receive 25 cents of land and INR 75,000 for building houses; 525 families whose land value was less than 5 cents were also to receive the same benefit. In contrast to the totally landless, these people owned unassessed lands which were mostly inhospitable. It was also agreed that land was to be given to the beneficiaries within three months.

The Chengara Package was thus introduced, and as part of the rehabilitation package, land was apportioned and titles were granted to affected families. In Kasargod district, for instance, 166.42 acres of land in the Periya region of Hosdurg *taluk* was handed over to the SC/ST Department for the benefit of 360 families (260 STs and the remaining others). As a further extension of the rehabilitation package, 11.37 crore acres were earmarked for the K.R. Narayanan Co-operative Village Settlement Programme. This package included the construction of houses, soil protection, provision of community facilities, milk production, supply of clean water, and so on (9 April 2013). There were two relief packages that were announced by the government – the Moolampally Package announced on 19 March 2008 and the Chengara Package on 24 August 2011. Between these two time periods, the government claimed that there were nine other projects that were in progress, beginning from 2010 onwards.

Land claimed by the Forest Department that is also suitable for habitation and cultivation should be utilized for distribution after requisite negotiations. The allocation of land in terms of districts was to be decided by throwing lots; arrangements were also made for assistance with the construction of houses and the setting up of various social infrastructure. The aim was to find a permanent solution to the Chengara issue; an effort was made to find suitable land in every district of the state, and the aim was to re-house the Chengara occupants within the next 10 days. This decision was taken on 5 October 2009. The order was issued on 2 January 2010.[11] In a response to a submission on the Chengara issue, the revenue minister, K.P. Rajendran, reiterated that the government's policy in general was 'land for the landless'; in addition, the occupants of Chengara were guaranteed their little piece of land. As the lands in question were under dispute, it posed a practical difficulty in the way of resolving the issue. The government's policy would be to grant land to eligible families among the Chengara occupants. However, it was pointed out by the opposition member Thiruvanjoor Radhakrishnan that the area also was home to nearly 22,000 poverty-stricken people. He argued that the government's policy was to create strife between the local estate labourers[12] and the families that occupied Chengara. Rajendran retorted that since the government had come to power, 2,100 SC families and 824 ST families (6,749 in total) were granted surplus lands.

As the Chengara occupants and the opposition insisted on 5 acres and INR 50,000, the government proceeded with its Chengara Package, distributing 4–50 cents in various locations, which, however, turned out to be a failure for more than one reason (Sreerekha 2012). One major reason was that unlike those who got the land in southern Kerala, including the midlands, who found it almost acceptable and began their occupation, most of those who got the lands in northern Kerala found it distant, as they originally belonged to the southern parts of the state; further, most of them reported that the lands assigned to them were not habitable or cultivable, and hence they even returned to the picket line, which was not a welcome step as far as those who continued to remain and struggle in Chengara were concerned. This led to new forms of fragmentation in the Chengara site. In short, the rehabilitation package that was announced by the government proved to be a mere window dressing as the distributed land was either uninhabitable or inhospitable, an aspect that we shall return to soon[13].

Plantation Village in the Making

The government and the opposition did agree most of the time on the planning and execution of the package; however, very little was actually being achieved on the ground. There were quite a few contradictions between their approaches. The opposition and the occupiers were of the opinion that the fallow lands over and above the measured area of HML should be apportioned to the protesters. However, the government pointed out that the occupiers had encroached on the actual plantation itself and not on the surplus lands. The whole issue between the government and the opposition was that when the opposition was in power, they did not take a particular interest in the measurement and demarcation of the surplus land in plantations. This was never a part of their ideological agenda. The state maintained that since the occupation was not on government land and was disputed land anyway, it could not accept the suggested plan of the occupiers. It was of the opinion that the occupiers were free to stay on government land.

After six and a half years of occupation, the SVSV was determined to take up some developmental efforts in the occupied area. One of the most important acts was the erection of a concrete wall – 6–7 feet in height with 1 metre width for about 7 kilometres, covering around 500 acres – all exclusively done by the Dalits and their labour. While the initial reason cited was that they wanted protection from wild animals, it was often articulated as a wall of commitment in response to neglect and deprivation. They sent their children, more than 25, to the neighbouring tribal school. They themselves started *anganwadis* (courtyard shelters) for their kids. They opened their own tea shops and reading spaces, and the entire space became a new signal for a new collective life. The initial strength of the occupiers dwindled, owing to many reasons. There were those who left as they found the struggle ineffective. Another category left as they got lands as part of the agreement. It was pointed out that the initial agreement was to offer land to 1,495 families. However, the state succeeded in providing land to 74 families, who left for nearby areas such as Kollam, Moovatupush, Malappuram, and Kannur. The remaining families, who numbered around 750, decided to settle, and they developed a reasonably good holding – less than an acre on average – where they grow annual and long-term crops, and the holdings are rich in fruit trees as well, and thereby are involved in ecospatializing the otherwise enclosed monoculture plantations. The model village underwent a drastic transformation: huts got improved with better building materials and consumption items improved, including huts where TVs could be seen. Children regularly go to schools, 6 kilometres from the village, by collectively arranged vehicles.

As a result of the struggle, the government appointed one committee after another, beginning with the High-Level Committee headed by Nivedita P. Haran (2007). Since the committee believed that HML's own title was doubtful and the transactions were illegal, the possibility of collusion between government officials and the company was not ruled out. Following this, the legal advice given by Justice Manoharan (2008) highlighted the reason for the government to investigate the transactions made by the private company, how to reclaim the land from the company, and how to restore the land to the government. After examining HML comprehensively, a special investigation team headed by Sajith Babu (2010) stated categorically that the company had no legal right to continue ownership because the lease agreement had ended and so much land was available for redistribution (also see Prakash 2002; Sunil 2019). There have been a number of instances of gross mismanagement with HML and plantations in general, including non-reporting of the information on actual land owned to the government, not paying taxes on plantations, and also encroaching on forest lands, all of which have led to the government not being able to redistribute surplus land and losing revenue. According to the team, more than 10,000 acres were illegally transferred or sold to individuals and firms in Kerala. In fact, the team suggested that the government should restore not less than 40,975 acres controlled by the Malayalam plantation and 15,786 acres controlled by the UK partner of the company. It is evident that this much surplus land could meet the needs of both the struggling communities and the plantation workers, who are also landless and in need of support. A similar position was also taken by the Rajamanickam Committee (2020). All committee reports and judicial reports were against the company and its claims, proving that it did not occupy private land but government-owned land. In the larger context of postcolonial conditions, this also raises the knowledge question of who owns the Harrisons' plantation or the Tata Tea land. This did, in fact, involve knowledge controversies with varying positions within the state bureaucracy and civil society, which have yet to be resolved.

In Chengara, at the moment, nearly 500 families own 50 cents of land each; the remaining land, however, was not properly acquired, nor distributed. The surplus lands of HML alone would be enough to resolve the Chengara struggle; and if land were left over, it could be distributed to those who occupy Arippa and other sites of struggles, gradually achieving the state's claim of zero landlessness in Kerala. Those who were part of the struggle in Chengara had to face a large number of problems, which they still face in one way or another: they had to collect water for cooking from the nearby streams; they had to transport groceries and vegetables by head load from distant places; women were particularly disadvantaged owing to the lack of any private spaces; children had to miss their regular schools. They lost at least full academic years, and this also led to dropouts in the remaining years. A quick enquiry into this issue convinced the author that at least 10 per cent of the children who were with the struggling families in Chengara could not return to school when some families had to leave Chengara, either voluntarily or on the state's promise of fresh lands. Jean-Jacques Rousseau gave an answer well before the French Revolution, let alone the Bolshevik one: those who are unequal in their access to material goods can never be equal in the eyes of the law.

The agenda of the state was to offer *pattayam* (title deed) in nine villages of 1 acre each, but the SVSV found most of the lands identified not cultivable or livable. At a later stage, they found that those 74 families who got *pattayam* were given lands that were cultivable, but the rest were not. As they found that the lands identified were not cultivable, they decided to boycott the *pattaya mela* (title deed fest) for them, but those who accepted had to leave the occupied lands. History shows that those who got such lands were disappointed with the quality of such lands, and they also spearheaded new struggles, either in front of the state secretariat or by becoming part of some of the ongoing land struggles such as that of Arippa in Kollam, primarily led by the Adivasi Dalit Munnetta Samithi (ADMS), an aspect I shall turn to soon. The Ambedkar Bhavan as the state secretarial office of SVSV was constructed in Pathanamthitta, which also was subjected to criticism, given the nature of the building. It was alleged that the building cost was high and Laha Gopalan manipulated accounts towards the same, showing the emerging divisions within the movement.

In a shocking revelation, and based on the reports of district collectors, 996 of the allotted plots as part of the Chengara package are inhospitable and 499 are inhabitable, negatively impacting the government. There are several reasons why the lands assigned are either uninhabitable or uncultivable. In the Thiruvananthapuram district, land was granted to 225 families in Uzhamalakkal village of Nedumangad. As a result of objections raised by the Department of Forest and Wildlife, no one has been allotted land so far. However, four families from the list of 225 were reallocated to the Pathanamthitta district and now own and occupy land at Enadimangalam village in Adoor. Most of the remaining plots were uninhabitable as well. Idukki in Devikulam was identified for allotment among 657 families; the parcel was rocky and unsuitable for habitation. In addition, the area lacks basic amenities such as water, roads, and so on. According to revenue officials, the area is threatened by wild animals too, so the entire area comprising the village is inhospitable.[14] In addition, the fact that the situation was the same in the remaining seven districts also shows how pathetic the procrastination politics played out by the regime in power was and how the state failed to comply with their own agreement.

New Struggles amidst Suppression?

The state unleashed suppressive forces on the protesters in Muthanga and Chengara, but this did not make the Dalits stop their struggles. In both Chengara and Arippa, outsiders, including the trade unions, raised barricades for not allowing either the protesters to go out or civil society agents to come in. Media persons were not permitted to enter on many occasions. They were not allowed to go to nearby medical institutions like the district hospitals. On several occasions, hooligans forcefully entered and consumed alcohol within the protest lines. When this was challenged and blocked by the protestors, they were often threatened. In one case, Kunjumol was undressed and beaten, that too in front of her son. It was very difficult for her to express her feelings of marginality when this author requested her to speak about the unspeakable.

Throughout Kerala, instead of transferring land to those who had been cultivating on it, they were deprived of the same. Further, the lands went into the hands of those who did not require land as means of production, as those caste groups have been gradually climbing the ladder of economic and social progress. This was the beginning of absentee landlordism in the state. This has taken an alarming proportion as, at one level, economic expansion increasingly included those who owned land but were not cultivating it as they were being drafted into the emerging middle class and, at another level, land itself was changing its utility – from a cultivable asset to a speculative asset. The moment land entered into the speculative mode, it became all the more difficult and virtually unimaginable for the Adivasi and Dalit families to enter the land market and buy a piece of earth. Contrary to expectations, tenancy cultivation was restored in the state, and now it is the Adivasis and Dalits who take more interest in such practices. But it is clear that the Dalits in the state are still landless and hence one could infer that they were not making any surplus to the extent of buying land, save a few. This could have been the beginning of a debate on second land reforms in the state. However, this debate was debased and it was distant to the critical concerns of the Dalits (Janu 2011, 2013).

Kerala's land question continued to take different strides in the form of group farming, organic farming, and so on, with the consequent impact of marginalization of the genuine issue of land distribution to the landless. More than that, with the introduction of group farming, what the communist party and the state did was to legitimize further the way in which tenancy cultivation was practised. All those participants of group farming, first of all, were those who owned land but were absentee landlords. Second, they continued to receive a premium on their pre-existing fallow land, and thereby increased their power over wealth. Third, land, though it became more productive, remained valued at higher and higher levels, particularly as a means of speculation, which made the land more inaccessible for Dalits. What remains is subsistence tenancy (see Ajith 2003), which remained insulated from discourses on land reforms, including the provision for legalization of tenancy. Social relations of production remained unchallenged as part of the reproduced forms of social relations of state power. The state was reluctant to acting as an agency on behalf of the Dalit *bahujans*. The outcome was the absentee-landlords-turned-middle-class with overlapping identities of intermediate and upper caste Hindus and Roman Catholics reaching the top of the power structure.

Land struggles with massive levels of support began with Muthanga. It continued with Chengara. It also continued with the struggles in Ninankonam. While this chapter is being written on Chengara, the struggles went beyond Chengara – now in Arippa, for instance. The idea of land ownership was transformed with the Arippa struggle. Until this protest, the slogan raised by the strikers was that they should be given land, but now it is not just land but cultivable agricultural land that they demand. This is a big value addition that this struggle offered to the larger sympathizers of Chengara: they search for new spaces in economic and ecological domains, so also in terms of spatial relations of power.

It was on 31 December 2012 – five years after Chengara and nine years after Muthanga – that with the Dalits, essentially from the Kollam district, the Occupy Arippa was born. Nearly 40 Dalits families occupied 54 acres of 'surplus' land in Arippa and began living with the land. It was led by two persons, one a Muslim woman, Sulekha Thatha, and the other a Dalit schoolteacher, Sriraman Koyyon, from north Kerala. It was highly imaginative in the sense that Occupy Arippa began after midnight, and by morning several Dalit, Adivasi and Muslim families had joined the movement. They were around 4,500, and they pitched more than 1,000 huts in the revenue land, which was otherwise occupied by rubber plantations. Those 500-odd families with children remain on bare minimum existence (Sudhish 2020). There is no electricity or public tap as the residents are denied all access to basic facilities, an extended ordeal they have been enduring for about a decade. Sreeraman Koyyon, the president of the Adivasi Dalit Munnetta Samithi (ADMS), a collective that spearheads the struggle, explained to this author:

> By diverting a stream, we made water available for paddy cultivation. In several seasons, we cultivated paddy by hand as we were unable to afford modern machines or bullocks. Despite the fact that the authorities continue to block us with rules and regulations, forest laws, etc., we are ready for yet another season. However, subsistence ethics require us to survive. Also, we want to celebrate harvest festivals … and remind people what we do with this land when we occupy it which is surplus land … our motto is colony *vittu krishiboomiyilekku* (leaving colony for farmland).

This resembled the Chengara struggle in many ways. As in the case of Chengara, this also happened in the rubber plantation, reminding the larger public and the state that many of the colonially evolved plantations were built not only on encroached lands but also with many acres of surplus land. As in Chengara, the families who occupied included both the Adivasis and the Dalits; those who were outside of any particular caste but struggling to find a place to live also joined the occupiers.

There is, however, a major difference between Arippa and Chengara and, for that matter, Muthanga as well. While the Chengara monoculture plantation was owned by an Indian corporate, Arippa was an estate that had already been confiscated by the state from another private planter. The owner was Thangal Kunju Musaliar, from whom the state confiscated the land long back but kept it idle.[15] As in the case of Muthanga and Chengara, Arippa occupiers began humanizing the uncultivated land with paddy, and they harvested with a festive mood. Through the cultivation of rice in a state where paddy cultivation has been dwindling and dependency on neighbouring states is escalating, the Arippa radicals offered a new way of occupying and making the land more sustainable, both economically and ecologically.

Concluding Remarks: Hope and Despair?

While the 'land-broker state' (Levien 2013) was the order of the day under neoliberal conditions, the state in Kerala, by remaining silent on the lands colonially encroached by HML and other such plantation empires, in effect, produces the same outcome. The struggles from the margins to such neoliberal conditions have also come up throughout Asia, and the Chengara and Muthanga struggles belong to that category. Studies reveal that Kerala continues to experience high rates of social and economic inequality when it comes to land ownership: while the caste Hindus and Christians have the most land ownership, Dalits and Adivasis are at the bottom of the land ownership ladder. In comparison to SCs, forward castes have access to land five times more often in the case of land owned, and more than eight times more often in the case of cultivated land. Despite the passage of time, the land–caste nexus remains (Yadu and Vijaysurya 2016; Deshpande 2000). In a major way, such land deprivation inhibits Dalits' emergence as a middle class and also their participation in mainstream society; they are ecospatially trapped without any significant upward mobility. For them to be fully involved in the development process, cultivable and habitable land ownership becomes a prerequisite. If Muthanga was occupied exclusively by the Adivasis, it was the Pulayas and Cherumas of the Dalit castes and the converted Christian Dalits who re-enacted the drama of liberation in Chengara. Land deprivation and the consequent poverty and undernourishment was equally shared by the Adivasis and the Dalits, even after more than half a century of state formation in 1956. Neither the left nor the Congress-led governments, who alternated in power since the Chengara occupation, could resolve either the land question or the livelihood associated with landlessness, not to speak of its connections with caste and religion in the state.

Thirst for a piece of land, for the vast majority of Adivasis and Dalits in Kerala, is nothing less than a thirst for survival. If the state has to become modern, it must be able to erase spaces of exclusion, which in the case of land, should be translated in terms of ownership. The Kerala High Court in 2021 observed that the state government is bound to honour an agreement, signed in 2010 – this was with respect to Chengara alone – to provide land to landless tribals and SC and ST families at Chengara in Pathanamthitta. Justice Devan Ramachandran made the observation while hearing a writ petition filed in 2013 by the ADMS in relation to the land allotment agreement. The court said that the claims of the Adivasis and SC/ST families remained unresolved either because they had not been given the land promised or because the land offered to them was unsuitable for living. Nothing was placed on record by the government on how the claims of the 1,495 families had been dealt with. The issues remained without a complete solution for the last two decades, and if such status was allowed to continue ad infinitum, 'the unrest of the past may hold up its head again and escalate in future'. The transverse solidarity among the landless Dalit *bahujans* grew to the point where not only did the two battlegrounds of Chengara and Arippa unite – spatial coalescence – but they also jointly organized creative protests under the banner of Chengara–Arippa Bhoo Samithy – agential coalescence – such as a 101-hour sit-in at the state secretariat as recently as 7 January 2022. While the demonstrators were successful in enlisting the support of political figures, such as Congressman V.M. Sudheeran and non-governmental agencies, they were also successful in mobilising legal support, with the verdict from the Kerala High Court, with Justice Devan Ramachandran pointing out, 'It is State's sovereign obligation to honour pact signed with families' (see *The Hindu* dated 26 August 2021).

The ambiguous stand taken by the left and non-left governments that alternated in power recently was apparent from its handling of this issue. The whole land question reached an impasse when most of the state-sponsored committees and commissions came in with the assertion that all these lands should now rightfully be under the government from the time of Indian independence (Devika 2013). The government was of the view that land should be awarded to the landless in keeping with current laws. The state was of the opinion that the cases against these occupants should be settled in an amicable fashion. Interestingly, the state in itself had never been successful in delineating the surplus lands. And so the protesters were caught between the claims and counterclaims of the government and the opposition. The occupiers were struggling for their own survival and livelihood and were only too aware of the surplus lands under the privately owned plantations. As far as they were concerned, they were looking for a small piece of land each that they could put to use in order to provide food and sustenance for their families in an otherwise expanding market economy oriented to the commodification of life (Patnaik 2003). Polanyi (1944) demonstrated how capital was liberated from the control of society and now enables capital to control society, a process of disembedding, but this makes the 'double movement' inevitable: 'self-protection against the commodification of life', a lesson that constantly reminds us of the landscapes of ecospatial struggles.

Notes

1. A few years before the Chengara occupation, HM disposed of part of its estates: the disposal of nearly 3,500 acres of the Cheruvalli Estate to the Believers' Church was a case in point. It was alleged that the local CPI(M) also supported the selling of the estate. In another context, the Congress member of legislative assembly (MLA) Adoor Prakash declared that the land in the Kumbazha region of HM should be surveyed and any land coming under government jurisdiction should be redistributed amongst the plantation workers who were rendered jobless; no progress was made even when the Congress was in power.
2. The government made claims about confiscation of land or identification of surplus land but nothing concrete has been reported. On 25 June 2008, for instance, the government reported in the assembly that in Ernakulum district alone, 1,957,072 hectares of land were confiscated. It was also reported that action had been taken against 635 encroachers in the district alone. While

the state confirmed that the confiscation of land for distribution has been in progress, no substantial change has been found in the final analysis.

3. For more details, see Raman (2010).
4. Notification of Travancore government, July 1906, in Proceedings of Foreign Department.
5. While on a tour of the high ranges in 1907, for instance, the Dewan of Thiruvithamkur was approached by some European planters demanding more land, roads, and judicial facilities. The Dewan, however, did not accept these demands. This quite predictably annoyed the Europeans, one of whom is reported to have followed the Dewan on horseback in an attempt to obstruct his tour. Though a police case was filed against the offending planter, nothing came of it as the planter refused to submit himself to the law of the land. Further, any attempts at imposing restrictions on the release of land by the local rulers were thwarted by the planters. For instance, it was quite common for the planters to purchase lands from local landlords in addition to the land acquired through the state; the government demanded the sanction of such purchases from the state.
6. Laha Gopalan was the chairperson of the Sadhujana Vimochana Samyukta Vedi (SVSV) and Thattayil Saraswati served as the secretary of the same. Later, Prakkanam became the secretary of SVSV. However, she even had to quit the movement afterwards; to this we will return soon.
7. Question and answers, Kerala Legislative Assembly (KLA), 25 June 2008.
8. In August 2008, it was reported in the press that women were raped in the estate in which trade union activists were accused. The women approached the media and also the public agencies, including the National Commission for Women and the National Human Rights Commission for Scheduled Castes. The SVSV also asked these national bodies to visit the protest site.
9. Interviewed on 21 August 2021 in Pathanamthitta.
10. Question and answers, KLA, 25 June 2008.
11. KLA, 4 March 2010.
12. Labour organizations registered their protest with the government against the occupation of the plantation lands. Several rubber tappers and field workers were rendered jobless. They claimed that they had a huge loss of wage and income, turning their livelihood options uncertain.
13. LR/736/2021-LR(J8), Revenue Department, Government of Kerala, 1 December 2021.
14. Government of Kerala, Office of the Land Revenue Commissioner, Thiruvnanthapuram, LR/736/2021-LR(J8), 2 December 2021.
15. For details, see John (2013a, 2013b); Mohan (1999).

References

Ajith (2003). *Bhoomi, Jaathi, Bandhanam Keralathile Karshika Prashnam*. Eranakulam: Kanal Prasidheekarana Kendram.

Bhaskar, B.R.P. (2008). Mass peaceful squatting: Chengara challenges the grammar of protest. *Kerala Letter*, 14 April. http://sanhati.com/news/937/(accessed 21 April 2011).

Bijoy, C.R., and K. Ravi Raman (2003). Muthanga: the real story. *Economic and Political Weekly* 38 (20): 1975–1982.

Bijuraj, R.K. (2021). *Keralathinte Rashtreeya Charithram*. Kottayam: DC Books.

Deshpande, Ashwini (2000). Does caste still define disparity? A look at inequality in Kerala, India. *The American Economic Review* 90 (2): 322–325.

Devika, J. (2013). Contemporary Dalit assertions in Kerala: Governmental categories vs. identity politics? *History and Sociology of South Asia* 7 (1): 1–17.

Franke, R., and B. Chasin (1992). Kerala state, India: Radical reform as development. *International Journal of Health Services* 22 (1): 139–156.

Ganapathy, M. (1978). *Malayalam Plantations: An Era of Planting in South India*. Madras: Malayalam Plantations.

Gregory, D. (2004). *The Colonial Present*. Oxford: Blackwell Publishing.

Harrisons Malayalam Limited (HML) (2017). *Annual Report 2016–2017*. Kochi: Harrisons Malayalam Limited.

Herring, R.J. (1983). *Land to the Tiller: The Political Economy of Agrarian Reforms in South Asia:* Delhi: Oxford University Press

Ilaiah, K. (1996). *Why I am Not A Hindu*. Kolkata: Bhatkal & Sen.

Isaac, T. (2008). *Bhooparishkaranam Ini Enthu?* Thiruvananthapuram: Chintha Publishers.

Iyer, D. (2018). *Examining 'Land Occupation Movements' in Corporate Plantations in Kerala: A Case Study of Chengara*. New York: Cornell University.

Janu, C.K. (2011). We need to build huts all over Kerala, again and again. In *No Alphabet in Sight*, ed. K. Satyanarayana and Susie Tharu, pp. 429–451. New Delhi: Penguin Books.

———(2013). Adivasis cannot survive without their land: C K Janu (G. Kuruvilaroy, Interviewer). Round Table India, 14 March. https://www.roundtableindia.co.in/adivasis-cannot-survive-without-their-land-c-k-janu/ (accessed 15 May 2023).

John, Baiju (2013a). Kuthakakalkku vanabhoomi, bhoorahitharkku paarakkettu (Forests to the corporates and rocks to the landless). *Madhyamam* Weekly, 21 March, pp. 68–70.

——— (2013b). Porattaveeryam kedathe arippayile samarabhumi. *Madhyamam Weekly*, 8 July, pp. 8–15.

Kapikkad, Sunny (2008). *Kerala Bhoo Parishkaranam: Dalit Paksha Vimarshanavum Vibhavadhikara Prashnagalum*. Kottayam: Chengara Bhoosamara Aykyadardya Samiti.

Krishnaji, N. (1979). Agrarian relations and the left movement in *Kerala*: A note on recent trends. *Economic and Political Weekly* 15 (9): 515–521.

——— (2007). 'Kerala milestones: On the parliamentary road to socialism. *Economic and Political Weekly* 42 (23): 2169–2176.

Laclau, E., and C. Mouffe. (1985). *Hegemony and Socialist Strategy. Towards a Radical Democratic Politics*. London: Verso.

Mohan, Sanal P. (1999). Dalit discourse and the evolving new self: Contest and strategies. *Review of Development and Change* 4 (1): 1–24.

Mohanty, B.B. (2001). Land distribution among Scheduled Castes and Tribes. *Economic and Political Weekly* 36 (40): 3857–3868.

Namboodirippad, E.M.S. (1981). *Keralam Malayalikalude Mathrubhumi* (Malayalam). Thiruvananthapuram: Kerala Grandhasala Sahakarana Sangham.

Omvedt, G. (2006). Kerala is part of India: The Kerala model of development, Dalits and globalization. In *Kerala: The Paradoxes of Public Action and Development*, ed. Joseph Tharamangalam, pp. 188–214. New Delhi: Orient Longman.

———. (1993). Land reforms and economic change: Experience and lessons from Kerala. In *Essays on Kerala Economy*, pp. 1–22. New Delhi: Oxford University Press and India Book House.

Patnaik, U. (2003). Global capitalism, deflation and agrarian crisis in developing countries. *Journal of Agrarian Change* 3 (1): 33–66.

Polanyi, K. (1944). *The Great Transformation: The Political and Economic Origins of Our*. Boston: Beacon Press.

Prakash, P.K. (2002). *Anyadheenappedunna Bhoomi Adivasi Bhoomi Rasnattinte Charithravum Rashtriyavum*. Kozhikkode: Pappiyon.

Prakkanam, S. (2013), with O.K. Santhosh and M.B. Manoj. *Chengara Samaravum Ente Jeevithavum*. Kottayam: DC Books.

Radhakrishnan, P. (1981). Land reforms in theory and practice: The Kerala experience. *Economic and Political Weekly* 16 (52): A129–135.

Raj, K.N., and P.K.M. Tharakan. (1983). Agrarian reform in Kerala and its impact on rural economy: A preliminary assessment. In *Agrarian Reforms in Contemporary Developing Countries*, ed. Ajith Kumar Ghose, pp. 31–90. New York: St. Martin's Press.

Raman, K. Ravi (2010). *Global Capital and Peripheral Labour: The History and Political Economy of Plantation Workers in India.* Milton Park: Routledge.

——— (2020). Can the Dalit woman speak: How intersectionality helps advance postcolonial organization scholarship? *Organization* 27(2): 272–290.

Rammohan, K.T. (2008). Caste and landlessness in Kerala: Signals from Chengara. *Economic and Political Weekly* 43 (37): 14–16.

Said, Edward W. (1978). *Orientalism.* New York: Pantheon (New York: Vintage, 1994, with new Afterword; New Delhi: Penguin Books India, 2001).

Sreekumar, T.T. (2009). Randaam bhooparishkaranathinte velluvilikal. In *Chengara Aikyadardhyapushtakam* (Chengara Solidarity Souvenir), ed. T.M. Velam, pp. 85–101. Kozhikode: Solidarity Youth Movement.

Sreerekha, M. (2010). Challenges before Kerala's landless: The story of Aralam Farm. *Economic and Political Weekly* 45 (21): 55–62.

——— (2012). 'Illegal land, illegal people': The Chengara land struggle in Kerala. *Economic and Political Weekly* 47 (30): 21–24.

Suchitra, M. (2011). Chengara sheri, Muthanga thettu (Chengara is right, Muthanga is wrong). *Mathrubhoomi Weekly*, 10–16 April, 8–17.

Sunil, R. (2019). *Harrisons Rekhayillatha Janmi.* Thrissur: Keraleeyam.

Tharakan, P.K.M. (2002). Land relations in contemporary Keralam: A survey. In *Agrarian Studies: Essays on Agrarian Relations in Less Developed Countries*, ed. V.K. Ramachandran and Madhura Swaminathan, pp. 355–361. New Delhi: Tulika.

The Hindu (2021). Honour pact on land for the landless, Kerala HC tells govt. 26 August. https://www.thehindu.com/news/national/kerala/honour-pact-on-land-for-the-landless-kerala-hc-tells-govt/article36120039.ece (accessed 13 May 2023).

Thompson, E.P. (1991). *The Making of the English Working Class.* Toronto: Penguin Books.

Varghese, T.C. 1970. *Agrarian Consequences and Economic Change.* Bombay: Alliance Publishers.

Yadu, C.R., and C.K. Vijayasuryan. (2016). Triple exclusion of Dalits in land ownership in Kerala. *Social Change* 46 (3): 393–408.

7

Pombilai Orumai

Plantation Dalits, Intersectionality, and Power

Kuppathotti nankalku
Kottum suitum ungalku

Katikanni nankalku
Chickendosa ungalku

Pottulayangal nangalku
AC banglaow ungalku

Kolunthu nullathu nankai
Kasatikathu ninke

We are clothed in rags and
You are in suits

For us, plain gruel
You feast on meat

We are shack dwellers.
You live in AC bungalows

We pluck the leaves
You pocket the money[1]

—Slogans raised in the Munnar agitation

Alain Badiou points out that subjects become political when they create events – events as trans beings (see Hallward 2003; Badiou 2005, 2009) – even without the mediation of an agency. Badiou (see Hallward 2004) would also constantly remind us that what is important is post-eventual declaration: to quote Lisy

Sunny, one of the Dalit woman leaders of Pombilai Orumai in Munnar, '[A]t least now we have a union of our own.'[2]

The protests that rocked the Kanan Devan tea plantations, formerly Scottish James Finlay, in Kerala in 2015, led by the historic Pombilai Orumai – the women's unity – and later a parallel state-wide struggle spearheaded by the mainstream trade unions had been called off following what could best be described as mixed outcomes. While the plantation management has had to shift its position with regard to its decision not to increase the bonus or wages, the workers had to content themselves with a 30 per cent hike in wages as against their original demand for a 100 per cent increase. Yet the struggle has been path-breaking as it helped bring to light the harsh living and working conditions on the colonially evolved plantations. The company's claim that it 'ranked No. 1 in the category [of] best company for employees' involvement and participation in India' and 'featured among the 100 best companies to work [as per] its employees in India' was exposed as an untruth. In fact, the observations made at the second All Kerala Thozhilali Sammelanam (All Kerala Workers' Meet) held at Trichur in 1937 under the leadership of veteran communists including P. Krishna Pillai, N.C. Sekhar, R. Sugathan, and A.K. Gopalan, that of all the workers it was the plantation workers who suffered the most (see Raman 2010), remains true to this day – after nearly seven decades of Indian independence – with hardly a change in the historically evolved plantation-based patriarchal forms of exploitation/oppression. Further, it helped expose the state, the trade unions, and plantation capitalism, the first two for their political absence and ideological depoliticization and the third for its globally integrated exploitative practices in the global commodity chain.

The chapter explores how the emergent Dalit *feminitude*[3] – in the Kanan Devan plantations in Munnar – challenged the traditional understanding that workers themselves are not self-representable and are hence to be represented, and through this how they challenged the capitalist and patriarchal forms of exploitation/oppression. It has been argued that the new 'destituent power' (see Agamben 2014) first challenge their own trade unions by peeling away from them, thereby opening up a new politics of becoming, simultaneously taking on the Tata-controlled Kanan Devan Hills Plantation Company Private Limited (KDHP). The chapter also explains why the claims made by the company for its refusal to offer higher bonuses and wages do not stand scrutiny and how corporate capital transfers crisis to the workers while refusing to share their prosperity with them. More importantly, it makes an argument that in order to understand the Dalit womens' struggle in Munnar, one should bring in 'intersectionality' (Craenshaw 2014; Nash 2008; Spivak 2014; Vogel 1983; Walby, Armstrong and Strid 2012; Yuval-Davis 2004), an aspect that was not given adequate attention by Marxists who are otherwise preoccupied with the class question alone. The chapter concludes that there has been an erosion in the right to have rights in the plantations, but the present struggle brings hope through self-assertion at a time when the trade unions have depoliticized themselves and corporate capital intensifies its exploitation/oppression.

While it is true that oppression operates through a series of interlocking systems of production and power relations that cut across identity categories (Cohen 1997), what is important is not to treat all oppressions and resistance with equal importance as they vary in terms of caste, gender, everyday livelihood, and social reproduction of labour. The oppression as experienced by white women cannot be treated as that of black women, and so is the difference between a caste Hindu woman and a Dalit woman, as the latter has, first of all, been historically oppressed, and second, there are multiple 'layers of oppression' with respect to black or Dalit women, as this chapter will reveal. This necessitates the location of 'subaltern counter publics', the possibility of a subaltern counter-discourse and a recognition of their 'identities, interests, and needs' (Fraser 1997: 81, 69–98; Fraser 2014: 8–42, 129–156; Olson 1965), thus releasing their 'emancipatory potential' (Fraser 1997: 82) and addressing the 'unspeakability' and 'unrepresentability' of the subalterns. Further, the Dalit women show how they can organize and speak for themselves, driven by intersectional life experiences over 'time, and thereby they respond to the Spivakian challenge regarding 'Can the subaltern speak?' (Spivak 1988). It represents the power of collective agency within the social realm of differences, operating through what Laclau and Mouffe would call 'chains of equivalence' (1985) and what Yuval-Davis (2004) and Crowley (1999) would call the 'politics of belonging' through 'transversal' (Yuval-Davis 2004) and transverse solidarity politics (Raman 2010b), erasing the concern of intra-group differences as outlined by intersectionality scholars.

The Struggle(s) and the Settlement

It was on 25 August 2005 that the KDHP unilaterally declared the bonus – without discussing the matter with any of the recognized trade unions – for the fiscal year 2014–2015 at 10 per cent, as against 19 per cent in the last year. All the major trade unions in the KDHP – the All India Trade Union Congress (AITUC)-led Devikulam Estate Workers' Union, the Indian National Trade Union Congres (INTUC)-led South Indian Plantation Workers Union, and the Centre of Indian Trade Unions (CITU)-led Plantation Workers Union decided to refuse the bonus as they were demanding 1 per cent higher than the previous year at 20 per cent. The management tried to come to a consensus, but their offer was refused by the trade unions, which served strike notice, adding yet another demand that the minimum daily wage should also be revised to INR 500 from the current wage of INR 232. As the women workers were closely following the development of negotiations, they took the decision to *go-slow* with plucking leaves, the main operation in the industry. The unions, however, jointly rejected the women workers' response and directed them not to practise any such go-slow practices. This was the first provocation for the women workers who were already disheartened by their trade unions' lackadaisical approach to their question of livelihood and responsibility. Discussions amongst themselves, both at home and on the estates, led to their decision to represent themselves: the already organized women workers split away from their trade unions, challenging them and the company, and keeping all the trade unions, save a few, out of their protest domain, including the Devikulam Marxist MLA, S. Rajendran. With two rounds of talks with the labour minister, Shibu Baby John, having failed to resolve the issue, the chief minister was forced to the negotiating table mainly with the striking workers without any union representation, and an agreement was reached: a bonus of 8.33 per cent with 11.67 per cent ex gratia as a one-time payoff, thus in total meeting the workers' demand for the bonus of 20 per cent.

The second demand, an increase in minimum daily wage to INR 500 from the current INR 232, however, remained contentious with the Pombilai Orumai continuing their struggle and the mainstream trade unions entering afresh on indefinite strike, including a hunger strike in front of the company headquarters in Munnar. The basic daily pay of an estate worker engaged in plucking tea leaves was INR 232, including basic pay and dearness allowance, for a standard minimum output of 21 kilograms per day, in addition to housing and medical facilities. The labourer gets 60 paise per kilogram for an additional 14 kilograms and a further 85 paise per kilogram for the next 14 kilograms. An amount of INR 1.10 per kilogram was being paid for every extra kilogram of output up to a maximum of 100 kilograms of leaves. More importantly, as in the colonial past, the measured weight of the leaves is often reduced to adjust for the weight of water, on the grounds that the leaf plucked during the rainy season weighed more than they did in summer on account of being wet; paradoxically enough, this deduction was applicable during summer as well (Raman 2010). It is also evident from their wage slips, as verified by this author, that there is a considerable deduction of money from their monthly income towards such adjustments. Neither the firewood nor the electricity they get from the estate is exempted from the deduction.

The failure to resolve the issue of wages led the mainstream trade unions to launch an indefinite strike in parallel with and independent of the strike by the Pombilai Orumai – the second phase of the struggle – which has now been called off after a 17-day-long resistance and chaos in the plantation sector: the workers initiated a relay hunger strike, they blockaded traffic in the hill tracts, and the loyalists of mainstream unions even attacked the Pombilai Orumai workers; a woman worker even attempted self-immolation while the protest was going on, and the trade union leaders also decided to go on a hunger strike, thus forcing a settlement by the management. As per the new settlement, the basic daily pay of an estate worker engaged in plucking tea leaves would now be INR 301 as against INR 232 with dearness allowance and basic daily pay, which would also be applicable for workers in coffee estates; this is an increase of 30 per cent from the existing minimum wage, higher than what the trade unions managed to bargain in 2013 at 23 per cent. The minimum wage for cardamom has been increased from INR 267 to INR 330, and for rubber, it increased from INR 317 to INR381. It has been worked out that with the statutory benefits added, the tea and coffee workers would altogether get a daily wage of INR 436; this would be INR 478 for cardamom and INR 552 for rubber estate workers. Though no change has been made with respect to task wage rates, which at the moment is not that progressive, the trade unions could at least claim that they successfully bargained for a higher rate than the management's offer of 23 per cent. However, considering the fact that INR 301 is still only half the agricultural wage in various parts of Kerala and even a migrant worker gets more than INR 500 for a day's work in the plains, the increase in the cost of living in the high ranges, particularly in terms of provisions, education, and health care, makes the gap between money wages and living wages more pronounced. Interestingly enough, the Pombilai Orumai was not in agreement with the new settlement, and they have publicly expressed their dissatisfaction with it, but they have nonetheless withdrawn their struggle, owing to the extreme deprivation caused by the lack of daily earnings for over a month.

Lessons and Non-lessons from the Munnar Struggle

The Question of Power and Representation

The first phase of the Munnar struggle – the struggle solely led by the Pombilai Orumai –represented the new politics of becoming, which reflected the outburst of nearly a century and a half of oppression and exploitation of generations by old and new forms of capitalism and patriarchy, the outburst of what Giorgio Agamben would call the 'purely destituent power', 'a power that was only just overthrown by violence will rise again in another form, the incessant, inevitable dialectic between constituent and constituted power' (Agamben 2014: 70). In the case of Munnar, it was the changing forms of corporate and trade union agitation – first by the Scotland-based James Finlay, then Tata Tea, and now by the combined corporate power of Tata Tea and its employee buy-out organization form, the KDHP, in collusion with the conventional trade unions – that was challenged by the generationally reimagined destituent power: the direct producers of wealth who cannot either be captured or co-opted by the hegemonic forces. Plantations, in general, represent peripheries within peripheries; the Dalits and other depressed communities – who are also the descendants of the nineteenth-century outcastes and ex-slaves – constitute the majority of the workers; most of the workers are Dalit women, who are also mostly the descendants of migrants from nearby Tamil Nadu villages. The socially hierarchized plantation system has been reproduced over generations without any significant forms of socio-economic mobility within and outside the plantations, and whatever changes occurred were confined to relations between capitals without an alteration either in the basic nature of the labour process or relations of power. The labour process remains exhausting as the women tea pluckers rise from bed at 4.30 or 5 a.m. to do their household chores and reach the field at 8 a.m. to work until 5 p.m. and after. One of the protestors from Pombilai Orumai said, 'When one of us dies, our body is carried in a tractor. We want to change this animal-like life.'[4] With theirs being a story of continual misery and exploitation, it needed no mediating organization to drive them to an organized agitation but their shared existence.

It was pointed out that the workers joined in their hundreds in the various *layams* (line houses), communicating amongst themselves with the help of mobile phones and gathering early in the morning in the town and in front of the company headquarters. A few estates became a major source of inspiration with their meetings and discussions about future strategies. The leadership for the protest was gradually building up from below: though in the first few days, there were only hundreds of workers involved, within no time, it grew to thousands, many of them being women, both young and middle-aged. None of them failed to repeat why they had taken to the streets: they owned nothing, 'neither a house nor land; everything was company owned'.[5] Earlier, they had been allowed access to common lands for the raising of milch animals; however, this had been barred of late as part of the rose cultivation project of the company: 'Medical facilities are utterly poor, and what is more, the caesarean and hysterectomy rates among us are very high, and we were kept in darkness; why it is so?' Did all this have anything to do with the use of machines for plucking?[6] This was a question they asked of this author as well.

The Pombilai Orumai's demand thus seems quite simple, as they repeatedly stated to this author – a level of income that would support a decent living standard, allowing them to keep their children in schools, and ensuring the health of the family.It is worth remembering the suicide of Velankanni, a ninth-class student, who hanged herself in October 2002 at her parent's workhouse in the Ram Bahadur Thakur Group (RBT) estate, which had remained closed for the previous year, as she found herself unable to comply with the headmaster's orders to come to school in a new uniform.

> We were shattered to hear that our daughter Velankanni hanged herself when she found that we could not afford to buy her a set of school uniform in spite of repeated warnings from her school authorities. She was only 14 years. (Mariyammal, Velankanni's mother, 2003)[7]

Had the struggle been continued under the sole leadership of Pombilai Orumai, a better deal could have been expected for the workers, although this would also have prolonged their suffering even further.

The 'protest power' unleashed in this context was that of Dalit women who declared that they would no more be open to the patriarchal forms of exploitation that they have been suffering over generations. While the workers in general suffer from various forms of exploitation, it is specifically the Dalit women who form the core of the workforce as tea pluckers who were subjected to generations of patriarchal forms of exploitation and oppression. The four major forms of capitalist and patriarchal oppression that they historically suffered include: (*a*) the unequal gender-segregated labour market, with women occupying low-paying plucking jobs and men in factories with higher wages, (*b*) in the field, with the male representatives of the KDHP at the top and the mass of bilingual (Tamil and Malayalam) Dalit women at the bottom, with male supervisors most often from the middle and caste Hindus, (*c*) in the trade union domain, a new patriarchal form was added to plantation capitalism, with the upper caste, male trade union leaders imposing both economic and disciplinary strategies on the workers, and (*d*) the very reproduction of patriarchy at home with the women workers, after long hours of hard work, having to bear the additional burdens of household work as well as childbearing.

Like any other tea plantation, the KDHP also represented a system wherein labouring women were reined in by the patriarchs of class, ethnicity, and caste, and the accumulation has thus not been merely economic; apart from being patriarchal, it was ethnic-cum-caste hegemonic (or Brahminical) as well, thriving on the traditional caste hierarchy in the life of Dalit women (for details, see Raman 2010). It is worth noting that the woman multitude in Munnar challenged all four patriarchal forms of exploitation/oppression simultaneously, both as a strategy and practice: apart from waging the struggle against the KDHP, they kept both the trade union leaders and their appendages away from the imaginary picket line; they made sure that their husbands stayed out of the negotiations as well, having lost faith in them for being bribed with money or liquor into succumbing to the management and trade union interests.

The workers have invalidated the traditional Marxian understanding of representation, which maintained that workers are inherently not self-representable and hence are to be represented. The woman multitude has blazed a unique trail, vehemently rejecting all traditional forms of representation, including the leaders rallying the workers; instead, they have carved out a novel representation of their concerns. This is not the first time that women workers alone have come into the protest domain. Kerala has been recently witnessing several such protests, such as the one by Penkoottu, which fought for the right of the textile workers to sit during work in Kozhikode in May 2014 and the *irikkal samaram* (right to sit [in the workplace] protest) staged by women workers in Thrissur in January 2015. In contrast to these struggles that remained in the unorganized sector, the Munnar struggle was launched by those who had already been historically organized; this was a peeling away of the frustrated workers from organized networks by simultaneously putting a halt to the pseudo-history of trade unions and fashioning a new history of liberatory politics. They became the leaders and the followers: a new possibility of convergence of workers and leadership which challenged the various traditional hierarchical forms of organizing labour. This new politics of emergence provides hope for the toiling masses and presents a crisis for the established trade unions. While the agitators half-heartedly welcomed a few of the local representatives, all other local leaders were barred entry into the protest area, including the local legislative assembly representative. The only political leader who was welcomed with a warm acceptance was the left opposition leader V.S. Achuthanandan, who spent hours together with the protestors, discussing their everyday miserable life, and this was a reminder to the larger public that it was time for a change in trade union politics as well as the conduct of mainstream political parties.

It is worth noting that there was a workers' struggle in Munnar against James Finlay and Company, the forerunner of Tata Tea and the KDHP, on the same issue of an increase in wages, bonuses, and improvement in living conditions in October 1958, 17 months after Kerala first came under communist rule. However, the Scotland-based James Finlay, which had always been preoccupied with the labour question and even attempted to block the emergence of trade unions in its territory (see Raman 2014, 2010), refused to pay higher wages and bonuses; they also chose to ignore the agreement reached at the tripartite conference in the erstwhile princely state in the mid-1940s to pay bonuses. The strike organized by the joint trade unions, but largely by the communist union, and sponsored by the state was initially democratic but later turned out to be chaotic and violent. However, it failed to yield any significant benefits and further led to the death of two communist party workers – Papammal, a Dalit teenager, and Hussain Rawther, a middle-aged Muslim worker, in the police firing that ensued. It is worth noting that it was the militancy of the workers that was one of the reasons – apart from the fear of nationalisation of foreign-owned plantations by the communist government – that prompted the planter lobby to work for the toppling of the first communist government, in which they succeeded, along with the caste-communal forces in the state (see Chapter 8). The 1958 struggle failed with the workers' own communist government in power whereas the current protest has succeeded with the Congress government in power. However, the success of the struggle was specifically due to the imaginative form of its self-representation and the relentless power of agency unleashed through the woman multitude.

The Question of World Capitalism and Crisis

History is replete with examples to prove that whenever plantation capital was in crisis, the planters spared no means to transfer it to the workers, but in times of prosperity, they refused to share the profits with the workers. This has been so ever since the 1930s Depression when the decline in tea prices was transferred to the workers by way of massive levels of retrenchment and wage cuts. During 2000–2008, there was yet another steady decline in prices, which again was transferred to the workers by the closure of the estates, leaving them in the lurch (see Raman 2010). Now in 2015, there has been yet another decline in prices, and the management, including that of the Kanan Devan plantations, transferred it to the workers by halving the bonus from 19 per cent to 10 per cent, which was the immediate cause for the agitation. They remained trapped within the global commodity chain with a low share of wages and bonuses to the retail prices, the lion's share of the value generated in the chain going to the upper nodes in the profit hierarchy. Most of the small tea-estate owners persistently complain in south India that the auction price is not even one-third of the retail market price of tea, which, in turn, leaves small tea producers at a disadvantage. Instead of addressing the question of cartelization/buying concentration in auction centres and monopoly in retail markets, and the oversupply of tea into the world market leading to a consequent fall in prices, the plantation management and their associations, including the Association of the Planters of Kerala (APK), appear to take a position that they would not be able to meet the workers' demands, neither the wages nor the bonuses, which, however, was challenged.

It is worth noting that it was specifically during such long and short periods of crisis, with the management transferring the burden to the workers, that the latter were driven to revolt in varying forms. The very organization of the first trade union in the plantation belt, which occurred in Mundakkayam under George Kakkanadan, was in response to the planters' manipulation of the workers during the world depression of the early 1930s. It is no small wonder that the struggle in Munnar too has occurred in such a contemporary context. However, the difference this time was that when the organized workers found out their 'own' trade unions had depoliticized themselves, they have themselves been forced into self-assertion mode, demanding their 'right to have rights', even as hegemonic power relations and the state continue to erode their rights.

The Question of the Depoliticization of Male-led Trade Unions

The elite caste dominated plantation unions demonstrate that the unions were depoliticized. The fact that women were not given any representation in trade union leadership devalues the trade union system as a whole. While the labour unions under contemporary conditions fail to represent the workers adequately, they spare no effort to collect monthly donations from their members in favour of the political parties. The workers interviewed by this author repeatedly emphasized the lack of interest shown towards them by the trade unions, who would not intervene even when the workers fell ill and were in need of medical care. The absolute power unleashed by this bottom-up resistance is clear for all to see; the shock waves had spread to other 'tea forests', as they are often called, due to the very hostile conditions obtained in what mainstream society calls 'tea gardens': a strike had already broken out in the neighbouring Goenka-owned Harrisons Malayalam Ltd (HML) plantation; it had also spread to the tea estates in Wayanad and to remote areas such as Bonacaud in south Kerala and Nelliampathi in the north. More importantly, the strike had crossed the crops, now leading the workers in coffee, cardamom, and rubbers estates on agitation as the state-level marathon meetings of the Plantation Labour Committee (PLC) failed to adopt a practical solution to settling the wages. All the main trade unions were driven to an indefinite strike, which led to a 'movement of movements' (Wallerstein 2002). The struggle had taken a new form with local unions orchestrating the idea of occupying the estate as a means of livelihood as at one level the consecutive meetings of the PLC failed to resolve the issue and at another level there were occasions when plantation companies themselves threatened to declare industry-wide lockouts.

Further, the women workers were suffering from the multiple kinds of collusive deals in the plantation system. Two major collusive deals were almost exposed by this struggle. The first collusive deal was between the trade union leaders and the management, as is evident from the fact that various trade union leaders, irrespective of political differences, received the patronage of the management in various forms. A few of them have had the benefit of gaining nepotistic benefits, as well as service facilities such as free houses and cars. At the peak of the struggle, the workers even brought out the list of those leaders who enjoyed such benefits, unilaterally breaking the trust between the workers and their trade union leaders. The second major collusive deal often involved the supply of winter clothes such as blankets and other basic provisions to the workers, wherein the workers alleged that the trade unions made profits by selling them to the workers at prices higher than the market rates. Collusive deals between the management and the trade union leaders were raised even in the context of supplying firewood to the workers at high prices, which, in fact, was collected from the areas earmarked in the estates which are exempted from ceiling provisions, and should have been given free of cost to the workers. In contrast to the decadent trade unionism, the Pombilai Orumai started building a union on their own strength; moreover, they were fielding their own candidates in 39 wards in the elections for local self-government institutions in November 2015. Their triumph in two *grama panchayat*s and a block *panchayat* has further opened up new spaces of hope.

Minimalist State, Minimalist Trade Unions

Throughout the world, there is a move towards a minimalist state as part of neoliberalism, and this, in turn, demands greater responsibility from the trade unions. However, instead of accepting higher levels of responsibility, the trade unions have also become minimalist, and have either been appropriated by the state or constituted by it. In Kerala, as in many other states, trade unions have been reduced to appendages of alliance politics. They have failed to develop an independent historic bloc, independent of political parties and their sectarian interests, and thus incapable of developing an autonomous 'war of position'. They have failed to represent the workers as an autonomous force, a force that was supposed to liberate the workers from various oppressive forces. This is not to say, in contrast to their portrayal in mainstream media, that the trade unions did not take any interest in the question of bonuses and wages, but their intervention was slow and lacking in conviction, and this frustrated the workers even more, particularly the women workers both in the plantation and the non-plantation sectors.

The Plantation Labour Committee (PLC) – the state-level tripartite forum consisting of the representatives of the government, trade unions, and management – should have protected the workers' rights by ensuring a stringent implementation of the statutory welfare measures mandatorily provisioned in the Plantation Labour Rules. There are around 14 estates in the state that have been closed for over two decades; many welfare provisions remain redundant or ignored for the workers in the closed or abandoned estates (Raman 1986, 1996); benefits such as provident fund and gratuity remain undisbursed by many estates.[8] From the fear that they would lose their gratuity and other monetary benefits which are due, these workers are trapped in the estates with poverty-stricken lives (Raman 2004). This proves to be a false hope where their lives are enmeshed in everyday forms of discrimination and deprivation.[9]

A quick enquiry into the management staff of some of the plantations in the state convinced the author that those who had served as plantation inspectors of the government now got employed as human resource managers in the private plantations, and to the surprise of many workers, their behaviour is more often stricter than the actual owners; it is only natural to expect similar behaviour from the state labour commissioners' office as at least a few of them would be likely to imagine themselves getting a job in the estates once they retire from government service. A recent visit to the estates and a detailed conversation with the agitating workers in Munnar led this author to observe that the Indian replicas of the shorts-clad European masters still lord over the workforce, so much so that they put the colonial masters to shame.

A Wrong Model of Tata Employee Buyout?

Tata Tea, which earlier acquired its property in Munnar from the Scotland-based James Finlay in 1987, had ventured to unbundle its properties to the newly floated company called the KDHP in 2005, responding to two sets of crises, internal and external. Internally, Tata Tea was subjected to a legal challenge from the communist-led government for its alleged illegal ownership of estates spreading to thousands of hectares. Externally, like any other tea company in the country, it had to face declining prices in the world market. One of the measures to tide over the combined crises was to transfer its properties, including all fixtures (factories, offices, bungalows, and so on), to the new company by co-opting the workers as shareholders. Tata succeeded in creating an impression that it continued to honour its version of corporate social responsibility by distributing the shares; the trade unions also created the impression that the plantation was going to be their property, and the workers, by and large, were also given the confidence that they were the owners of the newly born company. Tata Tea, renamed as Tata Global Beverages Limited, had first of all resorted to a policy of what they termed 'labour rationalisation', de-linking production from marketing in a manner that dissociated them from the management of plantations altogether. The acquisition of one of the world's largest tea companies, the UK-based Tetley, made its dominant presence felt in the world tea market. The company left the back-end operations to the employees but retained strategies to control.

During the time of the formation of the company itself, the distribution of shares was heavily skewed: Tata Global Beverages Limited retained nearly 28.52 per cent; the KDHP Welfare Trust, in which Tata has a significant stake, owned a share of 8.95 per cent, and the rest was left for the employees and workers. It is learnt that out of the 63 per cent of the shares they own, it was, by and large, owned by the salaried staff and executives, leaving a meagre share to the 10,000 plus workers. It was said that the workers were asked to take a maximum share of 300 at the rate of INR 10 per share; lower-level staff were offered 1,200 shares; the executives were offered virtually limitless shares, and it was widely reported how some of them even bagged shares worth lakhs of rupees.

Tata also played the role of a financial capitalist by offering INR 2,400 lakhs as a term loan, with a fixed and a variable portion of interest (which appears as high as 8.5 per cent); the remaining working capital was raised through the issue of new equities from employees and from commercial banks; the KDHP also availed a loan from Tea Board of India with an interest at 12-month LIBOR. While Tata is confident in the interest accruing from such a big loan and the dividends from its single largest equity, the amount that goes to the workers in the form of dividends – around 10 per cent has been announced for the last three years – would be marginal, hardly INR 300 in a year as against huge sums to the executives and higher-ups. The nominal share that the workers held as owners did nothing to empower them, in terms of either control or dividends. What was glorified as an employee buyout or participatory management, in fact, turned out to be a Tata-controlled re-composition of capital and managerial staff and executives, the circuit of control getting completed with Tata and a few oligopolistic firms exercising control on the auction centres and the retail market.

Some of the statistics that the company revealed through its balance sheet are also not fully convincing. First of all, the legitimate question that arises – and one which many workers, in fact, raised informally – is: how did a 15–20 per cent decline in prices lead to a 66 per cent decline in profit? This is also when the company's own records show an increase in output and productivity. Had there been an increase in capital expenditure or statutory benefits, this decline in profit could have been partially explained, which, however, had not taken place, leaving certain questions unanswered. A quick analysis of the balance sheets reveals that there has been an accelerated depreciation of 23 per cent, which was also responsible for the low figure in net profits. Interestingly, this was when the value of tangible assets declined from INR 5,227 lakhs to INR 4,994 lakhs. More importantly, the earnings before interest, taxes, depreciation, and amortization (EBITDA) profit, the real indicator of business sustainability, had not declined if not registering a marginal increase over the years. A decline in profit by 66 per cent should not have, for an enlightened management, led to a dividend of INR 1 per share, but rather a suspension of the dividend itself; it also reveals the fact that the major shareholders would be less affected by both a dip in prices and the decline in profit than those who own fewer shares, as in the case of the workers.

Refusal of 'Right to Have Rights'

Two major absences leave plantations in Kerala vulnerable to exploitation by a corporate capital regime: the absence of the state and the trade unions, which have both encouraged plantation managements to turn their estates into mini-empires. While the absence of the state is a colonial continuity with the colonial plantation managements themselves admitting that they were a 'state within state' (Raman 2010: 146; Mackay 1984), a fact often acknowledged with contempt by post-independence political leaders, the situation with respect to the trade unions is different. Though the trade unions are physically present, they are confined to fostering the interests of the political parties they are affiliated to, which would include the collection of money from the workers, renewal of membership fees, and so on; their absence has been conspicuous in terms of political effectiveness and addressing the concerns of the workers (see Bhattacherjee 1999; Ahn 2010).

As has been noted earlier, what we have been witnessing in the plantation life-world in the post-1991 liberalization phase is a repetition of history, with the crisis being transferred to the workers and the prosperity retained. Critically examining Arendt's notion of the *right to have rights* (Arendt 1994: 292), Seyla Benhabib (2010) argues that the word 'right' has different meanings in each half of the phrase. The first 'right' implies the familiar conception of a 'right' as a recognized claim, which implies a duty on the part of humanity and hence primacy in all other rights; the second right in the phrase, for Benhabib, is more juridical-political. What we find in Munnar is the loss of both the rights.

Agitated women, descended from Tamil families, repeatedly told this author to what extent they have been treated as second-class citizens in Munnar. Their children are not often admitted to a school run by the Tatas; their health rights are not honoured in any standard manner; the male-oriented trade union leaders, who are mostly upper caste, pay the least attention to their everyday concerns; the state is no more visible except in times of elections; and procrastination politics continues whether it is with respect to land, housing, or their ethnicity (see Raman 2010, 2020; Raj 2018). Each of these deprivations adds up to a loss of belonging to the wider community of Kerala, as they expressed through many of their deliberations, which, in turn, makes their struggle for a new citizenry. The first 'right' in the phrase also has critical links with the notion of international law and rights, as Arendt implies only the 'community of nations' could protect their interests, the interests of refugees, migrants, poor workers, and so on. The protection of rights was absent in the plantations as well: the International Labour Organization's Decent Work Agenda with a focus on freedom, dignity, security, and equity, which was launched in 1999, still remains an illusion for the workers.

The substitution of bonus by ex gratia is a classic example of this removal of the second right in the phrase. It is no longer mandatory for the management to offer the same in the forthcoming years; the right they enjoyed was taken out of the legal safety framework as the management became increasingly insulated from the welfare provisions of the state. As it has been constituted by social relations of power, the state resolved the crisis by ultimately lending its support to the plantation management by accepting the idea of ex gratia payment. However, the state failed to strengthen the legal right of the workers to claim more bonuses, which, in fact, was hardly 1 per cent higher than the previous year. Both the state and the participating trade unions, including the agitating workers' representatives, failed to counter the management view that a decline in profit does not allow them to increase the bonus conveniently, keeping under cover the fact that bonus need not be based on profit alone but could also be based on production and productivity; in either case, the workers could have won the legal right as well. Given the fact that the established trade unions did not represent their interests implies that political rights as represented by trade unions were lost, thus completing a circuitry of lost juridical-political rights.

Dalit Experience of the Kerala Model of Development

The Munnar revolt – as also the other struggles narrated in the preceding chapters –offers a from-below critique on the otherwise glorified Kerala model; while applauding the Kerala model of social development, our social scientists failed to ask how social this development has been. The key aspect of the developmental manifestation as it has panned out in the state is that it does discriminate across communities, and this truth has once again been brought to the fore: the Dalit experience within the Kerala model does not affirm the success of the much applauded socialist state. Land reforms in the state have worked to the disadvantage of all the Dalits, including plantation Dalits, as has been evident in the case of Dalit land struggles going on in the state and their deprivation of other resources with an overrepresentation of those below the poverty line. This has many implications. First, the very formation of James Finlay & Company in 1879 through two successive acquisitions of 215 square miles of land – 1.37 lakh acres – which was equivalent to one-tenth of the forest area of Travancore, testifies to the extent to which the princely state was subordinated to British colonialism. The land was acquired at throwaway prices: the sale was made for an outright price of INR 5,000.[10] Second, the land reforms passed in the post-independence state kept the plantations, including James Finlay, exempt from ceiling provisions, thereby defeating the very idea of identifying surplus land for redistribution to the landless. Third, almost all the plantation companies continued to sequester lands by dispossessing the Adivasis and Dalits and retaining vast areas of land illegally.

Even a day after the KDHP was forced to concede the demands of its protesting workers in Munnar, the state had to report to the Kerala High Court that the company had no right over lands in its possession as the title deeds were fraudulent. The studies conducted by the court found that in the post-colonial context, the land belongs to the government. The court made this remark in the context of the KDHP and its predecessors claiming vast swathes of land in Munnar on the basis of two title deeds registered in 1976 between the associated companies of James Finlay and Tata Tea. However, the matter is not settled yet.[11] The government took the position that the transaction could not be given legal backing as the succession was not in keeping with the Companies Act and was not approved by the Reserve Bank of India.[12] The move by the State Human Rights Commission to initiate a police-aided verification of the legality of the ownership of various plantation lands and how they were transferred to Indian hands from British planters since the early twentieth century appears to provide fresh insights into the massive encroachments and illegal sequestering of land in the plantation belt, and this may benefit the plantation workers if the requirements of landless families are prioritized. Earlier interventions of communist leaders like V.S. Achuthanandan brought the encroachments of corporate plantations to the public, including those of TATA, and were successful in confiscating some of the surplus land, though concrete results were absent.

Paradoxically enough, the state decided to allow, in the midst of the workers' agitation, the utilization of 5 per cent of land in plantations for non-plantation activities to a maximum of 10 acres. The plantation management now makes use of their lands for high-tech farming, medicinal plants, floriculture, dairy farming, and, more importantly, tourism. The state had taken the view that this kind of conversion should be permitted as the plantations were currently in crisis, and the workers were also bound to benefit from this; it was further stated that this was a decision approved by the trade unions themselves. This decision, however, had already been challenged by the striking workers; some of the trade unions who earlier agreed with the above proposal now retraced their steps, largely in response to the new struggle.

Concluding Remarks

When does the subject become political without any pre-mediating agency? In the case of the Munnar struggle, it is true that the women workers rose up without the help of any organized pre-mediating agency, but challenged them from within, and through this a new politically charged Pompilai Orumai has been created. Given the fact that they do not challenge the idea of trade unionism but rather their manner of conduct, they are only co-electing a new collective with a politics of becoming. And every event that unfolds on the edge of the void throws open its own window of truth – and produces its own truth. What Badiou calls a truth is one that, sparked by a break with routine, persists in an affirmation whose progressive imposition transforms the very way things appear in the situation. None can predict the outcome of such events; what carry authenticity are the post-evental declarations. The much-discussed Arab Spring, for instance, has now been replaced by autocratic and religious fundamentalism in most of the regions involved, in place of a new era of democracy with political pluralism and freedom of the press, and this must be attributed to an absence of ideological clarity and enlightening imagination.

Given the fact that Munnar borders Tamil Nadu and more than half of its population are Tamil-speaking, the allegations that the workers were also influenced by certain Tamil radical groups promoting Tamil nationality issues[13] may bring in new forms of ethnic and geopolitical conflict. This would also complicate the issue in the future, particularly when one finds that the presence of such groups in Munnar was first felt during the Mullaperiyar dam controversy when the demand that parts of the district be joined with Tamil Nadu first arose. The spokespersons of the Pombilai Orumai, however, denied such connections, but were firm that they would spare no means to challenge any kind of exploitative and oppressive forces in the future, offering sparks of hope for the Global South under neoliberal capitalism (Mertes 2004).

The arguments in this chapter complement the postcolonial organizational approach to workers' protests in the management and organizational discourses and politics in three ways. First and foremost, this struggle addresses the 'unspeakability' and 'unrepresentability' of the subalterns and shows how they can organize and speak for themselves by deriving insights from intersectional life experiences over time. The second is the strategies of dissent that are organized at two levels: On one level of self-organization – breaking away from the non-representational and hegemonic organizational forms – ultimately self-organizing by the misorganized by refusing to comply with the traditional

Marxist understanding that workers cannot represent themselves, but are to be represented. At another level these women workers dared the male-led trade unions and the patriarchal structures of accumulation. In this process of political assertion by these workers, they challenged both the male-led trade unions and the state and its apparatus. Third, challenging not just the management, but the very constituted hegemony in which other hegemonic forces such as the state and trade unions participate in regressive roles, and, therefore, becoming politically aware of their own acts of resistance and unleashing their own agency. Women from Dalit communities had to engage in both recognition and equality politics simultaneously (see Fraser 1997, 2000). These are aspects of Dalit feminism and subaltern identities that call for a focused attention in intersectionality and postcolonial studies. This provides an integrated narrative of intersectionality, labour process, and postcolonial discourse, an issue with which critical scholars have yet to engage seriously.

Notes

1. Author's own translation.
2. Personal interview, Munnar, 4 and 5 September 2015.
3. The notion of multitude as a theory of political subject was critiqued from feminist perspectives on grounds of 'gender-blindness' and an implied violence to empirical realities (see Quinby 2004) as also for a failure to 'foreground gender' (see McRobbie 2015; also see Balakrishnan 2003) (for details, see note 1 in Chapter 1).
4. Lisy Sunny, personal interview, Munnar, 4 and 5 September 2015.
5. Gomati Sebastian, personal interview with the author, Munnar, 5 September 2015.
6. Interview with the women workers, Munnar, 12 September 2015.
7. These words were spoken to an audience worldwide through Doordarshan, the national television channel, in early 2003. It was before a unique studio audience that this experience was related. It included planters, trade union leaders, and scholars; the author, too, was part of the television programme, and thus the on-the-spot ethnography indeed.
8. Interview with Vazhoor Soman, state secretary, AITUC, 12 September 2015, Munnar.
9. Vazhoor Soman, a communist trade union leader and the current MLA from Peerumedu, confirms that the living conditions in most of the tea estates are

deplorable, and even worse in closed estates without any sign of revival (personal interview, state secretary, AITUC, 4, 5, and 12 September 2015, Munnar).

10. For more details, see Raman (2004).
11. For more details, see Haran (2007), Rajamanickam (2016), Sajithbabu (2010), and Sunil (2019).
12. Interview with Susheela Bhatt, government pleader, Kerala High Court, Kochi, 2 September 2015.
13. Though the state-level CITU secretary made a statement that agitation by women had the backing of a Tamil extremist group, the CPI(M) leadership in the state refused to accept the same.

References

Agamben, Giorgio (2014). What is a destituent power? Translated by Stephanie Wakefield. *Environment and Planning: Society and Space* 32 (1): 65–74.

Ahn, Pong-Sul (2010). *The Growth and Decline of Political Unionism in India: The Need for a Paradigm Shift*. Bangkok: ILO DWT for East and South-East Asia and the Pacific.

Arendt, Hannah (1994). *The Origins of Totalitarianism*. New York: Harcourt Books.

Badiou, A. (2005). *Being and Event*. Translated by Oliver Feltham. New York: Continuum.

——— (2009). *Theory of the Subject*. Translated by Bruno Bosteels. New York: Continuum.

Balakrishnan, Gopal, ed. (2003). *Debating Empire*. London: Verso.

Benhabib, Seyla (2010). *Politics in Dark Times: Encounters with Hannah Arendt*. New York: Cambridge University Press.

Bhattacherjee, D. (1999). *Organized Labour and Economic Liberalization India: Past, Present and Future*. Geneva: ILO.

Cohen, C.J. (1997). Punks, bulldaggers and welfare queens: The radical potential of queer politics. *GLQ: A Journal of Lesbian and Gay Studies* 3: 437–466.

Crenshaw, K. (2014). *On Intersectionality: Essential Writings*. New York: The New Press.

Crowley, J. (1999). The politics of belonging: Some theoretical considerations. In *The Politics of Belonging: Migrants and Minorities in Contemporary Europe*, ed. A. Geddes and A. Favell, pp. 15–41. Aldershot: Ashgate.

Fraser, N. (2014). Transnationalizing the public sphere: On the legitimacy and efficacy of public opinion in a post-Westphalian world. In *Transnationalizing the Public Sphere*, ed. N. Fraser and K. Nash, pp. 8–42. Cambridge: Polity.

Hallward, P. (2003). *Badiou: A Subject to Truth.* Minnesota: University of Minnesota Press.

———, ed. (2004). *Think Again: Alain Badiou and the Future of Philosophy.* New York: Continuum.

Haran, N.P. (2007). *Unnathathala Committee Report.* Kochi: Harrisons Malayalam.

Hardt, Michael, and Antonio Negri. (2009). *Multitude: War and Democracy in the Age of Empire.* London: Penguin Books.

Laclau, E. and C. Mouffe. (1985). *Hegemony and Socialist Strategy: Towards a Radical Democratic Politics.* London: Verso.

Mackay, W.S.S. (1984). The Kanan Devans. In *United Planters Association of Southern India,* ed. S.G. Speer, pp. 338–339.

McRobbie, Angela (2015). Reflections on feminism and immaterial labour'. *New Formations* 70: 60–76. http://research.gold.ac.uk/6012/1/Dec201006_nf70_mcrobbie.pdf (accessed 5 October 2015).

Mertes, T., ed. (2004). *A Movement of Movements: Is Another World Really Possible?* London: Verso.

Nash, J.C. (2008). Re-thinking intersectionality. *Feminist Review* 89 (1): 1–15.

Quinby L. (2004). Taking the millennialist pulse of *Empire*'s multitude: A genealogical feminist diagnosis. In *Empire's New Clothes: Reading Hardt and Negri,* ed. Paul Passavant and Jodi Dean, pp. 231–251. London: Routledge.

Raj, J. (2018). Tea belts of the Western Ghats, Kerala. In *Ground Down by Growth: Tribe, Caste, Class, and Inequality in Twenty-First Century India,* ed. A. Shah, J. Lerche, R. Axelby, et al., pp. 49–81. New Delhi: Oxford University Press.

Rajamanickam, M.G. (2016). *Report of the Special Officer & Collector.* Thiruvananthapuram: Government of Kerala.

Raman, K. Ravi (1986). Plantation labour: Revisit required. *Economic and Political Weekly* 21(22): 960–962.

——— (1996). Planter at large, labour at crossroads. *Economic and Political Weekly* 21 (51): 2214–2215.

——— (2004). Of peripheral labour: Trajectories of the Dalit labour in southern India plantations, 1820s–2001. *Indian Journal of Labour Economics* 47 (3): 497–509.

———. (2010). *Global Capital and Peripheral Labour: History and Political Economy of Plantation Labour in India.* New York and London: Routledge.

——— (2014). Business, ethnicity, politics and imperial interests, UPASI. *Business History Review* 88 (Spring): 73–95.

——— (2020). Can the Dalit woman speak: How intersectionality helps advance postcolonial organization scholarship? *Organization* 27 (2): 272–290.

Sajithbabu, D. (2010). *Special Team Report*. Thiruvananthapuram: Government of Kerala.

Spivak, G.C. (1988). Can the subaltern speak? In *Marxism and the Interpretation of Culture*, ed. C. Nelson and L. Grossberg, pp. 271–317. Urbana, IL: University of Illinois Press.

Sunil, R. (2019). *Harrisons-Rekhayillatha Bhoomi*. Thrissur: Keraleeyam.

Vogel, L. (1983). *Marxism and the Oppression of Women: Towards a Unitary Theory*. Chicago, IL: Haymarket Books.

Walby, S., J. Armstrong, and S. Strid (2012). Intersectionality: Multiple inequalities in social theory. *Sociology* 46 (2): 224–240.

Yuval-Davis, N. (2004). Borders, boundaries and the politics of belonging. In *Ethnicity, Nationalism and Minority Rights*, ed. S. May, T. Modood, and J. Squires, pp. 214–230. Cambridge: Cambridge University Press.

8

Ecospatiality

Right-Making/State-Making

With the Occupy protests in the West, which have lately been superseded by the Black Lives Matter movements, we started telling the stories of protest movements in the Global South, with a focus on Kerala. It would also imply that right-making/state-making dialectics ought to be applied to understand and assess state formation and state performance, including that of the Kerala model of development. After the post-independence state formation, the historical landscape of Kerala, by and large, validates the right-making/state-making thesis despite shortfalls; it appears that after state formation, and until recently, there have been tendencies on the part of the state to put constraints in the process. It strengthened the case for why the confluence of class and race/caste, with its gender expressions, matters for appropriate politics, particularly in leftist groups. Furthermore, research has shown that different communities have been negatively impacted by global crises like the coronavirus pandemic, with the most marginalized members of society bearing the brunt of this burden because they lack access to adequate healthcare, are malnourished, and live in poverty. Neither the exploitation and oppression of global capitalism nor the pandemic is caste- or class-neutral. All the more important is the livelihood and environmental vulnerability of the marginalized in a state which is otherwise known for its social developments and socialist experiments which in turn demands what has been described in this monograph as political ecospatiality.

Threats and enclosures are additional features of the current world, and the pandemic has made individuals who defend their rights even more vulnerable. Countries of the Global South such as Colombia, Niger, Indonesia, and the Philippines are used as examples of neoliberal predations (Burns and LeMoyne 2001; Lucas and Warren 2003; Iwilade 2012; Quimpo 2009). In the case of

India, as argued elsewhere, the modalities of emerging power is by and large constituted by the Hindutva–corporate regime; this is further contrasted with the 'graduated social democratic state' as in Kerala (Raman 2023). As we describe the problems of the excluded, the future seems as hazy as ever. Yet the ecospatial struggles we narrated so far are optimistic, and so is ecospatiality in its totality, which is in and of itself politics proper.

Kerala's left-led government in power does not fit into the neoliberal predatory institutional and political systems in the Global South, and that is particularly one of the reasons why voters in 2021 chose to elect a second consecutive term for the first time in history (Raman 2021). In contrast to many other states, Kerala's left-wing government has been very careful to allocate budgetary resources for SC/ST population at a rate greater than their population share. However, if the state's socially disadvantaged groups are to participate in a society with egalitarian values and an ethical state, they still have a long way to go. In today's times of crisis and globalized, predatory neoliberal capitalism, the question I raise in the monograph, 'What is politics proper?' is more important than ever. Further, the 2018 deluge, the worst ever flood in a century since the 1924 floods (Raman 2020), and the global pandemic make it even more compelling as to why political ecospatiality matters.

As I described the conflicts and demonstrations, I was continually thinking about the issues raised in the first chapter, such as what constitutes proper politics. Why does ecospatiality matter? How can livelihood and environmental conflicts and transverse solidarity transform into political ecospatiality: the mirror image of the future state? Which perspective – spatial, temporal, or agential – is the most effective for understanding this? What new perspective on modernity might there be? What kind of dimensional shift might one anticipate in the relationships between politics, society, and the state? How did the democratic state respond to environmental and livelihood struggles led by socially oppressed groups? And to what extent was civil society able to lend support to such struggles? The on-the-spot ethnographically focused accounts – narratives, struggles, and revolts – provide us with answers to some of these issues. I have also been incorporating some of the conversations made, from their own voices, while moving forward with the manuscript, using a wide variety of disciplines such as political ecology, political economy, social and cultural anthropology, and historical sociology. As neither of the issues is constrained by boundaries, so too the journey towards post-disciplinary paradigm, celebrating the diversity and multiplicity of perspectives but with an ecospatial agenda: locating livelihood-environment struggles and the politics of identity towards egalitarian and ethical existence, aspects that become more relevant as the world faces an existential crisis unlike anything humanity has ever experienced. Thus, almost two decades have passed since the Subaltern Studies project was abandoned or derailed into cultural studies, and the question of how communities with weak lobbying power continue to organize themselves to defend their honour or their daily livelihoods is once again relevant. Returning to the question of writing a non-elitist history of those with little political clout and their movement trajectories for subsistence ethics is what has been narrated as ecospatial struggles.

Most of the movements in the Global South that have been briefly explained in Chapter 1 involve ecospatial aspects of politics, livelihood, and identities. It is claimed in this study that it is by assembling certain key ideas and premising the same in post-disciplinary framing that we get a comprehensive understanding of the landscape of the struggles. In other words, this study assembles three key ideas and applies them as analytical tools to form an overall framework, *ecospatiality, transverse solidarity*, and *epistemological coalescence*, to build up the narrative of ecospatial struggles and to open up the right-making/state-making practices possible. Ecospatiality refers to the rationality of the struggles – why they are being fought, how they are being organized, and what is to be imagined – through which I understand the concrete forms of struggles. The events and resistance movements are covered throughout the book chronologically. One would be able to observe how the various state modalities of power – under the left and liberal Congress coalitions – responded to the struggles and how the state itself was being increasingly conscientised in this process. Additionally, one would also be able to observe how the movement itself has taken new directions and departures, with victories and defeats as part of larger transformative changes. If not a Dalit critique in the truest sense in terms of livelihood, environment, and identities, the study provides a Dalit/subaltern reading of the Kerala model of development. Moreover, there have been a number of instances where employees, who are primarily from vulnerable Dalit and other backward groups, have directly clashed with subaltern communities with similar social backgrounds.

The contrasting positions of the capitalists and the subalterns, the former of which is frequently protected by the state and even by the mainstream unions, are two key characteristics of the six struggles studied in this book, the first of which was described in the 1960s. Whether those participating in the conflicts won or lost, the struggles and movements ultimately aided in the democratization of the state; therefore, it does not really matter how it was resolved. The process of conscientization of the state and a larger civil society was the primary factor that the subaltern opposition played in the democratization of the economy, society, and the larger environment. The trajectory, emotional reactions, and ups and downs of the struggles have been detailed in each chapter. Here I will conduct a more comprehensive examination of the themes involved, frequently relating Kerala's struggles to both conflicts in other parts of the world and larger theoretical debates.

Theme 1: Ecospatial Resistance as Politics Proper

Ecospatiality is all about ethics and egalitarianism. At the end of the day, it is a question of participating in the ecospatial struggles and taking a position. The struggle for ecospatial existence goes on whether it is successful or unsuccessful, sustained or abandoned. The main issue is why historically marginalized people should continue to resist through ecospatial struggles, how much of these efforts have been political ecospatiality/subaltern modernity, and where these struggles are headed in the future. The 'revolutionary republics' that the marginalized formed with the help of civil society are represented by Muthanga, Chengara, Plachimada, and so on. Since they stand for the Kantian 'becoming', which Deleuze rightly noted cannot be reduced to history, they are not reducible to history in the case of Kerala as well. Unlike many Occupy movements in the West, these republics contributed to the epistemology of humanizing the landscapes and recovering rights to one's means of subsistence and the larger ecological sustainability. These were also the moments of the inseparability of epistemology and ontology (see Barad 2007), with an emphasis on 'new materialism' of the social future as they continued to change the occupied lands into the sustainable forms of human–nature assemblage – blurring the nature–culture division (see Kirby 1997, 2017). The radicalized longing for change is another factor that makes the marginalized and the precariates the carriers of liberating forces. Further, transverse solidarity with an ecospatial agenda is constructed as a work in progress, moving through different historical phases, from anti-imperialism, to caste and social reform renaissance movements, to organized politics and the use of the institutions of the state. The communities were able to forge collective action from differences, differences of historical and contemporary origins, with the assertion that their voices be heard by the larger civil society and the state.

In many respects, the local Mavoor communities bringing the state, the trade unions, and the Indian big bourgeoisie, the Birlas, to their knees simultaneously serves as a symbol of ecospatial resistance, as subaltern modernity. To begin with, it sparked a discussion about the best course for state developmentalism and who should be in charge – the democratic government or the Indian big bourgeoisie or other alternatives. Second, the debate over the relative merits of the two social classes – the industrial proletariat and the socially backward communities – finally led to a scenario in which they could come together for a shared goal, or a process of creating collective meaning for a social future. Third, it marked a turning point in the investigation of the possibilities of movements that combined political and ecological principles with social justice and egalitarian forms of being. Since the Muthanga insurrection, underprivileged populations have been equally worried about tactics and strategies. The intervention of the federal government was to be avoided at all costs; thus, care was taken to avoid encroaching on forest areas. The search for counter-enclosure was more focused on private empires, such as the sizable plantations managed by Indian corporate capital, such as the Tatas/Harrison Malayalam Ltd, which remain as the symbols of 'post-coloniality' (See Dirks 2001; Prakash 1992: 31–32; Hall 1995).

The state-making exercise by the communist government (1957–1959) was toppled by none other than the British planter lobby, in alliance with the Kanan Devan Hill Plantation Corporation Limited (KDHP) which was later to become the Tata-owned plantations that still maintain its hegemonic position in the state. The planter authority posited that E.M.S. Namboodirippad 'met his Waterloo' in the Kanan Devan empire (for details see Raman 2010; Mackay 1984). The author has elsewhere supplemented that there were two reasons for the initiatives taken for overthrowing the communist government. First of all, they were afraid of the potential threats of the nationalization of the British-owned plantation, as it was already an agenda of the election manifesto of the communist government. The intervention of A.K. Gopalan for the nationalization of foreign-owned plantations and CPI's manifesto had already provoked the plantation forces. The narrative on the dissolution of the communist government in Kerala was until recently confined to the caste communal forces and the established parties such as the Congress and the Muslim League; however, the new narrative strengthens the debate on how the communist government was overturned by both the internal and external lobbying power in Kerala (see Raman 2010: 147–148; Anil 2023). Second, the workers became militant, owing to low wages and poor working conditions in the plantation sector. What one would find is that even after six decades of state-driven developmentalism and land reform, some of the issues and concerns raised under the first communist government remain unaddressed, an aspect we will examine again.

The post-land-reform protestors aimed for state-owned and privately enclosed surplus lands or a larger share of economic surplus, as in the case of the Pombilai Orumai in Munnar. This resulted in increased political support from a bigger segment of civil society as well as increased negotiating space with the state and flexibility with communities that are engaged in movements. When questioned why not forest lands, Laha Gopalan said emphatically, 'We don't want to repeat the mistakes done in Muthanga by the Adivasi Gothra Maha Sabha.' Gopalan continued: "[E]ven otherwise who wants to get lands in forest boundaries where there is constant wildlife threat?'1 In this context, strategy takes the front seat targeting a specific end. However, Muthanga became legendary due to Gramscian spontaneity and Badiou's truth event. The lessons learned from one site of resistance led to higher forms of imagining things for the next site in emergence: for instance, the land struggles in Arippa, Nilambur, and Aralam. These struggles also continue to remind us of the communist parties in the state abandoning its prior pledge to nationalize plantations and make lands available to the landless, including the plantation Dalits.

In other words, their struggle implies a simultaneous process of material improvement and collective empowerment. It also implies continuity and change – continuity of Muthanga and Chengara but change in terms of strategies. In fact, the very harvesting of paddy was transformed into a festival of all. It is the revolutionary struggles that appear to integrate on their own into the state, a state that historically was founded by renaissance movements, which was also a process of right-making and claim-making as state-making. Harvest celebrations take on great significance in states like Kerala. For instance, the Onam festival in Kerala is celebrated as a harvest festival, and it is important to keep in mind that, as described in Chapter 3, the Adivasis chose the timing of their protest in 2001 to expressly remind the public that the starving Adivasis were outside of the mainstream. Janu, at one stage, elaborated to this author what she had stated in public: '… who wants to be part of the mainstream? We don't want. It is the mainstream which is corrupt, casteist, and more than that undemocratic to the struggles of the marginalized.'[2] It goes well with Rancière, for whom the foundation of political is dissensus. It also implies that the Onam festival which is supposed to be 'universal' is reduced to the already counted mainstream, erasing the true meaning of the political. Reclaiming the political has become the subaltern agenda, as for ever. In the event of further neglect, Muthanga would inevitably occur.

Given that land remains the single most important source of subaltern livelihood and power, subalterns will continue to claim it. Arippa thus communicates messages regarding not only the past but also the potential for future harvests and the organizations that may carry out this in a joyous manner. Occupy Chengara, which came in between, was equally imaginative and strategic as many of the occupants were able to transform small pieces of land into livelihood plots, and the state was also reshaped while responding to such transformations: a process of right-making as state-making. This process is further enhanced by large number of struggles and protests carried out by marginalized communities – such as traditional workers (coir, cashew), fisherfolks, and so on – who all could become critical nodes in the transverse solidarity for claim-making/right-making.

While discussing the 'agrarian question', Lenin (1972) took a compelling stance that it becomes our responsibility to encourage the small farmer. That took a different turn in Kerala, where the middle class emerged from the castes that benefited from land reforms – in particular, the Ezhavas and Christians – who, with the caste Hindus, still own land but through absentee landlordism rather than as those who till the soil. As we asked earlier, how does one explain the Dalit land struggles in Kerala, despite decades of land reform right-making/state-making experiments? (see Chapter 6). Furthermore, in Kerala's plantations, ownership remained concentrated, notably on over-acquired lands owned by pan-Indian capital, while in the midlands both landlessness and reverse tenancy persisted. Land inequality has significantly reduced in Kerala since the state-driven reforms while this has increased at the national level. However, landlessness still persists among the Dalit and Adivasi population. Dalits and other backward populations that engage in lease farming are also denied access to finance because the larger institutional framework has not changed in their favour; the mainstream left turned a blind eye to the contemporary dimensions of caste, property relations, and politics proper, leaving the mainstream to celebrate Onam festivals with pomp and pleasure while compelling the marginalized to select the same day for their protracted resistance, they assert. It implies that the ecospatial content in such struggles is not meant for any kind of unilateral ecospatial inclusion per se, but an equal footing with the rest: an egalitarian and ethical existence.

As previously indicated, there has been a sharp drop in the proportion of landless households in Kerala, from 15 per cent in 1971 to 4 per cent in 2003. In contrast, many other states, including Gujarat and Rajastan, have seen an increase in the number of landless households. However, given that Kerala strives for higher levels of egalitarian existence, the state cannot be complacent about the low rate of landlessness in the state. This suggests that the state's experience with land reforms should not be over; if it has only implemented them in non-plantation areas up to this point, which is essentially one of their downsides, it is time to expand them to include plantation areas as well. According to information provided by the government, large plantation businesses that handle more than 50 acres each are in control of more than 2 lakh acres. Plantations continue to benefit from the ceiling provision, but the majority of their lease agreements have expired, and in many cases, planters themselves encroach on public areas.

It is worth noting that in response to the writ petition filed by International Union of Food and Agricultural Workers, Paschim Banga Khet Majoor Samity, and other tea garden workers' collectives, the Supreme Court appointed a one-man committee headed by Justice Abhay Manohar Sapre to look into the issues of payment and other relief packages to the tea garden workers across Assam, Tamil Nadu, West Bengal, and Kerala. The Sapre committee found that a total of INR 650 crores as dues payable to 28,556 workers of 25 tea gardens in Assam alsone; it also includes 15 gardens owned by the Assam government-owned Assam Tea Company Limited (see *India Today* 2023). Within the context of Kerala, the Sapre committee has had several rounds of discussions with the authorities and it appears that crores of rupees are due to the workers in the abandoned estates. The Sapre committee calculated an estimated figure of INR 49 crores in due to the workers of the abandoned estates in the state, of which around 28 crores have been admitted by the plantations themselves. While this amount has been paid by them, it is important to realize the remaining amount, for which active government action is required.

It is also worth noting that climage change and natural disasters had differential effects: it is the marginalized who become the major victims, an aspect that the state should take into account when any viable rehabilitation programme is undertaken. For the marginalized people of Kerala, for instance, the floods of 2018 and 2019, notably the landslides in Kavalappara (Malappuram) and Puthumala (Wayanad), were already bloody disasters that occurred back-to-back, and the Pettimudi tragedy in the Idukki district, a landslip that took place on 6 August 2020 during severe flooding, was tragic. The majority of the 70 people who perished when their line homes (plantation *layams*) were washed away were fifth- or sixth-generation plantation Dalits (Raman 2020). It is true that the Pinarayi Vijayan led government (2016–) played a historical role in managing various natural calamities in the state such as floods, Nipah (2018, 2019, 2021), and Ockhi (2017). However, no systematic risk transfer mechanism has so far been introduced by the state despite the fact that climate change has become a relaity and it is the poor who bear the brunt the most.

Theme 2: Intersectionality, Feminism, and Power

The Dalit feminist presence in Kerala's radical uprisings and other livelihood–environment struggles is also notable, and it is a subject that has not yet been discussed, save a few, in Kerala's otherwise rich research repertoire. Three well-known instances are Occupy Muthanga, Occupy Chengara, and particularly Occupy Munnar, although the anti-Cola protests in Plachimada were also an admirable experience. It was common to see Muslim women with children in both the Chaliyar/Mavoor and anti-endosulphan struggles. The Dalit woman was the main source of power in almost all of these conflicts, whether she was acting as the leader, as in the case of Muthanga and Munnar, or playing second fiddle. While Dalit women Gomati Sebastian and Lisy Sunny, sixth-generation plantation workers, led the women multitude/Dalit feminitude in Munnar, often to the spatial exclusion of male and male-led trade unions, Adivasi woman C.K. Janu led it in Muthanga, while another Adivasi woman named Mayilamma played a critical role in Plachimada. A young Dalit woman in her twenties, named Sabeena Prakkanam, was made to play second fiddle in Chengara, thanks to the patriarchal leaderhip of the struggle, despite the fact that she was the one who played a critical role in the movement. Prakkanam herself narrated several instances of patriarchal forms of domination within the movement while the struggles were going on (Prakkanam 2013), to the effect of marginalizing the core values of the struggle. It ought to serve as a lesson to the major political parties in the state, which have been dubbed the pinnacle of male culture in the past.

The concepts of feminism and intersectionality remained key components in almost all of these conflicts. It is equally crucial to recognize the meritorious work done by the media in bringing awareness of some of these conflicts to a wider audience, though the same media was not keen on highlighting the political importance of the female textile shop employees engaged in a 'right to sit struggle', which has been successful in the state! In Kerala, a huge proportion of elderly Dalits, especially Dalit women, are forced to work out of economic necessity and poverty. This reveals the functioning of caste elitism in which the Dalits are forced to toil in the labour market while the rest are placed in a better situation by the late years of lives.[3]

Intersectionality scholars take seriously not only the presence of consciousness and 'domination-subordination' but also the very expression of consciousness, representation, and identity, which cannot be limited to any type of implicit consciousness generated in autonomous domains and is frequently expressed in terms of caste, gender, and religion. It is specifically the social reproduction of labour and the precariousness of their daily existence, which are intersectionally sensitive to the historical roots of divisions of caste and gender, that trigger their protest and struggles, according to their own admission, and thus without elitist or external mediation. Additionally, they are the ones who decide to criticize the exact ways in which they are misrepresented and mis-organized and to emphasize the need for them to self-organize themselves (see Raman 2020). This self-organization by the misorganized serves as the foundation for opposing the constituted hegemony and creating a new subject position from which they could and did speak. The state's mainstream politics paid little attention to understanding identity politics or treating it as a new source of instrument for solving problems, despite the fact that it was one of the things that gave the struggles and revolts their strength. As the earliest feminist scholars also failed to engage with the question of caste and gender in terms of intersectionality of power relations, it becomes all the more important to integrate the idea of ecospatiality in everyday forms of state–civil society negotiations.

Theme 3: Divided Counter-publics: Workers versus Communities

In most of the struggles explored in this book, the workers and their organizations – the trade unions and their political parties – were, by and large, opposed to the struggles, essentially on the ground that such struggles led to further loss of jobs. In most cases, the workers and their unions negotiated between jobs of the few and the sustainability and livelihood of the many, and they failed to take a non-partisan approach. They not only failed to address the question of erosion in the environment as part of global developmentalism but also failed to extend their support to their local communities, who, in turn, struggled for livelihood and ecological sustainability. The very decline of the labour movement should also be attributed to their own pseudo-class position and its attitude to the rising struggles led by the emerging agencies, which, in fact, should have been supported by the labour unions to form some kind of social unionism and collectively leverage social power. However, it did not take place except in the case of Chaliyar, where the industrial workers and their unions, while continuing their own struggles against the management, also supported, though at a later stage, the struggles against environmental pollution. When asked about the complexities that could emerge out of the juxtaposition of both the struggles, environmental issues, and workers' protests, A. Vasu, the Maoist-turned-human-rights-activist, shared the feeling that it was a time of self-conflict. However, almost a decade later, on 16 November 1997, a mass public convention was organized by the Chaliyar Malineekarana Virudha Samithi. In the same convention, GROW representatives, especially A. Vasu and Moyeen Bappu, were present and they declared that if the management failed to resolve the pollution-related issues, they would also join the protesting masses and would fight for the closure of the company. This was in fact a historical moment where one would find a convergence of environmental and workers' struggles for sustainable forms of existence. This was a particular moment in Kerala's trade union history, with workers expressing high levels of political-ecological consciousness. The trade unions, in fact, lost a golden opportunity to reimagine themselves in many other contexts, such as Chengara, Plachimada, and Munnar, in particular. This is not without recognizing the fact that the immediate livelihood challenge makes historical consciousness a temporal myth.

A few examples are worth citing. Coca-Cola employed hardly 30 workers, 20 permanent and the remaining on contract, whereas Grasim in Mavoor employed thousands of workers, both men and women. Those employed as permanent workers were recruited from the local regions and also faraway places. In the case of Chengara, plantations had both permanent and contractual workers, mainly men, the descendants of historically marginalized communities. The workers and those who were part of the struggles were from the same communities, by and large, in terms of their social origins. When the anti-Cola struggle gathered momentum, the first resistance came from the workers, which was, in fact, expected. There was no common platform to discuss the larger issues. Workers formed their own unions and argued that the company should not be closed as it was a question of their livelihood. In other words, livelihood was a common issue as relevant for the anti-Cola agitators and the anti-agitators.

While both positions help the state to accelerate its process of right-making, only a philosophical understanding of social conflicts would help us resolve such issues. When there is a social conflict between the larger sustainability of the system (local in this context) and the immediate livelihood, a position in favour of the former would be desirable, assuming that the state would come forward with alternative livelihood options. There should be a state-form that should take care of the livelihood requirements of the agitators and the anti-agitators, though priority should also be given to those subaltern of subalterns. In the case of Plachimada, the indigenous people argued that it was not their livelihood that alone is at stake but also the larger sustainability of the local village system. A comprehensive compensatory package could have solved the issue to a large extent – a compensation for the villagers and the employees. Though the compensation for the former was discussed at various levels, the central government turned a blind eye to the same, a version of procrastination politics that has been playing out, as explained earlier (Chapter 4).

Theme 4: Identities, Violence, and Resistance

The Marxists' stance on 'state' has typically focused on how repressive it is. International experiences from the past and present have also supported this. Even in India's West Bengal state, where protestors and demonstrators clashed with the police, the Singur Krishi Jomi Raksha Committee (Committee to Save the Farmland of Singur) was put down by force (Nielsen 2008; Roy 2014: 160–167).[4] The state oppression was also shaped by the contours of the struggles, as they were different for different struggles. Additionally, Kerala has a different political history, as evidenced by police brutality against activists, particularly those who were radical Marxists. In the narrated fights, if one was more radical in nature, the other was more Gandhian. If Muthanga was catastrophic – in which a police officer and an Adivasi were killed – Chengara was unharmed, creating the framework for ongoing discussion and negotiation between the communities and the government. When the Congress-led state used police force to repress Muthanga in Kerala, state oppression was brutal. If the High Court had not made a wise decision, the conflict in Chengara when the left was ruling would have escalated into violence. The remaining conflicts in Chaliyar, Plachimada, Kasaragod, and Munnar were largely non-violent, leaving little room for police intervention; even when they did, the amount of violence was minimal.

Even after the horrific events in Muthanga and the local-level violence against Plachimada, there were numerous livelihood and environmental movements that occurred in the state. The struggles led by Dalit leaders in varying contexts particularly by highlighting the precarious livelihood conditions in the state's Dalit colonies, which was also a critique of the Kerala model of development, were instrumental in awakening the marginalized. The struggles that arose in February 1999 against the construction of 11KV electric lines across the Sachivotham colony, making Sreedharan the state's first Dalit martyr, were also historic in nature.[5] These activities were suppressed by the armed police during the neoliberal phase, as in the case of the Kathikudam struggles. A local businessman founded the Nita Jalatin in the early 1980s to make Ocin, which was then exported. Animal carcass bones and hydrochloric acid are the primary raw materials used. Similar to the accusations made against Mavoor, the Kathikudam villagers started their struggle by claiming that the Chalakudi river was contaminated by the factory's effluents (Binoy 2014). The people began their fight because the factory wastes contained nickel, cadmium, and other extremely carcinogenic elements, the same reason that forced Coca-Cola to leave the state. The police, at the Congress' direction, put an end to this.[6] Police attitude against Plachimada and Chengara protestors was a component of various forms of state persecution. The Pombilai Orumai was possibly the only conflict in which police involvement was minimal due to its uniqueness in having only female participants who were waging democratically acceptable struggles (Raman 2015).

In contrast to other Indian states, in Kerala explicit ways of caste discrimination is considerably less. Nevertheless, the state is not free from subtle forms of caste hierarchy and unequal social status, which in turn blocks the building up of any critical public sphere. This generates a counter-publics as a critique of Habermas (1977) and as a possible option for subalterns. So long as the power is skewed and reproduces in everyday hegemonic processes, it invariably generates new counter-politics by making use of new symbols and instruments. Identity politics offers a new means of social expression for them, both as strategy and tactics. It is by sharpening their identities that they unravel their culture, history, and pathways for the future; no authority could easily ignore such strategies, partly due to the fact that the authorities themselves are constituted and hegemonized by their own identities. Strategies should primarily be evaluated based on which hegemony the marginalized social sections fight against or oppose and not which symbols they employ or how they are shared and or how they come together to form a solidarity. So long as the struggle was against the hegemonic forces and also as part of negotiating with a social democratic state, the struggles were justified and legitimized. This may challenge the mainstream notion of the existing power relations. This notion of counter-mainstream was articulated by challenging the very foundations of mainstream and its constituents, often reinforced by caste elitism. Apart from land ownership and control, a stress needs to be placed upon social elements and other non-land indicators of development to assess the mobility and social position of Adivasis in Kerala.

Although Kerala has attained an exceptional achievement in the educational sector, there are stark discontinuities and disjunctures between various communities, especially among Adivasis. Kerala shows an excellent performance in the field of education, in terms of gross enrolment ratio, low drop-out rates, participation in the higher education sector, and so on. The average annual drop-out rate in the secondary level was only 9.14 in Kerala while the same was almost double (17.87) at the national level in the year 2019.[7] The general education department studies show that out of the 139,916 students who dropped out in the last 10 years in the state, 19,000 students belonged to the ST category. Confronted with multidirectional exclusions and heterogenous layers of marginalization, such as the unequal access to educational services, relativelyinaccessible health facilities, and land poverty, Adivasis stand at the back of the emerging economies in Kerala. Students are found to experience social exclusion on a variety of levels, in addition to having low levels of livelihood and economic status. Despite the alarmingly high rate of student suicides among Dalits and economically disadvantaged groups in the premier institutions in India,[8] Kerala is largely free of these problems. However, they encounter numerous social limitations on campus and in the workplace. State-level planning would also have to be reformulated to capture these processes. The planning process must be designed in such a way that it is ecospatial to the extent of bringing structural transformation in terms of economic, ecological, place-space dynamics, and power relations of the future generations. To capture such dynamics, the planning process should ensure that it is intersectoral, intersectional, and ecospatial in an all-encompassing manner with a temporally framed perspective. A few of the left initiatives are commentable: under 'Unnathi' overseas-education assistance scheme of the Department of SC/ST Development, students get financial support for studying abroad, they are given particular attention in foreign recruitment, and so on. As and when the jobseekers from Dalit/subaltern backgrounds enter the labor market, new modes of inclusion needs to be imagined and practised, including affirmative actions in private and state-aided institutions.

The study on ecospatial struggles and movements in Kerala, often embedded in identity politics against exclusion, is relevant at various levels in the larger context of the Global South. First, the movements and events that have been taking place in Kerala in the last 50 or 60 years remind us of the Landless Workers' Movement in Brazil and Zapatista/Chiapas in Mexico, all assertions of land rights. Equally powerful and comparable are the other Latin American–African resistance movements, such as those in Buen Vivir (Ecuador), Cochabamba (Bolivia), and Ogoni (Nigeria), which, in turn, attribute new and decolonized meanings to land rights, autonomy, food, water, environmental sovereignty, and identities. Further, the mode of resistance that has been employed in Kerala has several commonalities with the struggles in the Global South, including the way in which the struggles invoke iconic symbols of the history of resistance. For instance, Hugo Chevoz was successful in invoking Bolivarianism – the new socialist and pan-South American vision named after Simon Bolivar, the South American revolutionary leader who fought against Spanish colonial rule and established pan-Columbia (Spanakos 2011: 14); though not on such a massive scale, the Kerala Dalits too have had to invoke historic symbols, such as Ayyankali, who organized the first agrarian struggle in the state in 1907 by refusing to till the land owned by caste Hindu feudal lords unless they admitted Dalit children in their schools. In spite of the fact that the Maoist sections in Kerala articulated their agenda in the name of Ayyankalipada on several occasions, it was not sustained, as the very mode of resistance could not be mainstreamed or grounded democratically. Instead, Ambedkarism has had a lasting impact on the state across cultures, as Ambedkar, another great visionary architect of the Indian constitution, was a leading source of new forms of resistance, often alongside or against the non-violent means of Gandhi.

Kerala seems to be unique with respect to two major contrasting experiences: the livelihood–environmental continuum and the interface between the class-privileging left and the identity-driven subalterns with the multiple layers of power relations in the way of accessing and sustaining livelihood–environmental resources. As in the case of many other movements in the Global South, the symbols of resistance adopted in Kerala by the subalterns were devoid of mainstream Marxist markers; instead, the images adopted were those of social reformers, often in a strategic invocation of identity and shared values. Yet, as opposed to the traditional male- and trade-unionist-dominated movements, the main body of the subaltern resistance in the contemporary context consisted of women and children offering fresh meanings of resistance, agency, and identity. This also raises questions of ideology and practice, apart from agency and structure and how power relations are embedded and enmeshed, an aspect of agential coalescence, often overlooked by political ecology scholarship on the Global South. This also reinforces the necessity for transnational subaltern activism as has been happening in the case of Indian diaspora activism.[9] Such events have further accentuated the ambiguity in the role of the state and the strategic and contingent alliances in political-ecology-identity activism; it also necessitates an exploration of the reasons why Kerala is special in terms of such popular livelihood–environmental-oriented protests from below.

Finally, these movements in Kerala allow us to see a new and emerging notion of modernity with socialist perspectives, more specifically, ecospatiality, as subaltern modernity (Raman 2017). Far from signifying a 'lost modernity' (see Woodside 2006), they actually point to a vibrant future, leading to the creation of an ethical humanity, keeping history moving, although in an 'incomplete' fashion as in Europe (Habermas 1997). The history of modernity as a collective project is no longer in limbo in this part of the world, as is evident from the engagement with livelihood and environmental movements inviting debates on and a rearticulating of received knowledge and practices in the Global South. The chapters that followed thus narrated these movements, simultaneously challenging multiple authorities – the state, corporate capital, mainstream trade unions, and the legal regime, all constitutive of structure authorities – in order to legitimize the 'right to have rights' (Arendt 1951: 298) and contribute to resistance as modernity and thereby strengthen right-making/state-making processes.[10]

Theme 5: Problematizing Postcolonial Marxist Scholarship

First, the narratives made so far addresses the unspeakability/unrepresentability of the subalterns and reinforces their ability to organize and speak for themselves through insights from intersecting life-world experiences. They offer a response to the Spivakian challenge of 'can the subaltern speak?' and reaffirm that the subaltern as a Dalit can speak and as female is no longer in the shadow. Second, the strategies of dissent, which occur at two levels: First, as self-organizing, by splitting away from the non-representational and hegemonic organizational forms refusing to comply with the traditional Marxist understanding that workers and the subalterns cannot represent themselves but are to be represented. Second, the women workers dared the male-led trade unions and the patriarchal structures of accumulation. In this process of political assertion by the workers, they challenged both the male-led trade unions as well as the state and its apparatus. Third, enabling a new consciousness of the political subject's consciousness of their own acts of resistance and unleashing their own agency to challenge not only the management but also the ways in which hegemonic powers operate, such as the state and male-led trade unions. This advances intersectionality and postcolonial organization theory, because class, caste, and gender overlap such that women in revolt are subjected to multiple deprivation conditions (Omvedt 1993; Munshi 2019; Roy 2016). Dalit women have to engage with both the politics of recognition and the politics of equality along with economic reproduction, aspects of Dalit feminism and subaltern identity that require focused attention in both intersectionality and postcolonial critical scholarship. This helps us to provide an integrated narrative of the intersectionality of subaltern castes and communities, labour processes, and postcolonial state formation. The political power of Pombilai Orumai, which has weakened when compared to the days of their struggle, points towards the need for rethinking wider politics, along the lines of transverse solidarity. Organizations such as Kerala Pulaya MahaSabha (KPMS), Adivasi Gotra Maha Sabha (AGMS), and Dalit Human Rights Movement (DHRM), Indigenous People Collective, Adivasi Dalit Munnetta Samithi (ADMS), and so on, carry the political potential to take forward the subaltern struggles through transverse solidarities in Kerala.

The question of consciousness, which is more autonomous in nature in postcolonial scholarship, warrants scrutiny. Community consciousness, as Chatterjee (1993: 167) would argue, is not an alliance forged from the outside, but a unifying force, where 'the bonds of solidarity that tie them together already exist. Collective action does not flow from the contract among individuals; rather individual identities themselves are derived from membership in a community'. It is not sufficient for postcolonial scholars to mediate with resistance power by engaging with culture and cultural expressions – images and signs or through notions such as 'mimicry' and 'ambivalence' (see Bhabha:1984) – but with the actual material domains of everyday life as both caste-life and life as resistance; they are not dogmatic or Marxist economistic.

Identity questions and the use of identities as a weapon have not yet found recognition among communists. Rather than deterring communities from realizing their identities, the left should view caste/race/ethnicity as a binding factor rather than a barrier. Across the world, in peasant and working-class history, there are many instances of a community consciousness shaped by religion and caste. In England, for example, religious idioms became manifestations of the consciousness of the new class of workers, as Thompson (1963) has so beautifully described. Mapilla peasants of Malabar fought against feudalism and imperialism with a special sense of honour and solidarity in their anti-feudal and anti-imperialistic struggle. The early protest movements among the working class in Thiruvithamkur were also articulated through the ideology of caste (see Kannan 1987); Phule and Lohia's ideas could also be filtered in this way, as could Ambedkar's (see Roy 2017; Jaffrelot 2008; Ambedkar 1936). While debating the national question in Kerala, E.M.S. Namboodirippad (1952) himself had acknowledged that caste organisztions aided the political organisations in building up the structural forms. As many would argue (see

Kappikkadu 2017a; Kochu 2022; Salimkumar 2020a), identity reductionism is not what the subalterns are doing, but rather a strategy they are deploying to challenge oppressions and exploitation effectively, a point the left forces should acknowledge. This becomes all the more strategic as and when the left state, with its class reductionist strategies, find barriers in advancing the subaltern rights for a decent living. It embodies a reflexive global epistemology – on equal terms – when it comes to challenging oppressive historical legacies. What is important to recognize is that there is no 'lost cause' and 'if any lost cause can ever really be lost' (Said 2000: 428). Further, they are also cautious not to reify primordial identities such as caste/religion while advancing global solidarities.

At the end of the day, what multitudes would aspire is human emancipation and not merely the narrowly understood political emancipation (see Marx 1978 [1848]). Both the inability to comprehend identities and the lack of a state-making/right-naking process are reflected in the current instability and chaos in Manipur. It is not how the subalterns view their identities and the past that influences future power dynamics, but their economic positions and living conditions under the constantly evolving modalities of hegemonic power in India – primarily, the Hindutva-corporate regime – and how best the demos could challenge the same by making the state of their own and representing the whole society. This would imply the right-making/state-making process and the circuits become complete as and when the subalterns first claim the state and then represent the whole. As long as the corporate class interests remain dominant, everyday state conscientization and constructing an imaginative civil society–state synergy will be a task. Therefore, more sustainable political economic solutions are not something that is set in stone but rather something that evolves as voices of the transverse solidarity of precarious forms of existence from below are heard, raised, and enables alternatives.

Much as in the case of the Paris Commune, the failure/success of the revolts – 'antisystemic movements' (Wallerstein 2002) or 'movement of movements' (Mertes 2004) – does not lend itself to an easy interpretation. While the idea of the commune was praised by Marx and Lenin, they saw its failure as an inability to install yet another effective state. This failure, for both Marx and Lenin, is something that could have been corrected by an official communist party with durability. In contrast to this typically Marxist position, Badiou (1998, 2003) resists seeing it as a failure and instead sees it as a structural gap between true political invention and the state. In the post-Muthanga phase or in the case of the Pombilai Orumai,[11] many of the Adivasis and Dalits consider themselves with the thought that they at least have an organization of their own/an agency of their own, even if they do not have land of their own, and even if they do not have a house of their own – yet another post-evental declaration. When its meaning, or what Badiou calls the truth-event, transcends time and space, it becomes a universal principle (2004). The newly emerged agency questions and puts on trial not only the state (patriarchal) structures but also the communist structure authorities; it is how it grows beyond the limits of communist precepts as conceived and practised in contemporary times. Universal affirmation and a just society become a reality through subverting the concentrated wealth and power (see Piketty 2020) and by dismantling of the established notions of structure and agency. Yet a word of caution is needed when celebrating the poststructuralist/postmodernist position – whether it is that of Badiou, Hardt, and Negri, or Žižek.

The post-Marxist perspective is helpful in understanding Kerala's landscape of struggles, but it is also important to part ways with it as none of the struggles is supportive of the position that the state is not important for them in shaping their own future or a future state. Rather than engaging with mainstream political parties and male-led unions, the communities in struggle called for the state to intervene democratically and ethically and imagine right-making/state-making possible. Some of the struggles even challenged the mainstream ruling and opposition trade unions. The autonomy of the political – or the politics proper of the marginalized – was what sparked the struggles, which were supported by a number of civil society groups. The state was important to them since they were in negotiations with it, thus challenging the irrelevance of the state as envisioned by postmodern/post-structuralist Marxists become problematic. From Aristotle to Marx, the meaning of state has been constantly contested and rearticulated. However, the graduated social democratic state understood as potentiality remains, at least to this author. As the state exists in its potentiality and responds to the livelihood and environmental requirements of society, the state gets legitimized for its good reasoning. A social democratic route for change was not ruled out by Marx; a Marxist state like Kerala has been rich in demonstrating this ever since the renaissance struggles in general and in the post-independence state in particular.

Theme 6: Post-political? Knowledge Controversies, Democratizing Democracy

By locating the new practices of good governance, or consensus building as post-political conditions (Žižek 1998), Swyngedouw (2007) further argues that this post-political condition forecloses potential struggles for alternative political futures and proclaims the end of meaningful dispute about society as the 'end of politics'. However, this approach leads us to an impasse through a failure to incorporate the ever present struggles and state–civil society synergy, which admittedly remains contested as an idea and practice (see Cohen and Arato 1994; Gellner 1991; Gramsci 1971; Wui and Lopez 1997), with actual empirical examples countering some of the post-political claims. It is specifically in this context that I bring in a state and its governance not as 'governance-beyond-the-state' (Swyngedouw 2005), as post-political critics argue, but a state that not only engages with but also articulates practices of alternative politics and development: a key element in the right-making/state-making exercise.

A state becomes modern when it erases spaces of exclusion. It is by contesting from below – through ecospatial imaginations and struggles – that the subaltern carves out spaces of inclusion, whether the state was run by the organized left or the right. The striking marker of the struggles and the movements in the state, as in the colonial days of the region and contemporary times of the Global South, were not confined to their resolution of biological existence alone. They were the outcomes of sustained interest in politics: politics of living, representation, and environmental justce. This book does not tell us that the ethical left would build up an ethical state brick by brick, but what it does tell us is that subaltern ethicality would continue to come to the limelight to light up the global. No hegemonic force, howsoever powerful, could ignore the sparks of hope, both in the West and the Global South. The World Social Forum debate on 27 January 2005 provides us additional insights into our understanding of the situational state. In 'Can we change the world without taking power? The only way to find out is to do it', Holloway (Holloway and Callinicos 2005) explores further, and for him, becoming part of the state is not productive for the social movements advocating social liberation. Callinicos (2005), who engages with Holloway, makes it explicit that the process of self-emancipation of the collectives, on which both of them agree, would require us 'to confront and overthrow the existing state and replacing it with a radically different form of state power'. This would imply the 'oppressed and exploited' break the existing state and, in the process of doing so, create imaginatively new and democratic forms of power and managing society for themselves.[12]

If the state continues to bypass the marginalized, particularly in the context of emerging knowledge economies and digital domains, they will continue to contest the state and the state apparatus by sharpening their identities – identities and ideologies as strategies of rights assertion – as has been historically done on various occasions. While it is true that Kerala is unique, and since the left forces have been in power, Kerala's exceptionality has been even more apparent. So long as the subalterns claim the state with the greatest potential and turn it into reality in a way that allows them to serve as a representative of the greater society, the ecospatial struggles from below will continue unabated. It is long past time for the state to reassure the public that it is not enough for the state to achieve higher growth, but that an increasing share of every additional growth goes towards bringing the poor up to par, thereby strengthening an egalitarian state form. At that point, the right-making/state-making process will be complete.

Yet another challenge in everyday contestation politics is centred around knowledge controversies. In the case of the endosulfan movement, there is a knowledge controversy, which still remains unsettled. The landscape of the protest site has become complex. A 'dollar crop', as described by the State Planning Board,[13] contrary to intentions, made 'life cheaper than cashew'. More than two decades of aerial spraying of endosulfan, initially a state-driven development project, turned into an endosulfan tragedy, with a cost in terms of human lives and making life worse than death. However, it is equally important not to ignore the recently evolved knowledge controversies associated with struggles, though the larger middle-class public sphere in the state continued to ignore these aspects, save for a few.

Some of the earlier commissions also share some of these perspectives (see Dubey 2003; Mayee 2006). What this author would like to mention is that it is important for the state to engage with such knowledge controversies, and if it ended up being an 'endosulfan 'emocracy' – a culture of 'feelings matter more than reason'[14] (also see Raman 2021) – the state, led by the UDF and the LDF, was to blame because a lot of money was given out in the name of endosulfan victims. The poorest social groups received a considerable portion of this money, while the bigger social structures incurred significant costs that could have been avoided. The money invested on endosulfan may have also been used to improve society's overall health.

The knowledge controvery is not something confined to endosulfan alone. As we have seen earlier, this has always been a subject of contestation as in the case of other struggles. Equally significant is the fact that, in the broader context of politics proper, marginalizing such scientific findings in a state like Kerala, with its high literacy and past science movements, would be a costly and irrational mode of dealing with struggles. One wonders whether the governements have made the case of endsulfan a dogmatic tool of populism. But the question remains if this is done at the expense of scientiifc knowledge dissemination.

While scientific methods are the best way to learn about this, we should also acknowledge that there are other knowledge-gathering techniques that have the potential to enlighten humanity. Despite the lack of scientific proof linking endosulfan to specific diseases, the protest itself revealed how severely the state's local communities were suffering from a lack of access to healthcare (Sreekumar and Prathapan 2021). Furthermore, it is precisely these health disadvantages and sufferings that encourage the marginalized to adopt new strategies for lobbying the government and big businesses. This is not to come to a dead end to the question of 'whether scientific knowledge represents things in the world as they really are', particularly in the posthumanist paradigm (see Barad 2007), but to engage with the question incessantly, and thereby arrive at a democratically and ethically sustainable position.

Theme 7: *Ecospatiality* in the Making; State-Making Incomplete?

In his *Gundrisse*,[15] the young Marx talked about the effective state and the social democratic path to the welfare state. While elaborating on the critical features of civil society, Gramsci too was more vocal on the 'integral state', a state that has been evolved through the processes of the dominant groups under capitalism, constructing an 'organic passage from the other classes (dominant) into their own' (1971: 260), a process of 'internal articulation and condensation of social relations within a given state form' (Thomas 2009: 27–28, 140, 144). The state thus evolved will be in consensus with the larger social sections of civil society through discourses, legal institutions, and technologies (Thomas 2009: 144), but need not be with the marginalized social sections, who would also desire to be part of the larger civil society. Nehru and Ambedkar's ideas of a redistributive state and state socialism were more specific in their conception of the government's democratic responsibility. Right-making as state-making has been slowly forming despite some of the struggles that have taken place in the state, which have only been partially successful. In the event the right-making as state-making and the vice versa process fails, it will create yet another conscientization process for both the state and the subalterns, as the latter would also have to shift their demands strategically. Essentially, they should identify and claim enlightened forms of ecospatial existence, which will require an egalitarian, ethical state and a community-oriented big push for equal opportunity and social justice.[16] While each of the ecospatial sites of resistance demanding their fulfilment of their rights has the potential to bring in subaltern modernity, it would be the combined force of the various ecospatial struggles that would usher in the new ways of life . The lack of trasnverse solidarity across these marginalized groups may even result in the loss of what the subalterns have already gained through their historical struggles. An ecospatial resistance, with its overt realistic manifestations of ecospatiality advancing egalitarian forms of existence under the moral leadership of an ethical state, translates into an imagined future – the idea of Kerala for the twenty-first century.

If ecospatiality is a process that needs to be completed, which it undoubtedly is, only the subalterns have the capacity to take on the challenge. In this process, what I did generate was the possibility of what I would call global epistemology: the theory of knowledge that situates subaltern ecospatial struggles/resistance as modernity (see Raman 2017), whether in the Global South or the Global North. The agents involved in the transformation of society – the subalterns, social activists, intellectuals, and the social democratic state – should simultaneously engage with their own histories of renaissance combined with the European enlightenment ideals and thereby generate the global epistemology on equal terms. This process embraces mutually intelligible forms of knowledge, generating a global epistemology which simultaneously translates and transforms knowledge and power of the present on a global scale. If it is the absence of a shared 'social imaginary' between the Global South and the Global North that Fraser (2014) points out as a factor presaging the failure of the scaling up of the public sphere, then would this global epistemology help achieve that target? While the West has failed to generate any internal critique of its atrocities on a range of issues,[17] the Kantian coming of age is increasingly becoming a utopian ideal as it produces multiple reasonings for its discourse power.

There are, however, glimmers of hope in the subaltern emergences from the Global South that will push us to think and act locally in these most critical of times to light up the global towards a more just society for all. Politics done right is all about ethics and fairness. The key is bringing together communities that care about people, the environment, and each other. Politics proper, from a subaltern ecospatial perspective, is this notion of guiding group action away from disparities. Also in this way, the landscape of the protests remains alive, and thereby the politics proper; otherwise you have a society deprived of new sources of energy for change. To put it in another way, it is the interconstitutiveness of power that develops into the source of subaltern ecospatiality that its orientation for broadening the right making/state making practices, which have its own ups and downs. They produce their own agential identities and modernities through such collective ecospatial struggles. They act across a variety of domains that span spaces rather than operating inside a single realm of rights, and, more significantly, they aspire to benefit a community that is larger than just their own personal origins in terms of class, caste, and gender. Right-making state-making process is a democracy project, both individually and collectively, for all the pluralistic agents involved. From a subaltern ecospatial perspective, this notion of shielding collective action from distinctions is what is referred to as politics proper. In other words, it is the interconstitutive subaltern power that gives rise to political ecospatiality, which has the potential to enlighten global movements and political imaginations.

Notes

1. Interview with Laha Gopalan on 21 August 2021 in Pathanamthitta.
2. Janu told this to the author on 3 October 2003 in Thiruvananthapuram.
3. Reports show that 75 per cent of Dalit women and 40 per cent of Dalit men are driven to the labour market out of economic compulsion (James et al. 2013).
4. The left government planned to give 997 acres of farmland to Indian multinational Tata Motors in 2006 so that it could produce the Tata Nano, a reasonably priced Indian counterpart to the 'people's car', the left government's new showpiece vehicle in Singur district, West Bengal. Farmers, social activists, and non-governmental organizations (NGOs) like the Association for the Protection of Democratic Rights (APDR), the Institute for Motivating Self-Employment, the Food First Information and Action Network (FIAN), and the Medha Patkar–led National Alliance of People's Movements (NAPM) worked together to defeat the government's effort; however, neither the government nor the protesters could offer any alternative development projects taking into account the industrial backwardness of the country (see P. Banerjee 2006; S. Banerjee 2007; A. Guha 2015). In the end, the Trinamool Congress won what the Marxists had lost.
5. For some of these struggles, see Gopinath (2022).
6. On 21 July 2013, for example, the police in Kathikudom used violence against roughly 20 locals in the afternoon whereas there were hundreds of them in the morning. It seems that the police were waiting for the larger throng to disperse before concentrating on the agitators.
7. SDG-India Index 2020–2021.

8. As per the federal government's own admission, of the 122 students in central government higher educational institutions who died by suicide between 2014 and 2021, 68 were from SC, ST, and OBC communities (Deeksha 2023).
9. Several examples have been given where states, regional councils or institutions in the West (for example, Seattle and California) were moved by diaspora activism and, in certain cases, caste was treated as a protected category thanks to transnational Dalit activism.
10. This is also the time when we will have to have a wider understanding of right-making/state-making processes. When the Indian government, as part of neoliberal structural adjustment, goes for the privatization of public investments, Kerala's left forces oppose the same; the first Pinarayi Vijayan government, for instance, even acquired HNL and protected the rights of the workers and the state resources when the federal government was about to disinvest the same, and now the company is in the public sector of the Kerala government and was renamed as Kerala Paper Products Limited (KPPL) in 2021.
11. I recently had a thorough conversation with a few Pombilai Orumai struggle participants, including Gomati Sebastian who was a key figure on the then picket line. I am aware that the Pombilai Orumai has enormous potential and, if properly utilized from inside, has the capacity to effect change not only in the plantation society but also in the greater societal arena where gendered identities continue to fight for the right to a decent standard of living. Kerala still has a long way to go before acknowledging the power of women, regardless of whether they work as domestic workers or in any other low-paying industries like hospitals or schools. The moment Kerala's woman power assumes a rights talk attitude, the entire economy and society could come to a standstill for a social transformation; this would also be yet another space for right-making as a state-making process.
12. But this may not be equally true for Petras and Veltmeyer (2007) who argue that the question is the character of capitalism and the sort of state that it produces. Lebowitz (2006) reasserts that the first step in Venezuela was to gain control of the existent state. Yet things did not change much though the hope for change is still alive (see Santos 2002, 2007).
13. See Nair and Sreedharan (2004).
14. Niall Ferguson, Feeling beats truth in our indignant 'emocracy,' *The Times*, 27 January 2019.
15. Marx wrote this series of manuscripts between 1857 and 1861 mostly for his own clarification for his later works, which included *Capital* and *A Contribution*

to the Critique of Political Economy, which were published in 1859 and 1867, respectively.

16. The LIFE (Livelihood, Inclusion and Financial Empowerment) initiative of the first Pinarayi Vijayan-led left government, which focused on providing shelter for the homeless and a means of subsistence for the poor, was launched from an ideological springboard and is currently being rolled out with commitment. Though the state government is successful in delivering houses to the first and second categories, that is, completion of incomplete houses and building houses for those with land, there is a long way to go in the third category of those with no land or house, which has witnessed only meager progress. Availability of land remains a barrier and the government needs to take measures to overcome the same. Yet another imaginative and egalitarian intervention from the left government was the identification of extremely poor households – around 64,000 – and the steps taken for their dignified life; nonetheless, the state has not yet taken a definite position for ensuring that a larger share of each additional growth is allocated to the empowerment of those on the margins.
17. This would include the issues such as waste disposal to the Global South or dealing with the issue of human flows from the periphery to the core, and also the ongoing Russia–Ukraine war.

References

Arendt, H. (1951). *The Origins of Totalitarianism*. New York: Schocken Books.

Badiou, A. (1998). Politics and philosophy (P. Hallward, interviewer). *Angelaki* 3 (3): 113–133.

——— (2003). *Infinite Thought: Truth and the Return to Philosophy*. London: Continuum.

Banerjee, P. (2006). Land acquisition and peasant resistance at Singur. *Economic and Political Weekly* 41 (46): 4718–472.

Banerjee, S. (2007). Peasant hares and capitalist hounds of Singur. *Economic and Political Weekly* 41 (42): 5296–5298.

Barad, K. (2007). *Meeting the Universe Halfway: Quantum Physics and the Entanglement of Matter and Meaning*. Durham: Duke University Press.

Bhabha, H. (1984). Of mimicry and man: The ambivalence of colonial discourse. *Discipleship Special Issue on Psychoanalysis* 28: 125–133.

Binoy, P. (2014). Struggling against gendered precarity in Kathikudam, Kerala. *Economic and Political Weekly* 49 (17): 45–52.

Burns, T., and T. LeMoyne (2001). How environmental movements can be more effective: prioritizing environmental themes in political discourse. *Human Ecological Review* 8 (1): 26–38.

Chatterjee, P. (1993). *The Nation and Its Fragments Colonial and Postcolonial Histories.* Princeton: Princeton University Press.

Deeksha, Johanna (2023). A Dalit scholar's death and Brahmin dominance at India's premier science institute. *Scroll.in*, 24 May. https://scroll.in/article/1049603/a-dalit-scholars-death-and-brahmin-dominance-at-indias-premier-scientific-institute (accessed 24 May 2023).

Dirks, N. (2001). *Castes of Mind: Colonialism and the Making of Modern India.* Princeton: Princeton University Press.

Fraser, N. (2014). Transnationalizing the public sphere: On the legitimacy and efficacy of public opinion in a post-Westphalian world. In: *Transnationalizing the Public Sphere*, ed. N. Fraser and K. Nash, pp. 8–42, 129–156. Cambridge: Polity.

Gellner, E. (1991). Nationalism and politics in Eastern Europe. *New Left Review* 1 (189): 127–134.

Gopinath, I. (2022). *Keralathile Janakeeya Samarangalude Charithram.* Kottayam: DC Books.

Gramsci, A. (1971). *Selections from the Prison Notebooks of Antonio Gramsci.* New York: International Publishers.

Guha, A. (2015). Acting cleverly in the comfort zone of power and visceral resistance: A case of land acquisition in West Bengal, India. *Indian Anthropological Association* 45 (1): 15–29.

Habermas, J. (1997). Modernity: An unfinished project. In *Habermas and the Unfinished Project of Modernity: Critical Essays on the Philosophical Discourse of Modernity*, ed. M.P. d'Entrèves and S. Benhabib, pp. 38–58. Cambridge: MIT Press.

Hall, S. (1995). *When Was 'The Post-Colonial'? Thinking at the Limit.* Milton Park: Routledge.

Holloway, John and Alex Callinicos (2005). Can we change the world without taking power? A debate between John Holloway and Alex Callinicos, World Social Forum, 27 January 2005. *International Socialism* 2 (106). https://www.marxists.org/history/etol/writers/callinicos/2005/xx/holloway.html (accessed 19 May 2022): 2771–2774.

India Today (2023). Assam: SC orders payment of Rs 650 crores to workers of 25 tea gardens in state. 8 February. https://www.indiatodayne.in/assam/story/assam-sc-orders-payment-of-rs-650-crores-to-workers-of-25-tea-gardens-in-state-509343-2023-02-08 (accessed 14 September 2023).

Iwilade, A. (2012). 'Green' or 'red'? Reframing the environmental discourse in Nigeria. *Africa Spectrum* 47 (2/3): 157–166.

James, K., T. Syamala, S. Verma, S. Nair, L. Shylaja, S. Sureshkumar, et al. (2013). *The Status of Elderly in Kerala, 2011.* New York: UNFPA.

Kannan, K.P. (1987). *Of Rural Proletarian Struggles: Mobilization and Organisation of Rural Workers in South-West India*. London: Oxford University Press.

Kappikkadu, S. (2017). *Janathayum Janadhipathyavum*. Kozhikkode: Aman Book.

Kirby, V. (1997). *Telling Flesh*. New York: Routledge.

———, ed. (2017). *What if Culture Was Nature All Along?* Edinburgh: Edinburgh University Press.

Kochu, K.K. (2022). *Dalithan*. Kottayam: DC Books.

Lebowitz, M. (2006). *Build It Now: Socialism for the 21st Century*. New York: Daanish Books.

Lenin, V.I. (1972). *Lenin Collected Works.(Translated by Bernard Isaacs and Joe Fineberg).* Moscow: Progress Publishers.

Lucas, A., and C. Warren (2003). The state, the people and their mediators: The struggle over agrarian law reform in post-new order Indonesia. *Indonesia* 76 (October): 87–126.

Mackay, W. S. S. The Kanan Devans. In *United Planters Association of Southern India*, ed. S.G. Speer, pp. 338–339.

Marx, K. (1978[1848]). On the Jewish question. In *The Marx Engels Reader*, ed. R. Tucker. New York: Norton.

Mertes, T., ed. (2004). *A Movement of Movements: Is Another World Really Possible?* London: Verso.

Munshi, K. (2019). Caste and the Indian economy. *Journal of Economic Literature* 57 (4): 781–834.

Nielsen, K. (2008). Not on our land! Peasant struggle against forced land acquisition in India's West Bengal. In *Rights and Legal Empowerment in Eradicating Poverty*, ed. D. Banik, pp. 217–246. Farnham: Ashgate.

Omvedt, G. (1993). *Reinventing Revolution: New Social Movements in India*. London: M.E. Sharpe.

Petras, J., and H. Veltmeyer (2007). *Multinationals on Trial Foreign Investment Matters*. London: Routledge.

Piketty, T. (2020). *Capital and Ideology*. Cambridge: The Belknap Press of Harvard University Press.

Prakash, G. (1992). Postcolonial criticism and Indian historiography. *Social Text* (31/32): 8–19.

Prakkanam, S. (2013). With O.K. Santhosh and M.B. Manoj. *Chengara Samaravum Ente Jeevithavum*. Kottayam: DC Books.

Quimpo, N.G. (2009). The Philippines: Predatory regime, growing authoritarian features. *Pacific Review* 22 (3): 335–353.

Raman, K. Ravi (2010). *Global Capital and Peripheral Labour: History and Political Economy of Plantation Labour in India*. New York and London: Routledge.

——— (2015). Pombilai Orumai: Sthreesanchayam (Pombilai Orumai: Woman multitude). *Madhyamam Weekly*, 5 October, pp. 12–21.

——— (2017). Subaltern modernity: Kerala, the Eastern theatre of resistance in the Global South. *Sociology* 5 (1): 91–110.

——— (2020). Can the Dalit woman speak: How intersectionality helps advance postcolonial organization scholarship? *Organization* 27 (2): 272–290.

——— (2021). The opposition 'emocracy' exposed: Kerala's landmark left victory. *Monthly Review*, 15 October. https://mronline.org/2021/10/15/the-opposition-emocracy-exposed-keralas-landmark-left-victory/ (accessed 18 May 2023).

——— (2023). Hindutva–corporate regime; Emerging modalities of power. Paper presented at the Global Conference on Caste, Business and Society, 15–16 June, Judge Business School, Cambridge University.

Roy, Animesh (2014). In pursuit of development: land acquisition and the dilution of legal provisions. *Journal of Land and Rural Studies* 2 (1): 149–170.

Roy, Arundhati (2017). *The Doctor and the Saint: The Ambedkar–Gandhi Debate – Caste, Race and Annihilation of Caste*. Chicago: Haymarket Books.

Roy, I. (2016). Equality against hierarchy: Imagining modernity in subaltern India. *Focaal: Journal of Global and Historical Anthropology* 50 (1): 15–30.

Salimkumar, K.M. (2020). Dalit samudayathe tholpikkunnatharu? *Mathrubhumi Weekly*, 19 July, pp. 32–39.

Said, Edward W. (2000). *The Selected Works of Edward Said*. Edited by Bayoumi, M., and A. Rubin. New York: Penguin Random House.

Santos, B. de S., ed. (2007). *Another World Is Possible: Beyond Northern Epistemologies*. London: Verso.

Spanakos, Anthony Peter (2011). Citizen Chavez: The state, social movements and publics. *Latin American Perspectives* 38 (1): 14–27.

Sreekumar, K.M., and K.D. Prathapan (2021). An evidence-based inquiry into the endosulfan tragedy. *Economic and Political Weekly* 56 (41): 45–53.

Swyngedouw, E. (2005). Goverance innovation and the citizen: The Janus face of governance-beyond-the-state. *Urban Studies* 42 (11): 1991–2006.

——— (2007). Impossible 'sustainability' and the postpolitical condition. In *The Sustainable Development Paradox: Urban Political Economy in the United States and Europe*, ed. R. Krueger and D. Gibbs, pp. 13–40. New York: Guilford Press.

Thomas, P.D. (2009). *The Gramscian Moment: Philosophy, Hegemony and Marxism*. Leiden: Brill.

Thompson, E.P. (1963). *The Making of the English Working Class*. London: Penguin Books.

Wallerstein, I. (2002). New revolts against the system. *New Left Review* 18 (November/December): 29–39.

Woodside, A. (2006). *Lost Modernities: China, Vietnam, Korea and the Hazards of World History*. Cambridge: Harvard University Press.

Žižek, Slavoj (1998). A leftist plea for 'Eurocentrism'. *Critical Enquiry* 24 (4): 988–1009.

Index

abuse of power, 19
Achuthamenon-led government, 11–12
Achuthan, A., 134
Achuthanandan, V.S., 88–89, 113, 117, 139, 183, 192
Achuthan Committee (2001), 134–135, 146n8
Adivasi–Dalit activism, in Wayanad, 93
Adivasi Dalit Munnetta Samithi (ADMS), 166, 168, 170, 214
Adivasi Dalit Samara Samithi (ADSS), 16, 67–68, 76, 78, 84–85, 91
  demand for the inclusion of land from Adivasi projects, 90
  occupation of the Muthanga Range of the Wyanad Wildlife Sanctuary, 16
Adivasi Gothra Maha Sabha (AGMS), 68, 86, 88, 94n14, 203, 214
  formation of, 78–82
Adivasis, 9, 12, 158, 169. *See also* indigenous communities
  community ownership of resources, 69
  employed as labourers, 70
  as ethnic minority, 68
  historical processes of marginality among, 69–76
  as hunter-gatherers, 70
  incidence of poverty and starvation, 69
  infant deaths, 69
  Janu-Model (Adivasi mode of struggle), 79
  of Kerala, 67, 68–76
  land rights, 76
  life expectancy of, 68
  of Muthanga, 89, 92
  of Plachimada, 117
  police operation against, 89
  refugee huts, 67
  rehabilitation into farms, 76
  as Scheduled Tribes, 70
  self-employment category, 69
  sequestering of tribal ancestral domains, 70
  serving as slave labour, 69
  staging the *kutilkettysamaram*, 73
  struggles for restoration of alienated lands, 16
  zero landlessness, 69

Adivasi Solidarity Day (18 September), 77
Adivasi Welfare Committee, 88
Advani, L.K., 134
Agamben, Giorgio, 181
agential activism, 5
agential realism, 4, 6
Agrarian Relations Act (1959), 154
Agrarian Relations Bill, 11, 152
agricultural and pastoral castes, 70
aikya Kerala movement (United Kerala Movement), 10
Air Act (1981), 38
Air (Prevention and Control of Pollution) Act (1981), 140
Ajitha, K., 52
alienated lands, restoration of, 68, 73–74, 85
alliance politics, 187
All India Institute of Medical Sciences (AIIMS), 56
All India Trade Union Congress (AITUC), 10, 41, 49, 51, 178
All Kerala Thozhilali Sammelanam (All Kerala Workers' Meet, 1937), 177
Althusser, Louis, 147n20
Ambedkar, B.R., 212
Ambedkar Memorial Model Colony, 159
Amma, Gowri, 51–52, 75, 80
Amma, Leela Kumari, 138–139
anganwadis (courtyard shelters), 164
Animists, 70
Anti-Cola Peoples' Struggle Committee, 104
anti-Cola struggles, in Plachimada, 17, 59, 100, 102, 107, 113, 118, 119, 206
anti-endosulfan campaign, 131, 137
Antony, A.K., 74, 76, 78, 80, 87, 89
Appachan, Poykayil, 22n15
Arab Spring, 1, 14–15, 20n1, 193
Aralam Farm, 46, 90
Arendt's notion of ' right to have rights', 21, 190
Armed Forces Special Powers Act (AFSPA), 63n42
artisan communities, livelihood of, 48
Assam Tea Company Limited, 205
Association for the Protection of Democratic Rights (APDR), 221n4
Association of the Planters of Kerala (APK), 185
Avakasa Sthapana Yatra (Journey for the Assertion of Rights), 77
avarna leaders, 157
avarna women, in Thiruvithamkur, 9
  Channar revolt (*marumarakkal samaram*), 10
  right to cover their body, 9
Ayyankali, 10, 94n15, 159, 212
Azhikode, Sukumar, 57, 79, 115

Babu, Sajith, 164
Bachelard, Gaston, 126, 147n20
backward communities, 3, 9, 14, 157, 159, 202
backward tribes, 70
Badiou, Alain, 176
Balakrishnan, Kodiyeri, 117
bamboo forests, 31, 36
bamboo resource mapping, 32
Banerjee, S.N., 133
Bapu, Moyeen, 52
Barad, K., 4, 6, 142, 201, 219

Bardhan, Ardhendu Bhushan, 113
Basel Convention, ratification by India (1992), 112
Bava, Vadappuram, 10
belonging, politics of, 178
below the poverty line, 69
Benhabib, Seyla, 190
Bharathapuzha river, 101
Bharatiya Janata Party (BJP), 68, 85, 105
Bhaskar, B.R.P., 94n15
Bhopal disaster, 137
bio-accumulation, 143
biochemical oxygen demand (BOD), 43, 62n18
Birlakkoottam Workers' Union, 49
Birlas, in Communist Kerala
  access to softwood and firewood from private properties, 45–46
  agitation against, 37
  agreement with the Kerala government, 32
  arbitration demanding compensation worth INR 4 crores, 46
  bamboo resource mapping, 32–34
  ban on labour strikes, 34
  bonus payments, 51
  Chaliyar river, pollution of, 15, 31, 36–38
  compensation of the workers, 56, 59
  conflicts over
    natural resources, 45–48
    water pollution, 37–45
    workers' rights, 48–56
  conflict with the Forest Department, 34
  conversion of natural forests into eucalyptus jungles, 36
  emergence of the modern factory complex, 34–37
  environmental hazards stemming from the factory's operations, 38, 58
  Environmental Review Committee, 40
  eucalyptus plantations, 46
  exploitation of forests, 36
  extraction of resources at cheap rates, 34
  felling bamboo from additional contract areas (ACAs) in Nilambur valley, 32
  Grasim Industries, 35
  Hindustan Newsprint Limited (HNL), 34
  industrial plantation of eucalyptus, 36
  license to cut bamboo from the reserved forests of the Nilambur valley, 32
  permission to buy private forests from Nilambur Kovilakam, 33
  Ramanilayam Accord, 40
  rayon factory in the Kozhikode district of Kerala, 15
  strategy of closing down its factories, 46
  workers' struggle against, 34
Black Lives Matter movements, 198
block *panchayat*s, 186
Bolivarianism, 212
Bolivia, urban resistance against water colonization, 119
bonus payments, issue of, 51, 56
British Broadcasting Corporation (BBC) Radio, 110

British colonialism, 191
British Empire, 71
British-owned plantation, nationalization of, 202
British policy of collecting land revenue in cash, 93n5
Buen Vivir movement (Ecuador), 211
Bureau of Indian Standards, 40
Butler, J., 7

cadmium, 110–111
Calicut city, 59
Calicut Medical College, 133
Calicut water supply scheme, 36
capitalist depression of the 1930s, 72
carcinogenic pollutants, 38
Cashew Export Promotion Council, 137
cashew plantation. *See also* endosulfan pesticide
mass cultivation, 130
planting on the hills of Kasaragod, 130
supply chain, 128
caste, 3, 6, 8, 10, 17–18, 31n7, 35, 58, 119, 152–154, 157–159, 161, 167–170, 178, 181–185, 190, 198, 201–204, 206–207, 210, 212–215, 221, 222n9
agricultural and pastoral castes, 70
caste Hindus place-space exclusion, practice of, 10
chaturvarna (the four-fold caste order), 4, 9, 14
discrimination-based on, 210
divisions of, 207
land-based, 154
land–caste nexus, 154, 169
National Human Rights Commission for Scheduled Castes, 172n8
Scheduled Castes (SCs), 87, 90, 169
Scheduled Castes & Scheduled Tribes (Prevention of Atrocities) Act (1989), 79. 117
upper caste–landlord–chieftain hegemony, 153
C.D. Mayee Committee (2006), 134
Central Bureau of Investigation (CBI), 87–88
Central Food Laboratory, Kolkata, 105
Central Food Technological Research Institute (CFTRI), Mysore, 105
Central Ground Water Board (CGWB)
Dynamic Groundwater Resource of Kerala (2004), 107
Central Insecticides Board (CIB), 139
Central Insecticides Bureau, 133
Centre for Nature Studies, Thiruvananthapuram, 47
Centre for Science and Environment (CSE), Delhi, 108
Centre for Water Resources Development and Management (CWRDM), Kozhikode, 106
Centre of Indian Trade Unions (CITU), 51, 178
chains of equivalence, 22n11, 178
Chaliyar Action Committee, 53–54, 58
formation of, 42
Chaliyar Action Council, 56
Chaliyar Air and Water Purification Committee, 41
Chaliyar Human Rights Protection Samithi, 42
Chaliyar-Jala-Vayu Shudhikarana Committee. *See* Chaliyar Air and Water Purification Committee

Chaliyar Malineekarana Virudha Samithi, 208
Chaliyar river, pollution of, 15, 31, 36–38, 109, 140
  awareness against Gwalior Rayons', 42
  due to
    carcinogenic pollutants, 38
    discharge of untreated effluents, 42
  presence of mercury in, 44, 58
  public opinion against, 46
  rejuvenation following the closure of the factory, 58
  Save Chaliyar Campaign (2011), 46
  steps to control, 41
Chaliyar Samara Sahaya Samithi (CSSS), 42, 55
Chandanappalli estate, 159–160
Chandy, Oommen, 49, 63n36, 159
Channar revolt (*marumarakkal samaram*), 10
chaturvarna (the four-fold caste order), of the Hindu caste system, 4, 9, 14
The Chemical Free Century: Declaring a Toxic Free Future, 137
Chengara–Arippa Bhoo Samithy, 170
Chengara, case of, 137, 156–158
Chengara monoculture plantation, 169
Chengara Package, 161–163
Cherumars, 70
Chevoz, Hugo, 212
Chiapas, 1, 92, 118, 211
Chief Minister's Relief Fund, 88
child abuse, cases of, 88
Chipko movement of 1970s, 8, 18, 22n14, 119
Christian community, 154
chronic low-dose environmental poisons, cause–effect relationship of, 134
Chungapalli, 37, 40, 43–44, 54
Civil Forum, 78–80
civil society, notion of, 14
civil society groups, 144, 216
civil society organizations, 131–132, 138
civil society-state synergy, 2, 215
Coates, Peter, 59
Coca-Cola, 16, 105
  in Atlanta, Georgia, 100
  commissioned of its factory, 102
  forced out of India, 100
  functioning of, 108
  generation of
    hazardous waste, 112
    wastewater, 112
  Hindustan Coca-Cola Beverages Private Ltd, 116
  licence for the production of Coke, 113
  operations at Plachimada plant, 117
  in Plachimada, 100–102
  Plachimada Coca-Cola Victims' Relief and Compensation Claims Special Tribunal Bill (2011), 117
  political-ecological concerns, 114–118
  under purview of the Hazardous Waste (HW) Rules, 112
  scale of operations, 102
  shut down of plant, 115
  Virudha Janakeeya Samara Samithi (Anti-Cola People's Struggle Committee), 102
Cochabamba movement (Bolivia), 1, 119, 211

Cochin Refineries Ltd, 39
Coffee Stealing Bill, 93n7
Cola Quit India movement, 17, 103, 108, 111–112, 115
colonial plantation
  economies, 155
  managements, 190
Columbian Pacific, 92
coming community, 4
Committee on State Agrarian Relations, 74
Communist Party of India (CPI), 11, 50, 159
  election manifesto of, 202
Communist Party of India (Marxist) (CPI[M]), 42, 68, 113, 139, 143
  position on Occupy Muthanga movement (2003), 68
Communist Party of India (Marxist-Leninist) Red Flag (CPI[ML] Red Flag), 85
  solidarity with the striking Adivasis, 68
community consciousness, 214
community livelihood, violation of, 103
community of nations, 190
Companies Act, 192
compensation
  disputes related to, 117
  financial, 118
  money paid as, 59
  payment of, 117
conflict resolution, process of, 99
'Conflicts over Natural Resources', 44
'Conflicts over Water Pollution', 55
Congress Socialist Party, 11
constituent power, transverse solidarity of, 126
constitutional protection, 85
Coromandel Fertilizers Ltd, in Chennai, Tamil Nadu., 129
corporate and trade union agitation, 181
corporate capitalism, 2, 13, 18–20, 33, 91, 116, 119, 157, 177–178, 189, 202, 213
corporate social responsibility, 106, 188
Covid-19 pandemic, 19, 118
Crenshaw, K., 18, 22n11
cultural identity, 86, 120n3

Dakshin Kanara, 71
Dalit feminism, 194, 213
  presence in Kerala's radical uprisings, 206
Dalits, 3, 6–9, 12–13, 17–18, 20, 35, 58, 73, 75, 78, 84–85, 89, 91, 93, 99, 101–102, 152–154, 156–162, 164, 166–170, 178, 181–184, 191–192, 194, 199–200, 203–206, 209, 211–215, 221n3, 222n9,
  Adivasi–Dalit activism, 93n9
  Adivasi Dalit Munnetta Samithi (ADMS), 168, 170
  Adivasi Dalit Samara Samithi (ADSS), 16, 67
  bahujans (backward classes), 157, 168, 170
  Chengara Package, 161–163
  Dalit Christians, 157–159
  Dalit Human Rights Movement (DHRM), 214
  emergence as a middle class, 169
  epistemic agency, 7
  experience of the Kerala model of development, 191–192
  feminitude, 18, 177, 206

land struggles in Kerala, 168, 204
Moolampally Package, 162
new struggles amidst suppression, 166–169
occupy movements, 20
procrastination politics and the struggles, 158–161
Strike Solidarity Committee, 78
decolonizing movement, 11
Democratic Youth Federation of India (DYFI), 113, 143
democratization of the economy, 201
Department of Forest and Wildlife, 166
depressed communities, 108, 181
de-Stalinization, process of, 60n2
destituent power, 177
developmentalism
corporate-driven, 12, 119
left-oriented state, 12
Nehruvian, 11
state-led, 12, 32, 119, 202
Devikulam Estate Workers' Union, 178
Dewan of Thiruvithamkur, 172n5
Dharmajan, M., 53, 59
Dhebar Commission, 73–74
distributional injustice, 9, 19
district panchayat, 144, 147n18
divisions of caste and gender, 207
dollar crop, 218
domination, patriarchal forms of, 206
Doordarshan (national television channel), 194n7

earnings before interest, taxes, depreciation, and amortization (EBITDA) profit, 189
East India Tea Produce Company, 155
ecological sustainability, 100, 201, 207
economic liberalization, 54
economic loss, 57
ecospatial conflicts, in the Global South, 2
ecospatial exclusion, 10, 19
ecospatiality
in the making, 219–221
notion of, 200
subaltern, 220
ecospatial livelihood, 13
ecospatial resistance, as politics proper, 201–205
effluent treatment plant (ETP), 38–39, 112
egalitarianism, notion of, 151
Elamaram, 37, 40, 43, 47, 49
employment
loss of, 55
opportunity of, 57
endosulfan pesticide, 44, 218
aerial spraying of, 159
complaint against, 131
expert knowledge, arguments, and counterarguments against, 132–136
families affected by fatalities from, 142
harmful effects of, 133
health disorders due to, 131–132, 135, 144
by helicopters and small planes, 130
human impact of, 127–128
negative consequences of, 131
protest against, 126
to save labour cost of manual spraying, 130

on state-owned cashew plantation, 126
Stockholm conference on, 132, 134, 144
suspension of, 131
widening the protests against, 141–142
anti-endosulfan campaign, 131, 137
as chemical of high aquatic toxicity, 133
committee to review use of
Achuthan Committee (2001), 134–135
C.D. Mayee Committee (2006), 134
District Environmental Committee, 136
Fact Finding Committee, 135
Inter-ministerial Committee (10th), 133–134
O.P. Dubey Committee (2003), 134
Registration Committee (195th), 133
Sivaraman High Power Committee (2003), 135
contamination of food and water bodies, 143
disposal of obsolete stock of, 143
emergence of, 128–129
Endosulfan Poisoning in Kasaragod, Kerala, India (2002), 135
Endosulfan Victims Relief and Remediation (R&R) Cell, 144
financial compensations paid to the affected families, 140
impact on wildlife, 130
'Life Cheaper than Cashew' report (1981), 130–132
manufacturing in India, 129
as most commonly used pesticides, 129
movements demanding the ban on, 127
nations opposing the ban on, 144
panchayat-led mobilization against, 131
production and patenting of, 128
residues in the water samples, 132
sale of, 129
solidarity groups gathering, 136–138
study on health impacts of, 132
toxicity symptoms, 130–132
use of, 17
ban on, 126, 133, 135, 139–140
committees to review, 133–134
formation of committees on, 132
legal activism combined with local protests against, 138–141
movement against the use of, 136
punishment for violation of ban on, 141
recommendation on, 137
victims of, 126, 128, 135, 137
demand for adequate financial compensation, 141
financial compensations for, 140, 142
number of, 141
recommendations of the NHRC for rehabilitation of, 142
rehabilitation policy for, 141–145
writing off loans of, 141
Endosulfan Poisoning in Kasaragod, Kerala, India (2002), 135

Endosulfan Spray Protest Action Committee (ESPAC), 136
enlightenment, concept of, 6
Environmental (Protection) Act (1986), 117
environmental activism, 42
environmental and civil society organizations, 131
environmental conflict, 41
environmental debacle, Plachimada, 109
environmental justice, 6, 217
environmental pollution, 57–58
environmental protection, ethics of, 102
Environmental Protection Agency (EPA), US, 143
environmental sovereignty, 1, 211
environment and society-nature relations, 56
epistemological break, 3, 126, 142, 147n20
epistemological coalescence, 200
equality, politics of, 213
Estallido Social (Social Uprising), in Chile, 1
eucalyptus plantations, 46, 73
Eurocentric enlightenment project of modernity, 120n3
Excel Industries Ltd (Mumbai, Maharashtra), 129
ex gratia payment, idea of, 191
Expert Committee Report, 108
Ezhavas, 10, 35, 58, 153–154, 157, 204

Factories Act (1948), 117
factory jobs, 58
Fanon, Frantz, 7
farmer producer organizations (FPOs), 118
Ferguson, Niall, 222n14
Fertilizers and Chemises Travancore Ltd, Cochin, 39
'feudal' agrarian production, 69
Food First Information and Action Network (FIAN), 221n4
food sovereignty, 18
Foreign Exchanges Regulation Act (FERA, 1973), 155
foreign-owned plantations, nationalization of, 202
Forest Development Corporation, 45, 89
forest lands, 36, 72, 86, 145n3, 160, 165, 203
forest resources, loss of, 47
forest tax, 47
forest tribes, 70
Foucault's notion of 'biopolitics', 21n6
freedom of the press, 14, 193
free health care, 116

Gandhian workers' cooperative, 8
Gandhi, Indira, 74
Gandhi, M.K.
  hunger strikes by, 63n42
Gandhi, Sonia, 89
Gangadharan, M.P., 63n36
Geethanandan, M., 76–77, 84, 89, 94n16
gender-segregated labour market, 182
Giri, V.V., 35
global capitalism, 19, 71, 100, 103, 110, 198
  connection with state-driven developmentalism, 126
  neoliberal version of, 119

global developmentalism, 207
global epistemology, 121n15, 215, 220
Global North, 220
Global South, 3, 7, 12, 76, 211–212, 217, 220
  ecospatial conflicts in, 2
  issue of waste disposal to, 223n17
  movement politics in Kerala, 8–13
  under neoliberal capitalism, 193
  protest movements in, 198
  rural, 128
  subaltern struggles in, 1
Goenkas (RPG Enterprises), 156
Gopalan, A.K., 12, 49, 177, 202
Gopalan, K.P., 48
Gopalan, Laha, 157, 161, 166, 172, 203
Gopalan, Susheela, 58, 120n7
governance-beyond-the-state, 217
Government of India, 32–33, 74, 156
  ban on the use of endosulfan, 140
  Department of Science and Technology, 111
Government of India Act (1935), 70
Gowri Amma, K.R., 11–12
graduated social democratic state, 199, 216
grama panchayats, 38, 81, 121n10, 144, 186
grama sabha, 86–87, 122n21
Gramscian metaphor for politics, 95n17
Gramscian subalterns, 4
Gramsci, Antonio, 14, 85, 217, 219
Grasim Industries, 33–35, 39
  adoption of clean pulping technologies, 38
  campaign for the closure of, 39
  effluent-treatment plant, 39
  installation of effluent treatment system, 40
  movement against, 55
  paper plant, 35
  Ramanilayam Accord, 40
  rayon-grade pulp division, 35
  viscose staple fibre (VSF) division, 35
Great Depression, 72
Greenpeace, 57
Green Revolution, in India, 129
groundwater resources
  depletion of, 110, 112
  mining of, 102, 111
  overmining of
    problematizing the 'scientific knowledge', 106–109
    scientific knowledge vis-à-vis liberatory knowledge, 102–106
  of Plachimada, 109
  pollution of, 106, 112
  recharge of, 101
groundwater table, 109
GROW, 208
Gujarat Rayons Workers Union, 52
Guru, Narayana, 10
Gwalior Rayon Pulp & Fibre Factory Union, 55
Gwalior Rayons Employees Union, 55
Gwalior Rayons Pulp Factory and Construction Workers Union, 48
Gwalior Rayons Silk Manufacturing (Wvg.) Company Ltd, 31, 47–48
  management of, 41
  water pollution in Chaliyar, 42
Gwalior Rayons (Rayon Pulp Division) Taking Over of Management Bill (1978), 50

Habermasian universalism, 22n13
Haran, Nivedita P., 164
Hardt, Michael, 20n2
Harrisons Malayalam Ltd (HML), 154
Harrisons Malayalam plantations, 152, 186
harvest festivals, 168, 203
hazardous gas, leakage of, 51
Hazardous Wastes (Management and Handling) Rules (1989), 39, 109, 112, 117
heavy metals, 110, 112
hegemonic power relations, 11, 100, 185
High Court of Madhya Pradesh, 58
higher education, 211
High-Level Committee, 164
high-tech farming, 192
Hill and Forest Tribe, 70
Hindustan Coca-Cola Beverages Pvt Ltd (HCCB), 116–117
Hindustan Coca-Cola Company Pvt. Ltd. *See* Coca-Cola
Hindustan Insecticides Ltd (HIL), Kochi, 129
Hindustan Newsprint Ltd, 33, 46–47
  establishment of, 34
Hindustan Paper Corporation Ltd mills, 46
Hindutva-corporate regime, 199, 215
HML (Indian company), 155, 165, 169, 222n10
Hoechst, 128
honeymoon hideaways, construction of, 86
human consciousness, 151
human–nature assemblage, sustainable forms of, 201
Human Rights Commission, 40, 88, 138, 140, 172n8, 192
human rights, violation of, 11, 106, 119
hunger strikes, 52–53, 59, 63n42, 141, 159, 179–180
hyper-capitalism, 4

identity-driven subalterns, 212
identity reductionism, 215
imaginative geography, notion of, 92, 151
imperialist universalism, 22n13
imperialist war of the 1940s, 72
Indian Constitution
  Article 21 of, 139, 143
  Article 356 of, 60n1
  Vth Schedule, 82, 84–85, 87, 94, 122n21
  VIth Schedule, 94
  IXth Schedule, 74–75
Indian Council of Medical Research (ICMR), 133
Indian diaspora activism, 212
Indian Easement Act (1882), 118
Indian Forest Act (1878), 70
Indian Law Conference, 141
Indian Medical Association (IMA), 135
Indian National Congress (INC), 60n1, 63n36, 89
Indian National Trade Union Congress (INTUC), 41, 51, 55, 178
Indian parliament, 117
Indian Penal Code, 117
indigenous communities, 13
  agential plurality of, 6
  constitutional rights of, 16
  livelihood of, 15

process of decoding the social life of, 71
indigenous people, 3, 8, 36, 68–71, 77, 82, 86, 208, 214
Indigenous People Collective, 214
industrial accidents, 49
industrial and labour laws, 55
Industrial Development Act, 52
industrial disputes, 57
industrial plantation, 36, 73
Industries Development and Regulation Act (1952), 50
industry-wide lockouts, 186
Insecticides Act (1968), 132
Institute for Motivating Self-Employment, 221n4
Integrated Rural Technology Centre (IRTC), 111, 146n6
Integrated Water Resource Management, 120n2
Inter-ministerial Committee (10th), 133–134
International Labour Organization (ILO)
Decent Work Agenda, 190
International Programme of Chemical Safety, 143
International Union of Food and Agricultural Workers, 205
irikkal samaram (right to sit [in the workplace] protest), 183

Jacob, T.M., 63n38
James Finlay & Company, 71, 177, 181, 184, 188, 192. *See also* Tata Tea
formation of, 191
Janakeeya Jaladhikara Yathra (People's Water Assertion March), 116
Janakeeya Samskarika Samithi, 93n8
Jananeethi, 42
Janata Dal, 113–114
Janu–Antony pact (2001), 86
Janu, C.K., 67, 76–77, 81–82, 84, 206
Janu-Model (Adivasi mode of struggle), 79
Jayarajan, M.V., 88
job loss, 55
Jogi, Adivasi, 88
John, Baby, 74
Joint Parliamentary-Chemical Expert Committee (JPC), 105

Kakkanadan, George, 185
Kallar, River, 160
Kalleley Appooppan Kaavu (local temple), 161
Kanan Devan Hills Plantations Company Private Limited (KDHP), 18, 177–178, 181, 188–189, 192, 202
loan from Tea Board of India, 189
male representatives of, 182
Kanan Devan Land Resumption Bill (1971), 95n21
Kanan Devan plantations, in Munnar, 18, 71, 177. *See also* James Finlay & Company
strikes in, 18
Kannan, K.P., 12, 128, 214
Kannur Central Jail, 88
Kareem, Elamaram, 49
Karunakaran, K., 40, 74
Kayyur–Karivellur–Kavumbayi protests, 10
KDHP Welfare Trust, 188

Kerala
acceptance of Nehruvian developmentalism by, 11
Adivasis of, 67, 68–76
beginnings of Naxalite days in, 73
Birlas in (*See* Birlas, in Communist Kerala)
cancer mortality rate, 38
collapse of the economic activities, 59
Committee on Environment, 38
Communist Party in, 31
conflicts over
natural resources, 45–48
water pollution, 37–45
workers' rights, 48–56
Department of Agriculture, 130
emergence of the modern factory complex, 34–37
environmental and identity politics in, 13
Environmental Review Committee, 39
forms of resistance, 12
forum for science literature, 47
Government of, 54, 74, 131
High Power Committee, 117
history of workers' protest in, 50
Land Acquisition Act, 40
land reforms in, 11, 73
left-front government in, 126, 199
life expectancy of an average Keralite, 68
livelihood–environmental struggles in, 12
model of development, 12
movement politics in, 8–13
People's Science Movement, 47
Public Accounts Committee, 38
Public Works Department, 40
rates of unemployment in, 36
Sen Gupta Committee (1996), 38
social democratic welfare state, 36
state-driven developmentalism in, 31
state legislative assembly, 38
theatres of resistance, 15
Kerala Agrarian Relations Bill (KARB), 152
Kerala Agricultural University (KAU), 132
Kerala Congress(es), 90
Kerala Forest Department (KFD), 47
Kerala Forest Development Corporation, 45
Kerala Forest Produce (Fixation and Selling Price) Act (1978), 34
Kerala Ground Water (Control and Regulations) Act (2002), 118
Kerala Ground Water Department, 106
Kerala High Court, 63n35, 75, 104–108, 139, 170, 192
Kerala Land Reform Act (1969 and 1970), 154
Kerala Land Utilisation Act (1967), 102
Kerala Legislative Assembly (KLA), 87–88, 92n1
Kerala Legislative Committee
Estimate Committee (1977) of, 40–41
Kerala Panchyat Act (1994), 101
Kerala Paper Products Limited (KPPL), 222n10
Kerala People's Science Movement. *See* Kerala Shastra Sahithya Parishad (KSSP)
Kerala Pollution Control Board, 109

Kerala Pradesh Congress Committee, 10–11
Kerala Private Forests (Vesting and Assignment) Act (1971), 33
Kerala Pulaya MahaSabha (KPMS), 214
Kerala Reforms (Amendment) Act (1969), 152
Kerala Restriction on Transfer by and Restoration of Lands to Scheduled Tribes Bill (1999), 16, 67
Kerala Sastra Sahitya Parishad (KSSP), 6, 146n6
Kerala Scheduled Tribes Act (Restriction on Transfer of Lands and Restoration of Alienated Lands, 1975), 74
Kerala Scheduled Tribes (Restoration of Alienated Lands and Restriction on Transfer) Act (1975), 83
Kerala Scheduled Tribes (Restriction on Transfer of Lands and Restoration of Alienated Lands) Act (1975), 16, 67, 84
Kerala Scheduled Tribes (Restriction on Transfer of Land and Restoration of Alinenated Lands) Amendment Bill (1996), 75
Kerala Shastra Sahithya Parishad (KSSP), 47, 136
Kerala State Council for Science, Technology and Environment (KSCSTE), 132
Kerala State Drugs and Pharmaceuticals Ltd (Alappuzha), 39
Kerala State Electricity Board, 93n11
Kerala State Planning Board, 77
Kerala State Pollution Control Board (KSPCB), 37–38, 106, 111, 135, 140
Khrushchev, 31, 60n2
knowledge
  as emancipation, 100
  liberatory knowledge, 102–106
  production, 100
knowledge-based industry, 55
knowledge conflicts, 99, 103–104
knowledge controversies, 126, 142, 216–219
Kodagas, 133
Kondha tribes (Odisha), 8
K.R. Narayanan Co-operative Village Settlement Programme, 162
*kudikidapukar*s (hut dwellers), protection of, 11
Kumar, Mohan, 146n7
Kunhalikutty, P.K., 111
Kurichiar *lahala*, 93n5
Kurichias, 9
Kurumbas, 9
Kurup, O.N.V, 79
Kuthali, 46
kutilkettysamaram (refugee huts), 67–68, 76, 156
Kuttappan, M.A., 86

labour disputes, 34
labour market, 206
labour rationalisation, 188
labour, social reproduction of, 207
labour strikes, ban on, 34
labour unions, 58
Laclau, Ernesto, 7, 21n6, 22n11, 157, 178
land-based caste system, 154
land-broker state, 169

land–caste nexus, 154
land claims, notion of, 92
'land grab' struggles, 12
land inequality, in Kerala, 204
landless agricultural workers, 152
landless households, in Kerala, 89, 204
landless industrial workers, 11
landless labourers, 72
Landless Workers Movement, 1
landlordism, abolition of, 11, 70, 152–153, 167
land ownership, 153–154, 168–170, 210
land reforms bill, 12
land reforms, in Kerala, 73, 152–153, 202
land struggles, in Arippa, Nilambur, and Aralam, 203
Land Utilization Order (1967), 117
land-wars, 151
Latin American–African resistance movements, 211
law of restoration, 74
layams (line houses), 181
layers of oppression, 178
lead, 110–111
Left Democratic Front (LDF), 68, 74–75, 141, 159
left-wing governments, 56, 73, 131, 199
legal activism, 74, 138–141
LIBOR, 189
LIFE (Livelihood, Inclusion and Financial Empowerment) initiative, 223n16
livelihood ecosystem, 87
livelihood–environmental continuum, 212
livelihood–environmental resistance movements, 13
livelihood–environmental risks, 13
livelihood–environmental struggles, in Kerala, 12
livelihood–environmental sustainability, 19
livelihood–environment ecosystems, 32
livelihood sustainability, 56
local communities, mobilization of, 17
local self-government (LSG), 120n7
local self-government institutions, 186
Lokayukta, 78–79
Lok Sabha, 105
London Stock Exchange, 155

Madras Presidency, 11
Malabar forests, 45
Malabar rebellion (1921), 10
Malayalam plantation, 152, 154–155, 165
Malayalam Plantations Ltd, 155
Malayalam Rubber & Produce Co. Ltd, 155
male-led trade unions, depoliticization of, 185–186, 194
Manoharan, Justice, 164
Maoist movements, in the 1970s, 73
Maoist politics, in India, 73
Mapilla peasants, of Malabar, 214
mapping of resources, 32–34
marginalities of exclusion, 4
marginalized communities, 4, 154, 159, 204, 208
  livelihood and employment for, 56
marginalized groups, 14, 220
marginalized people, of Kerala, 205
Marxism, 31
Marxist version of 'state', 2

mass starvation deaths, protest against, 16, 67
Master, E.N. Peethambaran, 57
Master, K. Chathunni, 42
Mateer, Samuel, 71
Mavoor communities, 201
Mavoor factory, 51
Mavoor rayon factory, 56
Mayilamma (the Dalit woman leader of the anti-Cola water movement), 99
Medical Laboratory, Kozhikode, 111
Meenkara dam reservoir, 101
members of the legislative assembly (MLAs), 41
Menon, C. Achutha, 46, 74, 95n21
missionary activism, 9
  challenging the norms of the Hindu state, 10
Mobile Fair Price Shop (State Civil Supplies Corporation), 76
modernity, idea of, 10
  European-derived, 10
  as liberation, 4
monoculture plantations, 71, 164
Moolampally Package, 162
Moolathara barrage, 101–102
Mooply Valley Tea Co. Ltd, 155
moral economy, as traditional norms and mutual obligations, 59
Mouffe, Chantal 7, 21n6, 22n11, 157, 178
Moulavi, Vakkom Abdul Khader, 10
M/S Moonlight Chemfab Ltd Indore, 55
Muhammedaji, 61n10
Muhammed, Aryadan, 38
Mukkam *panchayat*, 41
Mukundan, M., 79
Mullaperiyar dam controversy, 193
Munnar struggle, lessons and non-lessons from
  corporate and trade union agitation, 181
  question of power and representation, 180–184
  workers' struggle against James Finlay and Company, 184
Murugappa Group of EID Parry (India) Ltd, 129
Muslim League, 42, 202
Muthanga–Chengara occupations, 18
Muthanga range of the Wayanad Wildlife Sanctuary (MWWS), 68, 86–88
  evacuation of the illegal occupants from, 87

Nadar women, 9
Nagda Rayon factory, Nagda, Madhya Pradesh, 40
Nair, M.T. Vasudevan, 79
Nair, P.K. Vasudevan, 43, 50
Namboodirippad, E.M.S., 11–12, 23n17, 31, 153, 202, 214
Narayanan, K.R., 75
Narendran, K.K., 62n19
Narmada Bachao Andolan (NBA), 8, 115
National Alliance for People's Movement, 115
National Commission for Women (NCW), 87
National Environmental Engineering Research Institute (NEERI), 44
National Human Rights Commission (NHRC), 40, 140

National Institute of Occupational Health (NIOH), 133, 135
National Rainforest Biosphere, 22n12
National Research Centre for Cashew (NRCC), 132, 137
National Water Policy, 105
natural resources, conflicts over, 45–48
natural teak forests, razing of, 71
Nayanar, E.K., 52, 75, 81, 120n7
Negri, Antonio, 20n2
Nehru, Jawaharlal, 31, 60n1, 74
Nehruvian developmentalism, acceptance by Kerala, 11, 31
neoliberal capitalism, 193, 199
neurotoxicity, 143
new-generation industries, idea of starting, 56
Nilambur valley, 32, 45
non-governmental organizations (NGOs), 7, 221n4
noxious gases, deaths due to inhalation of, 39

Occupy Chengara movement, 158, 160, 204, 206
Occupy Muthanga movement (2003), 156, 206
  agreement and its implementation, 83
  breaking new ground, 84–86
  CPI(M) position on, 68
  first phase of struggle, 76–78
  origins of, 68
  second phase of struggle, 78–82
  third phase of struggle, 86–91
Occupy politics of 2011, 1
Occupy protests, in the West, 198
Ogoni movement (Nigeria), 211
oligarchic capitalism, 4
Onam (harvest festival of Malayalis), 16, 67, 76, 203–204
  Onam celebrations and refugee huts, 76–78
Ongoni movement (Nigeria), 1
onsite/on-the-spot ethnography, 13–15

ooru kootttangal (Adivasi congregations), 86
O.P. Dubey Committee (2003), 134
organic pollutants, 134
Orissa Mining Corporation, 8, 134, 144
other backward classes (OBCs), 154
ownership rights, 92, 152, 154

paddy cultivation, 168
Panchayat Raj Act, 114
panchayats, 47, 53, 59, 77, 103–104, 111, 114, 130–131, 136, 142
Panchayats (Extension to the Scheduled Areas) Act, 1996 (PESA), 86, 122n21
pan-India corporate capital, 91
Paniyars, 70
paper and pulp industry, promotion of, 32
paper industry, in India, 36
Parambikulam–Aliyar project, 113
Paris Commune, 215
parliamentary politics, of legitimization and procrastination, 72
Parry & Co., 155
Paschim Banga Khet Majoor Samity, 205
Patkar, Medha, 79, 115
  National Alliance of People's Movements (NAPM), 221n4
pattaya mela (title deed fest), 166

Pazhassi rebellion, 93n5
peaceful coexistence, policy of, 60n2
peasant uprising, at Naxalbari, 73
People's Council for Social Justice, 139
People's Liberation Committee. *See* Sadhujana Vimochana Samyukta Vedi (SVSV)
People's Plan Campaign, 86
People's Science Movement (Kerala), 6, 47, 136
People's War Group (PWG), 85
PepsiCo, 16, 101, 103, 105, 113
persistent organic pollutants (POPs), 144
Perumatty *panchayat*, 101, 104, 114–115
Pesticide Action Network Asia and Pacific (PANAP), 135
Pettimudi tragedy, in the Idukki district, 205
Piketty, Thomas, 2, 216
Pillai, P. Krishna, 177
Pillai, Ramakrishna, 10
Pillai, V. Surendran, 123n29
place-bound proletarian/socialist revolutions, 5
place-space exclusion, practice of, 10
Plachimada Coca-Cola Victims' Relief and Compensation Claims Special Tribunal Bill (2011), 117
Plachimada movement, 17, 119
Plachimada Solidarity Committee, 103
Plantation Corporation of Kerala (PCK), 90, 128–130, 132, 138, 158
  aerial spraying of pesticides in all the cashew plantations of, 135
  campaign against spraying of the pesticide by, 131
  endosulfan pesticide (*See* endosulfan pesticide)
  five-year pesticide holiday, 135
Plantation Labour Committee (PLC), 186–187
Plantation Labour Rules, 187
plantations
  British-owned, 202
  capitalism, 177
  colonialism, 70
  development of, 156
  layams, 205
  management of, 190–192
  Tata-owned, 202
Plantation Samrakhana Samiti (Plantation Protection Committee), 137
Plantation Workers Union, 178
police raj, 93n8
political-ecology-identity activism, 212
political ecospatiality, 3–4, 157, 198
  conceptualization of, 2, 19
political pluralism, 14, 193
Pombilai Orumai, Munnar, 193, 203, 210
  attempt to self-immolation by Dalit women workers, 180
  Dalit woman leaders of, 177
  gap between money wages and living wages, 180
  hunger strike, 179–180
  Munnar struggle, 180–184
  political power of, 214
  protest power, 182
  struggle(s) and the settlement, 178–180
  trade unionism, 186

poramboke regions (land unassessed by the government), 77
postcolonial Marxist scholarship, 213–216
post-Covid-19 capitalism, 20
post development social movement, 100
poverty, 128, 158, 170, 198, 206, 211
  below the poverty line, 69
power inequality, 3
power relations, intersectionality of, 207
Prakkanam, Sabeena, 206
Prakkanam, Saleena, 157
Premachandran, N.K., 118
President of India, 74
private forests, nationalization of, 45
procrastination, politics of, 72, 89
procrastination politics of the state, 158
Public Accounts Committee, 38
public-sector industries, 39
Pulayars, 70, 157
Punalur paper mill, 46
Punchiri Sports and Arts Club, Muliyar, 136
Punnapra Vayalar revolts, 10
Puthusseri *panchayat*, 114

Radhakrishnan, Thiruvanjoor, 163
radical democracy project, 7
radicalized democracy, in Kerala, 153
Rahman, K.A., 41–42, 53
rainwater harvesting, 114
Rajamanickam Committee (2020), 165
Rajan, P., 93n8
Rajendran, K.P., 88, 159, 162
Rajendran, S., 179
Ramachandran, V. K., 12, 170
Ramanilayam Accord, 40
Raman, Ravi K., 7, 9, 13–14, 18, 34, 48–49, 52, 56, 70–72, 75, 100, 104, 106, 119, 127, 152, 157–158, 177, 183–184, 190, 199, 207, 218
Ram Bahadur Thakur Group (RBT) estate, 182
Rammohan, K.T., 12, 52, 152–153
Rancier, Jacques, 3, 5, 21n6, 69, 203
Ravunni, Murkoth, 35
Rawther, Hussain, 184
rayon pulp factory, in Mavoor (Kerala), 32
recognition, politics of, 213
redistributive state, idea of, 219
reflexive modernity, concept of, 127
refugee camps, 91, 94n15
refugee huts, 16
  dismantling of, 79
  Onam celebrations and, 76–78
Registration Committee (195th), 133
Rehabilitation Tribal Mission, 86
Relief Bill, 119
religious fundamentalism, 193
renaissance movements, 9, 22n15, 91, 201, 203
Reorganization Act (1956), 11
Reserve Bank of India, 192
reserved lands, 71
rice cultivation, 169
rice economy, 102
right-making, process of, 2, 11, 56, 198, 203–204, 208
rights assertion, strategies of, 217
right to have rights, refusal of, 189–191, 213
right to sit struggle, 206
right to water, denial of, 110
risk society, concept of, 127

river biography, 59
river pollution, 59
Roy, Arundhati, 57, 79
Roy, Tirthankar, viii
rubber plantation, in Chengara, 17
rubber plantations, 168, 169
Russia–Ukraine war, 223n17

Saboo, R.N., 44
Sadhujana Vimochana Samyukta Vedi (SVSV), 157–159
  occupation of undisputed state-owned lands, 160
  plantation village in the making, 163–166
Said, Edward, 151
sakhas (wings), 159
sales tax, 47
Samatha Law Society, 139
Santillo, David, 110
Sapre, Abhay Manohar, 205
Saraswati, Thattayil, 157
Sargam Metals Ltd, Chennai, 111
Sartre, Paul, 7
Save Chaliyar Campaign (2011), 46
Save Himalaya movement, 8, 119
Save Silent Valley Campaign of the 1960s and 1970s, 136
Scheduled Areas and Scheduled Tribes Commission, 74
Scheduled Caste and Scheduled Tribe (Prevention of Atrocities) Act (1989), 117
Scheduled Castes (SCs), 87, 90, 154, 169
Scheduled Castes & Scheduled Tribes (Prevention of Atrocities) Act (1989), 79
Scheduled Tribes (STs), 70, 90, 116
scientific knowledge
  dissemination of, 218
  problematizing of, 106–109
Sebastian, Gomati, 206
Seethihaji, P., 43
Sekhar, N.C., 177
self-determination, 82
  right to, 70
self-dignity, idea of, 9
self-emancipation, process of, 217
self-rule, notion of, 92
Sen Gupta Committee (1996), 38
setting fire to the forests, threats of, 88
settler cultivators, immigration of, 72
settler peasants, 72
Sharmila, Irom, 63n42
shifting cultivation, 71
Silent Valley campaign, 6
Singh, R.B., 133
Singur Krishi Jomi Raksha Committee (Committee to Save the Farmland of Singur), 209
Sivarajan, 32
Sivaraman High Power Committee (2003), 135
slavery, abolition of, 70
slum dwellers, 78
social and economic inequality, 169
social body politic, 2
social classes, involved in the cashew industry, 128
social conflict, 208
social democracies, 2
social democratic state, 220
social injustice, 11
Socialist Unity Centre of India (SUCI), 161
social justice, idea of, 6, 202, 219

socially backward communities, 202
socially hierarchized plantation system, 181
social movements, 100
identity politics, 1
social reform renaissance movements, 201
social reproduction
of labour, 7, 178
and sustenance, 156
Society for Environmental Education in Kerala (SEEK), 136
socio-economic mobility, 181
sociology of emergences, process of, 22n13
soft-drink industry, 101
solid wastes, 110
Soman, Vazhoor, 194n9
South Indian Plantation Workers Union, 178
spatial material inequality, 19
spatio-agential-temporal coalescing, 2, 5–8
Spinoza, Baruch, 20n2
Spivak, G., 7, 18, 177–178, 213
Sreekumar, T.T., 135, 142, 146n8, 152, 219
Srinivasan, P.S., 45
Stalin, Joseph, 60n2
state–civil society synergy, 217
state-driven developmentalist modernization, 6, 119
state-driven development projects, 32
state formation, political anthropology of, 14
State Human Rights Commission, 138
state-led developmentalism, 6, 13, 202
state-making, process of, 2, 11, 19, 56, 198, 203–204
state-owned lands, 90
State Pollution Control Board, 37
state power, social relations of, 168
state socialism, idea of, 219
state within state, 190
Sterlite Industries (India), 8
Stockholm Convention on Persistent Organic Pollutants, 132, 134, 144
April Stockholm Conference (2011), 144
Strike Solidarity Committee, 78
subaltern counterpublics, 4
subaltern identities, 194, 213–214
subaltern mobilization, 18
subaltern modernity, 4, 202
subaltern power
interconstitutiveness of, 3
transverse solidarity/ interconstitutiveness of, 6
subaltern social movements, 12
Subaltern Studies project, 200
subaltern womanhood, 7
Sudhakaran, K., 86
Sudheeran, V.M., 170
Sugandhagiri Project, 90
Sugathan, R., 177
Sunil, Omana, 161
Sunny, Lisy, 206
Supreme Court Monitoring Committee, 112
Supreme Court of India, 111
surface water, pollution of, 109
sustainable development, 15
sustainable livelihood, 59
Swadeshabhimani, 10
Swamikal, Chattampi, 22n15

Swaraj, Sushma, 105
Swatantra Thozhilali Union (STU), 41
Syrian Christians, 72

tata employee buyout, 188–189
Tata Global Beverages Limited. *See* Tata Tea
Tata Motors, 221n4
Tata Tea, 91, 165, 181, 184, 188–189
Tea Board of India, 189
tea forests, 186
tea gardens, 186
temple entry movement, in Thiruvithamkur, 10
tenancy system
  abolition of, 73, 152
  provision for legalization of, 167
terrestrial food-webs, 144
territorial sovereignty, 82
Tetley (UK-based company), 188
Thaliparambu, 90
Thamarakshan, A.V., 38
Thampu, K.M., 93
Thanal (a non-profit NGO), 136
Thiruvamkulam Nature Lovers Movement, 139
Thiruvananthapuram, 16, 57, 76, 89
Thiruvithamkur, Hindu state of, 9
Thomas, T.V., 42
Thompson, E.P., 59
Thozhilali (the Worker), 10
Tilly, Charles, 21n4
total dissolved solid (TDS), 109
toxic metals, 110
trade unions, 53, 57, 59, 184, 207
  in Alappuzha, 10
  All India Trade Union Congress (AITUC), 10
  industrial workers, 10
  male-led, 6, 18
  minimalist state and minimalist trade unions, 187–188
transboundary conflicts, 120n2
transverse solidarity (TS), 2, 7, 105, 157, 200
  notion of, 56
  politics, 22n11
Travancore Titanium Products Ltd, Thiruvananthapuram, 39
Tribal Advisory Council, 94n14
Tribal Animists, 70
Tribal Court, 86
tribal development programme, 76–77
Tribal Land Restoration Act (1975), 74–75
Tribal Mission, 83, 86
tribal population, encroachment/displacement of, 72
  from Muthanga, 73
Tribal Sub-Plans, 86

U.N. Dhebar Commission, 73–74
Unfinished Task in Land Reforms, 74
Union Ministry of Health and Family Welfare, 105
United Democratic Front (UDF), 74, 141, 159
United Nations (UN), 143
United Nations Environment Programme (UNEP), 144
United News of India (UNI), 87
universal womanhood, challenge of, 7
Unnimoyeen, B.P., 41
upper caste–landlord–chieftain hegemony, 153
uprisings, against the landlords, 73

urbanization, 12
Uzhamalakkal village, Nedumangad, 166

Varghese, A., 93n9
Vasu, A., 34, 52–53, 59, 208
Vazhakkad Grama Panchayat, 38
Vedanta Alumina, 8
Veerendrakumar, M.P., 57, 121n7
Velankanni, suicide of, 182
Venu, K., 53
Vijayamadhavan, K.T., 61n18
Vijayan, Pinarayi, 205, 223n16
Vijayan, Varkala, 93n8
village council, 87
village *panchayats*, 17
Viswam, Binoy, 118
vittu krishiboomiyilekku (leaving colony for farmland), 168

Wallardie Tea Estates Ltd, 155
Wallerstein, I., 4, 186, 215
war of maneuver, 94n17
war of position, 94n17
Warrier, C.B.C., 46
waste lands, 71
Water (Prevention and Control of Pollution) Act (1974), 37–38, 117, 140
water conflict, 99, 120n2
water pollution
  conflicts over, 37–45
  health problems, 110
  hidden truths, 109–114
water rights, privatization of, 17
water shortage, 105, 108, 114, 116
water table, 111, 113
water wars, 99
wealth inequality, 3
well water, pollution of, 110
Western Ghats, 32, 48
  loss of bamboo and other forest resources from, 63n33
Western Occupy movements, 20
workers' rights, conflict over, 48–56
workers *versus* communities, 207–209
world capitalism and crisis, 184–185
World Health Organization (WHO), 110, 133
World Social Forum, 115, 217
World War II, 72
World Water Conference, 115
Wyanad Wildlife Sanctuary, 16
  Muthanga range of, 68
Wynad Tea Co. Ltd, 155
Wyse, L.D., 21n5

Zacharia, Paul, 94n15
zero landlessness, 89, 165
Žižek, Slavoj, 30, 227